W9-ADB-200

SOAP OPERA AND
WOMEN'S TALK

COMMUNICATION AND HUMAN VALUES

SOAP OPERA AND WOMEN'S TALK

The Pleasure of Resistance

Mary Ellen Brown

SAGE Publications
International Educational and Professional Publisher
Thousand Oaks   London   New Delhi

For Kevin, Colin, Sean, Chris
and Marion, Rena, Ruth, Louise, Sue, Kirk, and Kelley

For information address:

SAGE Publications, Inc.
2455 Teller Road
Thousand Oaks, California 91320

SAGE Publications Ltd.
6 Bonhill Street
London EC2A 4PU
United Kingdom

SAGE Publications India Pvt. Ltd.
M-32 Market
Greater Kailash I
New Delhi 110 048 India

Printed in the United States of America

Library of Congress Cataloging-in-Publication Data

Brown, Mary Ellen.
  Soap Opera and women's talk: The pleasure of resistance / Mary Ellen Brown.
      p. cm. —(Communication and human values)
  Includes bibliographical references and index.
  ISBN 0-8039-4392-X (cl) — ISBN 0-8039-4393-8 (pb)
    1. Soap operas—United States—History and criticism. 2. Soap operas—Great Britain—History and criticism. 3. Soap operas—Australia—History and criticism. 4. Televison and women—United States. 5. Television viewers—United States. 6. Feminism.
I. Title. II. Series: Communication and human values (Thousand Oaks, Calif.)
PN1992.8.S4B76   1994
791.45'6—dc20   94-1473

94 95 96 97 98 10 9 8 7 6 5 4 3 2 1

Sage Production Editor: Astrid Virding

Contents

Acknowledgments

There are many people I would like to thank for their help and support as well as their intellectual work. My teachers and friends at Murdoch University in Western Australia: John Hartley, Krishna Sen, and Leslie Stern shared their insights and guided me through the research. My colleagues at Edith Cowan University, where I was teaching at the time I did the research, gave me special insights into this work from both a media studies perspective and a feminist perspective. I think particularly of Robyn Quin, Hilaire Natt, Lelia Green, and Sherry Saggers. Others who contributed intellectual work to this project were Linda Barwick of the University of New England, New South Wales; John Fiske of the University of Wisconsin, Madison; and Dennis Gray, then of the University of Western Australia. At the State University of New York, where I taught for 4 years, Fred Halley, Chad Skaggs, Beth VanFossen, and Sarah Miles Watts Green were immensely helpful. Sharon Welch and Elaine Lawless at the University of Missouri provided intellectual stimulation and a supportive environment. Len Hoiles has stuck with me through tough times. My longtime friends and supporters, who often took the time to discuss with me the issues related to this manuscript and life in general, are Maxine Hatcher, Nelda Holder, Judith Quick, Marilyn Meyerson, and Etta Breit. My children Kevin, Colin, Sean, and Chris Bowers have cheerfully supported my endeavors. Patricia Morrow has helped me immensely in the process of making the text readable and understandable. Ann West, formerly of Sage Publications, has been enthusiastic and supportive as has Sophy Craze at Sage. The editorial assistance of Robert White, at the Gregorian University in Rome, has in many ways been responsible for making it possible for me to say what I have wanted to say.

Some portions of this volume have been published in modified versions in Brown (1986, 1989a, 1989b, 1990a, 1990b, 1990c, 1990d, 1991) and Brown and Barwick (1987).

Introduction:
Questions of Identity

My women friends and I have gone over that cliff together so many times.

This is the comment of a female viewer of the film *Thelma & Louise* (Scott, 1991), one overheard and repeated by a friend of mine. When people ask me how I can claim that television programs or films can be empowering, I repeat this phrase as an example of the empowering process. Although *Thelma & Louise* is contested territory as far as media critics are concerned (see Baker, 1992), like *The Color Purple* and its black women audiences (see Bobo, 1988), among the women I know *Thelma & Louise* is an acknowledged feminist statement. We all identified with Thelma (Geena Davis) and Louise (Susan Sarandon) in their ultimate inability to negotiate a position for themselves in a world constructed in masculine terms; hence the metaphorical leap that we have all taken so many times.

The final scene of *Thelma & Louise* contradicts oppression by providing a final mythic level of escape from it for these two women and metonymically for all women. Rarely, however, do we have such a clear example of possible resistive pleasure for women. More often, women and other subordinated groups are forced to take what the culture has to offer and construct their own moments of resistance. In this volume, I attempt to chart the struggle for resistive pleasure for women whose everyday lives include the pleasures of watching soap operas. I intend to outline how after watching soap operas they use them to create and support a social network in which talk becomes a form of resistive pleasure.

These and similar arguments were not clear to me in 1985 when I began to look seriously at soap operas and what was happening in soap opera gossip networks. At the time, I was familiar with soap operas only through other people's conversations about them, so I decided to "read up" on the plots in order to choose which one to watch. I was shocked by my need to explain to the clerk behind the counter, as I was buying a copy of *Soap Opera Digest,* that I myself was not a fan but was an academic studying about soap operas.

I realized the contradictory position in which my own social position had placed me. As a woman in this culture, I had accepted the disapproving valuation of soap operas on an emotional level even though I intellectually reasoned that soap opera viewing is not a negative act. The act of becoming a part of the soap opera in-group, however, opened the door for me to a world that has given me immense pleasure ever since. For what became important to me was not so much the plots of the various daytime soaps but who else watched them. I eventually chose the soap opera I wanted to be "my" soap opera because it was the one most of my friends watched, *Days of Our Lives*. So I became a fan of that soap opera, and I "keep up" with several others through conversations with friends and students.

When I left the United States and discovered Australian and British soap operas, or "serial dramas," as many Britishers prefer to call *Coronation Street, Brookside,* and *EastEnders,* I learned that soap operas could include a wide variety of characteristics. As I began to follow and to chat about these British soap operas and the Australian ones available at the time (1986-1988)—*Sons and Daughters, A Country Practice, Neighbours, Home and Away,* and *Prisoner*—I was struck by the viability of the oral networks that exist around soap opera culture in each of these countries.

I had a long-standing interest in how women talked to each other in everyday life and had developed an idea of what I called *feminine discourse,* a term that academic feminists had begun using to discuss how television programs or films addressed women. My idea was that women could be addressed in (at least) two ways—as women structured by the dominant discourse (usually men's ideas of what women are like) or as women who understand their subordinate position in society. The idea of "woman" addressed in dominant discourse is the woman who does not see her feminine position as problematic. This hypothetical woman responds without complication to the notions of femininity and life choices represented by the media, particularly in the ads but also in much of the programming. However, television or film representations that challenge or problematize women's actions and choices provide an edge or a point of resistance where women and others can see themselves as oppositional to a cultural norm that oppresses them. Similarly, when women talk to each other, such an edge can also exist. Women's talk can problematize women's position in society by acknowledging their position as arbitrarily subordinate. I began to wonder if the elaborate configuration of soap opera networks into which I had entered was a site of such resistive feminine discourse, so I stuck around to find out.

Mine is an ethnographic study in which I am a member of the group, a fan, and also the researcher. Ethnography in general (Clifford, 1983; Clifford & Marcus, 1986) and in cultural studies in particular (Morris, 1990; Seaman, 1992) has come under criticism for projecting the stance of the researcher through the voices of the subjects. This is always a danger in ethnographic work, but no more so now than in the past. I feel that, to pay attention to the specific practices of participants in fanship networks and other television spectatorship practices, ethnographic work is necessary and valuable. Otherwise, audience theory is based on an audience of one, the author of that theory. What I hope I have done here is to situate the discourse of several groups of fans in the context of some of the discourses that they are potentially resisting.

No study of this type can make claims to universality. My observations are of only a few groups of television soap opera fans from English-speaking countries, and my claim is simply that these soap opera fanship networks have the potential for providing a space for resistive discourse about gender role expectations. New work on these once unworthy forms has led to a heightened interest in soap operas, *telenovelas,* and *feuilletons* throughout the world. Just as there is no fixed idea of women (Ang & Hermes, 1991, p. 324), there is also no fixed idea of soap opera. Although the form of this female-oriented melodrama varies just as the uses to which audiences put it varies, its importance is now well established.

The chapters that follow are arranged in the following manner: Chapter 1 gives an overview of the concept of the hegemony that has been used in the analysis of media in British and American cultural studies. It attempts to delineate how cultural studies is particularly supportive of feminist analyses and lays out the parameters of the research methods and of the theorization used in the rest of the book.

Chapter 2 outlines the precarious position in which women often find themselves: their work devalued, their voices unheard. It also delineates the power of talk that acknowledges their subordination, to establish a position of control amid the contradictions of everyday life. I discuss how women have had trouble speaking publicly; how our languages constrict the way we speak so that often there are no words for what we need to say; how, in conversations with men, women's ideas are often not acknowledged or are attributed to a man in the group; or the ways in which women are sometimes simply not talked to. All of this has caused women to develop an oral culture of their own. This oral culture thrives on gossip.

Chapter 3 develops a history of soap operas, taking into consideration how the hegemonic process works in terms of the desire of the producers to integrate the new form into the world of a hypothetical housewife either in rural America or later in postwar suburbia. The relationship of orality to soap opera in both its form and production conventions is also explored. The chapter begins to delineate how soap opera's relationship to orality and to women's constructions in dominant culture does not prevent it from bringing conventional ideas of woman into question.

Chapter 4 traces the research concerning soap opera audiences as well as recent work in audience ethnography and reader response criticism that has prepared the way for the study of the spoken text, that is, the conversations people have about television that integrate the medium into their lives. Interview material at the end of the chapter makes it possible to see specifically how some fans integrate soap opera fanship into their lives.

Chapter 5 explores the manner in which many women in fanship groups are able to set aside a space for their own discourses within the context of soap opera viewing and to use what I have called the spoken text to mediate their contradictory position in society. Also discussed here are the ways that soap opera fanship groups resemble or differ from other fanship groups that are predominantly female.

Chapter 6 looks at the way people can take a devalued cultural form like soap opera and, within their interpretive communities, co-opt the very terms of degradation that they use defiantly. *Trash,* for example, becomes descriptive of socially unacceptable but very useful and pleasurable media forms.

Chapter 7 describes the ways in which these audiences use humor and parody to mark social and stylistic issues within soap opera discussions through the examination of liminality, the carnivalesque, and laughter in soap opera gossip networks.

Chapter 8 looks at interviews from this group of fans for more politically obvious points of resistance. The means by which teenagers are able to dissect and understand the narrative conventions of their soap opera and the ways that an avowed feminist can find content in a soap opera supporting her ideological position are investigated. The manner in which such positions may be negotiated, or a progressive reading may be rejected, are also looked at in this chapter.

Finally, Chapter 9 attempts to summarize and integrate the ethnographic data into a more coherent perspective. Here I return to the issue of the place of the construct "resistive reading" in relation to the politics of feminist cultural studies.

This book explores how hegemonic notions of femininity and womanhood develop at one cultural site and the ways they can be accepted, resisted, and/or negotiated in the process of consumption. This book not only claims that hegemony is leaky but also attempts to explain how the leaks occur.

1

The Politics of Pleasure

Women cannot tell stories and . . . what they do tell are not real stories.

(Kalcik, 1975, p. 7)

The claim that soap opera gossip networks can spawn resistive discourse is similar to the statement quoted above. Although we know that women do tell stories, women often do not tell stories in the way that dominant culture expects them to. Women's stories are often circular, lacking a clear beginning, middle, or end. Thus, in dominant discourse, what women tell is not classified or recognized as stories. Hence women's stories go unrecorded and unrecognized. Soap opera gossip networks are similarly invisible. How, one may ask, recognizing only the dominant and trivialized notion of soap opera audiences as hardly worthy of notice, can such an apparently trivial or even exploitative genre as soap opera be associated with a notion of empowerment for its viewers? The answer lies in the invisible discourse networks it plugs into and helps to solidify. Such discourse networks, or gossip networks, are important for women's resistive pleasure.

The purpose of this book is to support the idea that much of the pleasure in soap opera fanship lies in the discursive network among women that builds around the viewing of a program that is designed for them. Seven distinct questions that shall be addressed deal with the issues that have become germane in the process of exploring this topic.

1. Why do women enjoy a genre that supposedly puts them down and is widely considered, even by its loyal followers, to be trash?
2. What, in the history and culture of women, makes the development of feminine discourse salient and a particularly resistive form in our culture?
3. How has this genre of television program been so successful in developing a style that fits well with women's discourse and problems?
4. How has a genre of television program, generally watched in the home alone, become such a force for social interaction among women?

1

5. Is the pleasure given by soap operas reinforcing women's dependency and subordination or can it be liberating?
6. Is existing audience theory able to allow for theorizing about soap opera and its audiences' practices?
7. What are the challenges that feminist theory and methodology bring to this project?

It can be said that soap operas in some ways give women their voice. The constant, active, playful discussions about soap operas open up possibilities for us to understand how social groups can take a somewhat ambiguous television text and incorporate it into existing gossip networks that provide outlets for a kind of politics in which subordinated groups can be validated and heard. Many programs have discursive networks— that is, networks of people who share their pleasure in viewing through discussion—but soap operas and their existing oral networks are particularly open to the creation of a spoken text: Women take advantage of soap operas' availability to them, in spite of the fact that many people think soap operas are banal or silly. Outside of soap opera gossip networks, no one would suspect that there was anything important going on, but if we look at them closely, we will discover that there exists a rich spoken text within these networks. It seems clear that the sense-making that people engage in when they talk about television may be as important as their actual viewing of the television program. It is in the investigation of this spoken text that we may find the answer to the question: *Why do women enjoy soap operas so much?*

I am suggesting that soap opera viewing, generally considered not only apolitical but also antipolitical, can, in fact, be political and the basis for a kind of empowerment. One view is that politics involves, within countries, only class struggles and, among countries, only national interests. Although the dictionary definitions of *politics* delineate the political as "the art or science of government," within this definition *politics* can include the affairs of a politician or political party or a government, engagement in political affairs professionally, the tactics involved in managing a state, or "a person's general position or attitude on political subjects" (*American Heritage Dictionary*, 1982). The political can also include "factional scheming within a group: as, office politics" (*Webster's*, 1964). However, feminist concerns, multiculturalist concerns, and ecological concerns have led us to consider politics in a much broader sense, hence gender, race, ethnicity, and global ecology have all become part of a much more general notion of politics, a notion of politics that includes the struggles people have in their everyday lives over their own consciousness. Such a notion of politics is nonvertical and relies on a negotiated concept of power. Similarly, whereas class was once conceptualized as purely an economic distinction that was thought to determine the political and ideological positions and interests of the membership in that class, newer conceptualizations of class have recognized the political and ideological as well as the economic in the formation of classes (Frow, 1993). In the case of both politics and class, the focus has shifted to the cultural sphere, where many different groups are seen to struggle over culture. In this chapter I will attempt to trace how an ideological struggle over cultural capital (knowledge) within the popular sphere may be interpreted as political. To do so, I shall discuss hegemony, gender and class, theories of women's inequality, gendered audience theory, and, finally, a theory of feminine discourse as it relates to soap opera audiences.

Hegemony

A crucial concept for understanding the idea of feminine discourse is the notion of hegemony. Taken from the Greek *egemon*, which means leader or ruler, sometimes of a state other than his or her own, *hegemony* was originally used in English to indicate that one state had political predominance over another. It has recently also been used to describe power politics in which one state intends to dominate others. In a more general sense, it means simply "predominant" or "master principle" (Williams, 1976).

The term has become important to twentieth-century cultural studies, particularly through the work of Antonio Gramsci (1971), who extends the notion of predominance to relations between social classes. The character of this predominance is not, however, limited to direct political control. Hegemony, in this sense, includes particular ways of seeing the world, ourselves, and others because of the power and dominance of those others. Thus hegemony is a form of class rule that exists not just in economic and political institutions but also in forms of experience and consciousness as well. This idea is particularly important in societies where public opinion and electoral politics are significant elements. Where the people themselves determine the laws and practices of the state, the struggle for hegemony is considered a necessary and decisive factor in terms of radical change in either society or politics (Williams, 1976) because people must believe they are acting in their own interests in order to perpetuate the status quo.

Gramsci carried out his work in a Fascist prison between 1927 and 1935 and, although much is debated concerning his concepts, this work is considered by many to be one of the major turning points in cultural theory. According to Raymond Williams (1977), the implications of this conceptualization of hegemony are so strong because it both includes and goes beyond the concepts of culture and ideology. It goes beyond *culture,* which Williams had defined as a "whole social process" (p. 108), because it takes into consideration the recognition of dominance and subordination within a society while still seeing that society as a complex integration of social, political, and cultural forces. Williams also feels that the term *hegemony* goes beyond the idea of ideology, as not only a conscious system of beliefs and ideas, to include the whole lived experience, which is organized by specific values and meanings. Hegemony then is not just the conscious and articulate formal meanings, beliefs, and values that a dominant class propagates, but it also includes other, more personal aspects of life. In the case of patriarchal power and dominance, notions of masculine superiority permeate all levels of consciousness. According to Williams (1977):

> Hegemony is then not only the articulate upper level of ideology, nor are its forms of control only those ordinarily seen as "manipulation" or "indoctrination." It is a whole body of practices and expectations, over the whole of living: our senses and assignments of energy, our shaping perceptions of ourselves and our world. It is a lived system of meanings and values—constitutive and constituting—which as they are experienced as practices appear as reciprocally confirming. It thus constitutes a sense of reality for most people in the society, a sense of absolute because experienced, reality beyond which it is very difficult for most members of the society to move, in most areas of their lives. (p. 110)

It is this sense of reality, buoyed by the notion of common sense, that causes people not to question unequal power relationships. Hegemony thus means that we consent to our own subordination. In other words, hegemony naturalizes ruling class, or in this case patriarchal, ideology and makes it seem like common sense.

In this way, power does not have to be maintained by force because the very ways that we make sense of ourselves appear not as dominant strategies but as natural parts of human nature. Oppositional strategies appear not only as unofficial but are, indeed, impossible to imagine, represented as nonsense or as incapable of being represented (O'Sullivan, Hartley, Saunders, & Fiske, 1983). Hegemony, however, can never be total.

According to Williams (1977), "No mode of production and therefore no dominant social order and therefore no dominant outline ever in reality includes or exhausts all human practice, human energy, and human intention" (p. 125). Hence there are always residual and emergent cultural elements that challenge the dominant sphere. Residual values and meanings represent "areas of human experience, aspiration, and achievement which the dominant culture neglects, undervalues, opposes, represses or even cannot recognize" (p. 124) but that are actually earlier social formations or cultural phases. Emergent culture is a new, radically different aspect of the cultural process. The emergence of a new class, or of the feminist movement, is an example of what Williams would call "emergent culture." Thus, although hegemony is very powerful, there are always alternative politics or counterhegemonic consciousnesses struggling for recognition and thus for economic and political power. These may in various ways be mobilized in opposition to hegemonic culture. This is the basis for the notion that hegemony is leaky. It is this leaky hegemony that allows a cultural form that appears to reinforce dominant conceptualizations of women to create gaps to which actual women relate. It is not that the women are necessarily succumbing to dominant expectations, but dominant expectations may change in order to hold viewers. It is hard for many analysts and critics to accept that women and other subordinated groups do, in fact, get pleasure out of the very things that dominant culture designs to give them pleasure. People can, for example, enjoy soap operas or *telenovelas* even though they may be ideologically consistent with dominant values. But, at the same time, they may take up these pleasures and use them to critique these same values.

Gender and Class

Because early cultural studies was concerned with class and not with gender, how does the concept of hegemony relate to present-day feminist concerns? To explore this question, we need to look at how class might be conceptualized. Traditional Marxist concepts of class see it in terms of economic relations; that is, class is determined by a person's relationship to the means of production. The owning class profits from the labor of the working class. The middle class helps the owning class exploit the working class. These economic relationships have been viewed as having the status of objective conditions while all other relationships are contingent; that is to say that class supersedes every other relationship whether it be race, gender, nationality, age, or sexual preference, for example. In this view, all relationships follow from essential class positions.

Working from the assumption that retaining the notion of class, even if complex, is important for the understanding of relations of power, John Frow (1993) suggests that class be conceptualized as a process, rather than a given, and that it be based on political and ideological considerations as well as economic ones. According to Frow (1993):

> If class formation is based on struggle in three dimensions, then interests are constituted by and within (and—crucially—between) the economic, the political, and the symbolic institutions of this formation. It is a question of the discursive *representation* of interests, of calculation and hypothesis. There is no class essence and there are no unified class actors, founded in the objectivity of a social interest; there are, however, processes of class formation, without absolute origin or *telos*, with definite discursive conditions, and played out through particular institutional forms and balances of power, through calculations and miscalculations, through desires, and fears, and fantasies. (p. 254)

From this formation of class, it is possible to see gender, race, and ethnicity as more than an "add-on" or an afterthought. These aspects may actually structure the relations of production. For example, within the production process, gender structures the division of labor by indicating what counts as skill and what doesn't and then assigning the valued skills to men (Game & Pringle, 1983). Gender also organizes different positions within kinship systems, such as whose blood line is considered in terms of inheriting positions of status or who is the decision maker in a family. Gender also supports the distinction between public and private, such as the consideration of the public world as masculine and the private as feminine, and organizes separate hierarchies for men and women in which, for example, men become managers and doctors while women become secretaries, sales women, or nurses and where aggression is good in a man and bad in a woman (Frow, 1993). Thus gender can be seen as a critical element in a primarily class-based analysis. However, the decision to analyze an aspect of women's lives in terms of class relationships, what Frow would call a class-gender system, is determined by the primary focus of the analysis. The centrality of class to social analysis, then, is an explanatory convenience. Class can just as easily become a subsystem under the primary systems of gender, race, or age. Thus social systems are dealt with from multiple centers or no center, according to Frow (1993, p. 253). Class, however, is itself a power relationship, and it has always included gender.

Class needs to be defined in terms of culture and meaning because power is never fixed but is continually renegotiated.

It is not just class that determines women's inequality with men. Within class boundaries in all classes, women's position is still subordinate to that of the men in their class, but it is manifested in different ways. Within racial boundaries, class and gender may mean something different than they do for other races or subcultures. The first women's movement in the late 1900s, like the women's movement of the 1970s, was largely a middle-class movement. Its goals were votes for women; the right of women to own property, which affected their ability to function in the world without being married; and the right to an education. The second women's movement pushed for equal pay for equal work and access to high-paying jobs, women's control over their bodies, freedom from role expectations, and access to the professions, that is, the lifting of quotas on women in medical, dental, and law schools and equal access for women to graduate schools. During the 1980s, the women's movement was thought by many people to have been dormant; however, many women were busy taking advantage of the increased educational opportunities and work advances that only became possible after the 1970s. The struggles encountered in this long journey are evident in the 1990s, when we see the inclusion of multicultural and environmental issues.

In this study I attempt to reconceptualize gender and class in order to broaden the concept of politics to define a political culture or a political popular culture. I am appropriating the concept of hegemony from its original class definition in order to look at how pleasure, and in particular pleasure in women's discourse, can shape a kind of gender hegemony. In other words, the notion of hegemony is incomplete if it doesn't include gender in its conceptualization of struggles over power. The dominant or hegemonic position for women is one in which the dominant both is masculine and fits the assumptions of capitalism. The mediation between these two is particularly acute when it comes to shaping a woman's genre like soap opera. Even though the genre is created for women, it is assumed to be keeping women in their place, in this case, hypothetically in the home for middle-class women, where they can be better consumers.

The first try at this, the selling drama that sold products overtly within the context of the fictional drama on radio (discussed in Chapter 3) failed because people didn't "tune in." The audience refused this level of exploitation. The second try, which was less about buying products and more about people's relationships, succeeded. It seems clear that hegemonic notions have to be couched in a form that people care about, for whatever reasons. Just as one of the classic dilemmas of Marxism is what happens when a class is not interested in what are assumed to be its "real" interests. In any hegemonic power relationship the first step in winning a group to the dominant position is to do it in such a way that the group is interested enough to pay attention: To be persuaded, women actually have to want to watch.

This does not mean that, once people do attend to a cultural phenomenon, its meanings are obvious and consciously received by those who participate; but even in the overdetermined, overlapping context of postmodern cultural involvements, it is necessary for a cultural product to hit a responsive chord. Hence the process of hegemonic struggle is messy, contains overlapping ideologies, and is contradictory and never pure. In the case of soap opera, although it was designed to cultivate women as consumers for their households, it also gives us something to like. It plays into our cultural fantasies and fears. It sells but it also gives us something we may not be getting in legitimate culture. Soap opera and its complex mediation with its audiences is a quintessential example of the hegemonic process.

To say that women's places in society are determined by discourse means that what a woman, or anyone, is able to do or say at any given point in history is determined by what she and others in the culture are able to conceptualize, both what language will enable us to verbalize and what common sense tells us is possible, what seems natural. Hegemony works in capitalistic cultures, for example, to make it seem natural to enjoy shopping, to use credit, to own things as a statement of status, to spend money to counteract depression, to look and dress in ways that require money to maintain one's appearance. Individualistic lifestyles require separate domiciles where each person or family group owns their own household appliances, furniture, and lawn maintenance equipment. One of the ways we do this is in families. The maintenance of this system often supports gender role differences while it encourages us to consume. Such role differences—economic, political, and ideological—form hegemonic positions for men, women, and children based on different expectations depending on which gender role one is perceived to occupy. Men are sometimes forced into the role of drone, devoting their lives to the world of work while women and children, particularly female children, are sometimes molded into psychologically, emotionally, and economically dependent people. These notions can permeate almost everything we experience so that we come to think of them as natural. Even when we intellectually know they are not desirable or in our self-interest, our affective or emotional responses are often so ingrained that we can't tell the difference. So here we find ourselves once again struggling with hegemony. The struggle is just that, however, a struggle. One social movement that has made this an easier task for women has been the women's movement of the 1970s. Out of this movement has emerged several points of view on the nature and origins of women's oppression.

Theories of Women's Inequality

Feminist social theorists and media analysts have classified approaches to feminism into four perspectives on women's inequality (H. Eisenstein, 1983; Kaplan, 1987; Steeves, 1987; van Zoonen, 1991). To understand the possible positions that feminist research may speak from, let us look at this range of positions from which feminist research and theory has evolved. These are radical feminism, Marxist feminism, liberal feminism, and dual-systems theory.

Although this volume is written from what has been called a dual-system feminist perspective, I would like to explain each of the four groups so that the reader will understand the differences within the feminist movement because, after all, not all feminists are the same. This analysis is necessarily simplified. Radical feminists introduced the slogan "the personal is political" in the early part of the women's movement of the 1970s, which is generally termed the second women's movement, the first being the suffragist movement of the late nineteenth and early twentieth centuries. Radical feminism analyzes gender inequality from the perspective that women as a group are dominated by men as a group, and it is men who benefit from this patriarchal system. Patriarchy here is not seen as deriving from any other system of social inequality. This branch of feminist thought has introduced a range of concerns to the analysis of social inequality, which had not been a part of earlier analytic perspectives, such as the politics of housework, who dominates whom in conversations, and particularly violence against women. Radical feminists differ in theoretical perspective, but the basis of male supremacy is often seen as involving the appropriation of women's sexuality and bodies. This can involve male violence against women, compulsory heterosexuality, and/or the construction of sexual practice around male notions of desire (Daly, 1978; Dworkin, 1987). Radical feminists have been accused of biological reductionism as well as failing to take into account divisions between women like those of ethnicity and class (Walby, 1990).

Marxist feminists consider gender inequality to derive from capitalism. Male domination over women is seen as an outgrowth of capitalism's domination of labor. The site of women's oppression is often seen as the family because of capital's need for women's domestic labor to provide the day-to-day care of workers and to produce the next generation of workers. However, Marxist feminists also argue that discourses of masculinity and femininity are too complex to be tied directly to the economic relationships within capitalism. Sex-based division of labor within the home as it is functional to capitalism, women's exploitation and alienation in the workplace where women fill the lowest slots in the economic hierarchy, the nature of housework as it relates to the labor market, women's status as wage laborers while they continue in unpaid domestic labor at home are all issues that Marxist (sometimes called socialist) feminist theorists have considered (Donovan, 1992; Z. Eisenstein, 1981). Feminist political economists who are interested in media have looked at actors as laborers (Clark, 1989), women as workers (Willis, 1990), or class and popular culture (Roman, 1988). Critics of this approach argue that gender dynamics are not simply reducible to capitalism (Walby, 1990).

Liberal feminism looks at the denial of women's rights in areas like education and employment but does not offer an analysis of women's oppression in relation to any overarching social structure. Rather, it concentrates on numerous independent deprivations and assumes that legal remedies within existing governmental systems will suffice to grant women equal rights and opportunities. Liberal feminists have succeeded in obtaining the right to vote for women in many countries and have formed organizations to influence governmental decisions in favor of stronger laws guaranteeing women's rights. The liberal feminist approach in media studies and otherwise has generated useful empirical studies on gender inequities but has been criticized for its lack of theory concerning the origins and social structure of gender inequity. Because liberal feminism is the most public manifestation of feminism, often dealing with legislative issues, one might assume that it is the most political branch of the women's movement. From my perspective, the opposite is true. Because liberal feminism deals with public issues, those that can be verbalized and publicly debated, it often leaves out the important step of changing consciousness so essential to social change. Similarly, a purely Marxist position that suggests that class is the only valid basis for political analysis limits the way we can conceptualize cultural politics.

On the other hand, dual-systems theory synthesizes Marxist and radical feminist approaches. It holds that both capitalism and patriarchy are important in the structuring of gender relations. Some dual-systems theorists consider the two systems to be so closely related that they virtually become one. Thus change in one part of such a capitalist-patriarchal system produces change in other parts of the system. For example, political changes that benefit women have come about because of contradictions and pressures raised when more women entered the workplace. Other proponents see the two systems as distinct entities. In either case, dual-systems feminist theory presents women's oppression as related to the use of power and ideological influence that supports male privilege and that also benefits capitalism in its exploitation of women's labor in both the marketplace and the home. As Zillah Eisenstein (1981) suggests, there is a basic contradiction in capitalistic countries like the United States and Australia between the ideology of equality and the inequality of its citizenry under capitalism because, in order to establish economic equality by paying equal wages, for example, the system would undermine itself by accepting lower profits. Sylvia Walby (1990) suggests that a synthesis is possible between the more personal aspects of gender analysis supported by radical feminists and the more systems-based theories of Marxist feminists. She suggests that a synthesis of the analysis of gender inequities should include housework, sexuality, waged work, violence, the state, and culture. The present volume uses the perspective of dual-systems analysis to investigate an important cultural commodity for many women: the soap opera and the genre's position and use as it relates to the other aspects of gender inequality suggested by Walby. Although I do not attempt to generalize to all women, the vectors of the social discourses involved, mediated by class, ethnic, and time differences, relate to many women.

   Walby (1990) suggests that patriarchy has moved from a private or home-centered variety in the late nineteenth century to a public form of patriarchy in the late twentieth century largely due to the first women's movement, which freed women from their dependency on marriage for their very existence by making both divorce and entry into the workforce possible. Women also gained the right to an education, which opened the doors to the professions. These gains, according to Walby (1990), moved the site of gendered inequality out of the private and into the public sphere. Contradictions for women have become more public and less obvious. Soap operas, concentrating as they often do on the home and women's private lives and a private view of public issues, are a particularly revealing narrative site of some of the contradictions involved. Hence it is necessary within feminist theory to look at the domestic context as a site of complex cultural negotiation.

Individual women sometimes watch for cracks in the system or windows of opportunity where they can resist dominant conditioning. These points of struggle hinge on their relationship to both public and private worlds. None of us can live only in the public or only in the private and, for women, our existence in the context of relationships with other people is particularly important. It is in this private world that the concepts emphasized by radical feminists related to the way people treat each other on a personal level gain importance. These are areas that cannot be ignored by feminists, yet institutional structure, the ownership of the means of production, and systems of political influence based on economic power are areas of equal concern. By keeping both of these major social influences in mind, women and other oppressed people are able to survive, sometimes with some autonomy. But one is always aware that the window of opportunity may close, that one's fate is never completely of one's own making; hence oppressed groups always push at the boundaries, always watch to see what is possible. This is one of the areas in which soap operas and their discursive networks function as a source of strength for women. They help women test the waters to see how far they can go in challenging social norms.

Gendered Audience Theory

It has not been possible to study television audiences from the perspective of hegemonic struggle until the field of audience analysis in communication studies opened the window a crack. By excluding nondominant perspectives from the field or devaluing such work, the very ways we think and the ways knowledge is constructed are naturalized in terms of hegemonic values. Conceptualizing a position of power for soap opera audiences effectively deconstructs more hegemonically acceptable ways of looking at audiences, as masses, for instance. Seeing soap opera audiences as thinking and rational people debunks the possibility of stereotyping any audience, particularly audiences composed of subordinated groups. However, in recent years more diverse perspectives on audience analysis have emerged. Audience theory has begun to advance the idea that meaning construction on the part of television audiences is itself a social process (Jordan & Brunt, 1988), moving from the position that texts construct defined spaces into which audience members are supposed to fit, to a more fluid notion of the audience as capable of many kinds of interaction with a text. This brings us to the insight that interaction does not stop with the moment of consumption of the text. Rather, a primary site of meaning construction has been posited as residing in the tertiary text. The term *tertiary text* has been used by Fiske (1987) to denote the conversations that people engage in about their television watching and the letters that people write about their shows. He also includes the conversations that ethnographic researchers record. In this study I have tried to narrow this broad range of activities to a smaller selection, which I call the spoken text. The important point about spoken or tertiary texts is that it is here that much of the meaning construction generated by television takes place. Here people talk about their lived experience in relation to what they have seen and heard on television. This book explores many of the facets of soap opera discourse networks, or gossip networks, by looking at the social context of women's talk and by considering how soap opera, as a genre of television and radio programs, developed around a preexisting women's culture.

The bases for this investigation have come both from cultural studies and from the feminist movement and its assessment of the relationship of power structures to research paradigms. Although recent feminist analysis of cultural studies separates cultural studies from feminist research and theory (Franklin, Lury, & Stacey, 1992; Lont, 1993), this approach ignores feminist work that has been taking place within cultural studies (e.g., Brown, 1990a; Hobson, 1990; McRobbie, 1992; Press, 1991), much of it ethnographic work on women's television genres like soap operas. Ethnographic research looks at an issue from the inside: It attempts an insider's point of view even though it is also tempered by the perspective of the researcher herself. Feminist ethnographic research in cultural studies uses a series of techniques developed originally by anthropologists and also used by sociologists of the Chicago School in the United States and their theoretical descendants (Agar, 1980; Spradley & McCurdy, 1988). In addition, reader response and reader reception theory and research are often seen as separate from cultural studies and feminism while, in truth, much of this emerging body of work centers on the reception of media and popular culture by women and other subordinated groups. Some reader reception work uses ethnographic methodology,[1] while much feminist work in cultural studies does the same.

From a cultural studies perspective, the media experience is seen by the researcher as a part of the lived experience of the audience; their whole cultural pattern, the socioeconomic context, and, above all, the political context in the broad sense of the term *politics* are seen not just in terms of the formal political institutions of voting, parties, and governments but also in the sense of the relative power to make decisions about one's future or the expression of one's own identity as a member of a less powerful group in our society. Of course the issue of who speaks for whom is always a factor in ethnographic research. Once an interview, for example, is transcribed, it becomes, to some extent, the voice of the ethnographer. Despite this issue, many feminist researchers prefer this method because it does not claim to generate truth or knowledge but claims to give salient insights into a research problem, and it seems to allow for a less hierarchical, more personal research environment.

The theorization of gendered audiences in the contemporary postmodern research environment has also come under attack recently because it often takes white, middle-class First World women (and presumably men) as a norm. In addition, the idea of gendered viewing seems to smack of biological essentialism. Gendered viewing, however, needs to be conceptualized in terms of certain specific cultural, social, and historical notions of what appropriately is viewed, enjoyed, and valued as masculine or feminine viewing practices and other practices of daily life and sensemaking. In other words, masculine viewing practices and feminine viewing practices are just that—viewing practices (see also Ang & Hermes, 1991, p. 312). They are not in any way a product of one's biological or essential position in the world.

Gender roles are commonly thought of as the learned behavior that goes with inherited biological classification, but gender role characteristics of one sex can be displayed by people of either sex. Sandra Harding (1986) defines *gender* "as an analytic category within which humans think about and organize their social activity, rather than as a natural consequence of sex-difference, or even as a social variable assigned to individual people in different ways from culture to culture" (p. 17). Gender is framed by existing power relations and is produced by discursive struggle. According to Harding (1986): "In virtually all cultures, whatever is thought of as manly is more highly valued than whatever is thought of as womanly" (p. 18). Of course the simple delineations of *masculine* and *feminine* are also somewhat inappropriate because they imply masculinity as centered and femininity as marginal (see de Lauretis, 1987). For the present, however, most writers continue to use the terms because they still have currency in our culture and historical moment.

Theorists and critics (Deleuze & Guattari, 1977; Grossberg, 1988; Radway, 1988) have also conceptualized the reading or viewing process and people's involvement with the text as the product of multiple layers of various discourses. This notion of what has been called the nomadic subject or the traveling subject posits that a reader does not interpret from a position that is clearly defined and stable. Rather, this subject (or person) changes over time and according to the multiple influences with which she or he comes in contact. Up to this point, feminist critics have used stable categories of gender; that is, they have studied the category of woman as if that category were unproblematic. However, there have been changes in the way the audience members have been conceived of by the critics, according to Charlotte Brunsdon (1993). She has looked at soap opera criticism since the 1970s, when soap operas began to be revalued by feminists critics working in the cultural studies tradition. Liberal and some Marxist critics meanwhile often continued to look at soap opera as simply and successfully perpetuating dominant ideology. Brunsdon has developed a method of looking at feminist culturalist criticism and research concerning soap opera audiences in which she differentiates critical responses based on the critic's relationship to women as social subjects. Her concern is how the critic conceptualizes the feminine audience within the boundaries of this body of work on soap opera audiences. Her categories are (a) transparent, (b) hegemonic, and (c) fragmented.

In the first category, the "transparent" relationship between the feminist critic and other women is an easy and obvious one. The feminist critic is one among the women and there is a shared enthusiasm for the cultural object in the case of the work on female fandom. The preferred authorial pronoun in this case is *we*, in contrast to Brunsdon's second, or "hegemonic," category, where the feminist critic differentiates herself from the female audience. Although, in this second category, there is a defense of women's culture, there is also, according to Brunsdon, the notion of women as other. The preferred authorial pronoun, in this case, is *they*. The last category, which Brunsdon has labeled "fragmented," is the contemporary mode, in which the earlier two categories have become problematic, and there is no "politically correct" definition of feminism. The authorial pronoun used here is *I*. Thus this branch of feminist criticism can be seen as having evolved through the critic's identification of herself as subject, of herself as separated by critical distance, and of herself as flexible—as wandering on both sides of the boundary that separates fan from critic (see also de Lauretis, 1990). Hence the postmodern feminist critic finds herself in the position of the nomadic critic. Her position is influenced by the discourse of criticism as well as the discourses that influence her as a gendered subject. The "fragmented" or postmodern critic also crosses boundaries between the separation of herself from other women and the alliance of herself with other women. This is like the reading position that Davies (1984) suggests belongs particularly to soap opera audiences: This position is called implication, where one identifies with soap opera characters until something happens that causes the audience member to back off and take a more analytical position. Most audiences enjoy the continuing contradictions of this perspective. Contrary to hegemonically uniform positions, actual reading positions are filled with diverse and contradictory subjectivities, for both critics and audiences.

Feminine Discourse and Soap Opera

The notion of feminine discourse implies a fusion of the position occupied by the critic, who is a gendered person, and members of the audience, who are also gendered. The research described in this volume attempts to delineate the multiple discourses that may intersect to create the responses of people who participate in soap opera gossip networks. As Michel Foucault (1980) states: "Discourse is not simply that which translates struggles or systems of domination, but is the thing for which and by which there is struggle" (pp. 52-53). The concept of discourse used by Foucault suggests that, of all the things that *could* be said, only certain things are actually spoken or even conceptualized. In his view, people are constrained from saying or conceptualizing other things because of the representational, institutional, economic, social, and cultural practices that structure the way that things can be said. Women's gossip, soap operas, and the like are a constant irritant to dominant culture because the valuing of talk as activity and performance defies goal-oriented definitions of preferred cultural practices. Both gossip and soap operas are perpetually in process, and their apparent aimlessness marks them as incapable of serving a "useful" message-bearing function. Both soap operas and gossip claim for women a space and time in which there is freedom to play with dialogue—dialogue that does not necessarily advance the plot but is simply there for pleasure. All of these aspects fly in the face of dominant conventions.

Because preferred cultural practices value goal-oriented activities, soap opera and the talk following it are devalued and are constant irritants. Within the serial and open structure of the soap opera lies the possibility of feminine resistance to, and even subversion of, the dominant classical narrative form, a form that subverts women's expression by its construction and ability to define masculine ego boundaries by voicing dominant and patriarchal rules and values. The tension between dominant discourse and subordinate discourse, in this case women's discourse, is exemplified in Linda Barwick's (1985) work on women's song in performance. Barwick describes a song in which the woman's voice is negated by the masculine perspective of the narrative:

> In fact it does not matter in narrative terms whether the woman is a willing or unwilling partner in the seducer's plans. Because of the woman's inability to express herself in straightforward terms, the plot develops the same way regardless of her intentions. Although Donna Lombarda is the central figure of the narrative, her actions are redundant, her speeches expendable, and her intentions are immaterial. (p. 247)

In this passage we see how dominant discourse, through its preferred narrative conventions, can effectively silence woman's voice by its willful closure of the narrative. However, this account does not take into consideration how the discourse of the audience—that is, the talk about the song—can create another oral text that is counterhegemonic and thus involved in another level of struggle. It is this talk, this oral text, that is at issue when we look at resistance to the dominant viewpoint in soap opera.

The struggle can be seen as a struggle to resist a confluence of powerful discourses in favor of a resistive discourse. This resistive discourse comes out of the terms of contrast with dominant discourse, much of it situated around women's everyday lives as social subjects. Sometimes the struggle is centered on countering the discourses put forth by the educational establishment. At other times it is more centered on family issues. All of these, of course, are ultimately economic issues and ideological issues. Ideology, while giving us a way to interpret our lives, also attempts to legitimate structures of feeling beneficial to dominant classes, sexes, and races.

Feminine discourse relates to the way women are structured into society. It recognizes and relates to dominant discourse. However, while the discourse of the powerful seeks to construct reality for woman in ways that suit the dominant, feminine discourse constructs reality for women in terms of her perceptions of the social order in which she is subordinate. Sometimes feminine discourse is what Rowland Barthes (1972) calls "inoculated" into dominant culture, or acknowledged by dominant culture in order to be dismissed or discounted. Such inoculation may take the form of, for instance, an independent woman on television who is left unhappy at the end of the story, her independence thus co-opted (and dismissed).

Often, though, the issues brought up by such dismissals continue to float freely in women's talk (and thus are not dismissed at all). This continuing talk is what I call feminine discourse. Feminine discourse is a part of a larger discourse system. Women, for many reasons that we will look at later, hold the key that unlocks and permits entry into this discursive meaning system.

Women and Pleasure

In dominant discourse, soap operas often still are spoken of as trash. Viewers understand that the choice of soap operas as their television genre is not a socially valued act, yet they continue to watch and talk about them partly because it is a communal activity. It is something they share with other women (and sometimes men). It gives them something to talk about, and they do this in much the same way that men (and sometimes women) talk about sports. Both groups predict future behavior based on past performances of the characters that make up the team or show. They pick favorites and take pleasure in knowing as much as possible about each character. These kinds of active pleasures are in evidence around soap opera viewing.

In addition, one may experience reactive pleasures—that is, pleasures that come from an understanding that one's ideological positioning is problematic in our culture. In this case, fans get pleasure from the conversations brought up by the discomfort they feel when the contradictions of their social positions are momentarily brought to the surface by the narrative (Fiske, 1990). This is the source of much of the feminine discourse in the group discussions we shall look at.

Their position in culture as a silenced majority has created for women individually and as a group an awareness of the pleasures of talk with other women. Some of their active pleasure comes simply from the freedom women have in many all-women groups to say what they please without censure. The contrast between the freedom of women's groups and the experience of not being heard or accepted can also bring up, for some women, reactive pleasures. Likewise, the difficulties that women often have with expressing their ideas and feelings in "man-made" language can mean that there is pleasure in simply seeing and hearing other women express their feelings.

Soap opera as a genre has been successful in creating a style that fits well with women's discourses and problems. Soap operas are designed to be talked about. They create gaps (Allen, 1985) where audiences fill in and mediate with pieces from their lives. If spoken texts, or the ways fans interact with each other around television, are the real sources of meaning, one can see that, although many people may watch soap operas at home alone, the solitary viewing experience is not the end of their involvement.

A continual point of debate about pleasure and popular culture centers on the idea that if people experience pleasure it will simply keep them happy rather than fostering unrest, which may ultimately bring about social change. That is why, in this view, Romans were given bread and circuses. Social change, however, does not always happen in the form of open rebellion but often is a product of people sharing their experiences of oppression. Often, talk of such experiences is silenced by the constraints on discourse discussed earlier. In addition, oppressed people are usually unaware that other people are oppressed in the same way. Once people can see that many others have the same problems, they can begin to deduce the structural nature of the problem.

Women, in the relationship established through gossip about the soaps, and in the affective pleasure of communal watching practices, can establish a solidarity among themselves that may operate as a threat to dominant ideological systems. This is because gossip, as well as the soap opera itself, defies boundaries having to do with what can be said and how it can be said. Like gossip, soap operas are open ended, and such openness challenges the cultural dominance of systems that close off, limit, and contain meaning for women such as language or the classical Hollywood narrative with its definitive endings.

Hence we can look at this example of soap opera audiences' talk in order to understand a notion of politics in which politics, including class struggle, has shifted to the cultural sphere. We can see that the notion of hegemony suggests that power is never fixed but is continually renegotiated on many levels at once, that our reception of media and other forms of popular culture is not passive but is mediated, often through spoken discourse. Gender alliances can be just as political as class alliances, and both are inserted into complex matrixes of identity that broaden and extend counterhegemonic possibilities.

If women's lives and women's stories are to be taken seriously, then women's genres need a serious look also. When we look at them soberly, not only can we see how difficult it is for people to shed hegemonic notions of what life is supposed to be like but also how, on the other hand, it is sometimes impossible to keep these hegemonic notions. Our ability to conceptualize notions of power, freedom, or emancipation is limited by what the culture allows. We cannot see class issues in relation to gender, race in relation to class, or culture in relation to politics because these are mediated in many cases by our own internalized oppression garnered from history and structures of feeling that we can barely discuss in academic circles. The logic of soap opera's insinuation into our cultural world by commercial interests playing off of the institutionalized and hegemonic romantic dependence expected of women is easy to see. The subsequent application of theoretical approaches to soap opera discourse networks as a political move might be less obvious.

The central question of this book is this: Why do women enjoy soap operas so much? Through this enjoyment, they create the opening that for them serves as a wedge into dominant culture. This is much more than a question about genre. By exposing an everyday, mundane, and generally devalued media form to serious scrutiny and by examining its hegemonic position in women's lives in certain parts of the Western world, I hope to connect this research to an international trend in which televised melo-drama and soap opera have begun to be examined and their serious contribution explored, not only in relation to gender-power issues but also to class-power issues (see Martin-Barbero, 1993). For many, the politics of pleasure begins at home.

Note

1. Ethnography can involve any or all of three research techniques. The first, participant observation, means that the researcher enters the group she or he is studying and becomes a part of that group or the observer may already be a member of the group. The researcher in such a situation acquires in-depth knowledge concerning the workings of the group impossible to attain from other, more impersonal means. From this vantage point, the researcher analyzes and describes what goes on within the group, organizing and developing theory from notes she or he has taken during the process of observation. A second technique relies on interviews. These are usually audiotaped and then transcribed in writing, at which point the data are sorted out and organized. In addition to categories that the researcher decided to look for ahead of time, additional codes become evident to the researcher as she or he listens to the tapes and examines the data. This is the foundation for what is called grounded theory (Glaser & Strauss, 1967)—that is, theory that evolves from the data collected rather than being superimposed on the data. After the data are coded, the actual analysis begins. The analysis involves the researcher's interpreting the data according to theoretical criteria set up at the beginning of the study. In cultural studies, one refinement of this technique has been referred to as ethnosemiotics (Fiske, 1990). In this case, the interview data are analyzed not entirely for discussion of topics but also semiotically. This means that the researcher looks at the interview as if it were itself a text and tries to determine how meanings are being

constructed within the text-data. It is this type of data analysis that is used in the present study. A third research tool often used in ethnographic research is a questionnaire. The questionnaire is useful for gathering data about the participants themselves in a form that can be easily compared in one of the following ways: across groups within the study, with groups from previous studies, or concerning specific issues. In the present study, the questionnaire (see the Appendix) was used to enhance our knowledge about the groups involved in the study rather than to make direct comparisons.

2

Saying the Unsayable

Unequal distribution of power works to suppress conflict. Ideas of what is normal make it appear that both dominant and subordinate groups share the same interests and experiences. Open recognition of inequality, conflict, or contradiction tends to threaten the status quo and with it all of the naturalized beliefs, values, and power relations underlying economic, social, and cultural stability. In a world conceptualized as having limited material and economic assets, only some can have power while others must remain in subordinate positions. Power relationships are determined by recognizable differences from or "otherness" to the most powerful group. These differences are often sex, race, sexual preference, class, ethnic, age, or appearance based. The most powerful group, given access as it is to the construction of vehicles of social control, but particularly the construction of knowledge, meanings, and language, is privileged to conceptualize "proper" thought, beliefs, and behavior for the culture. In this chapter I would like to explore further how women, here considered one of many subordinated groups in Western society, use feminine discourse to counteract their construction in dominant society as subordinate, invisible, irrelevant, and compliant.

Subordination

Let us look at some of the basic issues surrounding subordination and explain how women's oral culture offers a place where women's identities are confirmed even though their position in society is one of subordination.

The place of a subordinate group is precarious, according to Jean Baker Miller (1976):

> A subordinate group has to concentrate on basic survival. Accordingly, direct, honest reaction to destructive treatment is avoided. Open, self-initiated action in its own self-interest must also be avoided. Such actions can, and

still do, literally result in death for some subordinate groups. In our own society, a woman's direct action can result in a combination of economic hardship, social ostracism, and psychological isolation—and even the diagnosis of a personality disorder. (p. 10)

Thus subordinate groups resort to disguised and indirect ways of acting that are designed to accommodate the dominant group. These groups know more about dominant groups than the dominant group knows about them because a large part of their life is spent accommodating those in power. Subordinate groups do, of course, act on their own behalf, depending on the social climate for such actions, but Miller points out that such actions are often not reported at all by the press or are reported inaccurately, and quite often mainstream history books omit the presence of both actions and groups. Thus, even though subordinate groups may have acted on their own behalf, many of these actions are not preserved as history. Hence it is difficult for these groups to reference their own history, and members of such groups are thus denied some ways of understanding themselves. It is difficult for them to get feedback from their own or a similar point of view, what Miller (1976, p. 10) has called "consensual validation." In addition, public expertise about such a group is often constructed by the dominant group, which, typically, is not attuned to and has never actually understood the subordinate's point of view. Women's history, Black history, British working-class history, Native American history, and Australian aboriginal history offer examples of lost histories that require the revision of mainstream histories in order to include whole segments of the population whose past is lost to Western literate society.

This situation is compounded by the fact that languages, ways of speaking, the things that are considered of importance and worth knowing, are also put together from a dominant perspective. Feminist scholars, on the other hand, have been attempting to take apart naturalized assumptions about knowledge, research, and gender and to deal with aspects of the construction of race, class, age, ethnicity, and sexual difference in culture and society. In the process, many aspects of how women construct their identities and view their lives have been of particular concern. One area of concern, which has been previously mentioned, has been the relationship between patriarchy and capitalism. There are many situations where the relationship between the two brings up contradictions that are difficult to resolve, but it is particularly evident in the daily lives of women within the family. The position of these women is constructed by discourse within capitalism and patriarchy and is thus lived with by many women.

Women who, for one reason or another, live outside of the dominant model of family in Western societies are often still influenced by their position as outsiders in relation to that constructed notion of the family.

Women's Work

Recent feminist scholarship concerning the relationship of patriarchy and capitalism to the family includes the notion of the family as a location for struggle. Heidi Hartmann (1987) argues that the family "remains a primary arena where men exercise their patriarchal power over women's labor" (p. 117). In a capitalist system where products that people need to survive are produced outside of individual households, people who have no resources of their own must offer their labor power to capitalist enterprises. With their wages, people buy what they need for survival. Within the home, these commodities are transformed into usable resources. Food is cooked and made into meals. Clothes are made, worn, washed, ironed, and worn again. Someone performs the labor for these enterprises within the home. The division of labor by gender makes women responsible for this household labor and production (p. 114).

It appears also that it is in the state's interest to deal with families rather than kinship groups. One theory of the state's interest in promoting the family headed by male wage earners cited by Hartmann (1987) is that the state needs to undermine prior political units based on kinship. Whereas in prestate systems it is kinship groups such as tribes or clans who make fundamental political and economic decisions, state systems need to consolidate power under an authoritarian head. Kinship systems often delegate power to the group, and women sometimes share in that power. Such systems are often matrilineal, with mothers and mothers' brothers being responsible for the welfare of children.

The issue of women's place in the kinship and economic structure is not confined to women who work only within the home. Women who labor outside the home tend to be exploited both in the labor market as workers and also within the home. Women rather than men, for example, according to Arlie Hochschild (1989), are more likely to perform most of the domestic chores even though married and working outside the home. Official statistics like the U.S. census or Labor Bureau employment reports, however, ignore women's domestic labor within the home. Michele Mattelart (1986) analyzes the value of this labor:

Everywhere, in developed and developing countries alike, women form the mainstay of the *support economy* which makes it possible for all the other activities to be carried on. A woman at home performs a fundamental role in any economy: she services the labor force each day. This economic activity, carried on by most layers of the female population, is of great importance; but the indicators by which the socioeconomic position of each country is defined, and its development measured, conceal the economic value of housework. (p. 7)

Not only is the value of housework not measured or reimbursed, but, according to Arlene Daniels (1987), there is also a lack of validation not only for work within the family but also in traditional women's occupations and the volunteer work women do. All of this points to the disturbing conclusion that, whenever an activity is performed predominantly by women, that activity is devalued.

One position within feminist cultural studies holds that there is an uneven valuing of public and private issues within Marxist criticism that Leslie Roman (1988) calls "productivist logic," which Roman describes as

a logic which treats the domination of women by men as either secondary to or a consequence of the exploitation of workers (usually presumed male) in the sphere of commodity production and waged work. . . . Such a logic holds that the labor women perform in the family, such as childbearing, parenting, domestic maintenance, consumption, and the emotional servicing of family members—the so-called "reproductive sphere"—is separable from directly exploitative economic exchange relations and, hence, is outside the sphere of "production." (pp. 143-144)

Although the issue of the invisibility of women's unpaid labor is stressed in this instance, it does not make less important the exploitation of women in the workplace. The issue of the control of women's labor both inside and outside the family is central to feminist political economy. Although power struggles within the family have been a major emphasis in feminist critiques of capitalism, economic and historic pressures affect women in their roles in the public workplace as well as their personal lives, which for many women includes a family.

The nuclear family and its role, while having been the subject of severe critiques within the women's movement of the 1970s, can possibly be seen as a source of economic survival for women in the 1980s and 1990s in nonsocialist countries like the United States. According to Judith Stacey

(1987), feminism's critique of the effects of female domesticity on women, especially in classes that could afford an economically dependent housewife, was as infantilizing, stultifying, and exploitative. Even though the institutions of domesticity and its male beneficiaries were the targets of this critique, it also provided ideological support for the rise of families headed by a single mother caused by the soaring divorce rates. In 1987, according to Stacey, fewer than 10% of U.S. families consisted of a male breadwinner, a female housewife, and dependent children. At the same time, because of the need for a second income caused by a changing economic structure, marriage has become a major axis of stratification. The married female as wage earner can lift a working-class or middle-class family into affluence, just as loss or lack of access to a second income can force women and their children into poverty.

During the recessionary climate of the 1970s and 1980s, major changes have also taken place in the structure of women's work. According to Joan Smith (1987), it is during times of severe economic disruption that women's household activities are revealed as "central and necessary to the economy and historically situated" (p. 417). For example, while in the recession of the 1930s there was a decline in consumer demand, in the recession of the 1970s and 1980s, there was no such decline (U.S. Bureau of Census, 1984, p. 448, in Smith, 1987, p. 417) until the 1990s. Obviously, economic declines in different time periods are subject to different pressures. Smith attributes the continued consumer activity during the 1970s and 1980s to three factors: (a) the wage income of working wives, (b) increases in consumer credit, and (c) an expanded welfare system. Each of these, according to Smith (1987), "required a substantial rearrangement in women's typical taken-for-granted, most often invisible, household activities" (p. 420). Although women's work within the household made a clear contribution to the family in the earlier depression, in the depressed 1980s the nature of this contribution changed.

In the 1930s women in the home contributed to a family's economic stabilization by doing in the home things that the family could no longer afford to have done (e.g., washing clothes by hand rather than sending them out, or home canning); by the 1970s and 1980s laundry, for example, was usually done in the home with the help of an automatic washing machine bought by each individual householder who was able to purchase one because of expanded consumer credit. Further, according to Smith, between 1971 and 1981, families supported by Aid to Families with Dependent Children increased by 50% (U.S. Congress, House, 1985, pp. 343-357, as cited in Smith, 1987, p. 421). The relationship of women's work to the family and consumption is crucial in either the scenario where women work only inside the home or where women do two jobs—one inside and one outside the home. As Smith (1987) puts it: "Primary economic activities are absolutely dependent upon that which is defined ideologically, and treated politically, as merely incidental to the 'real' economy and totally outside the bounds of what is politically acceptable" (p. 421).

In the 1990s, then, individual women are often not completely isolated within their homes but exist as part of the paid work force as well as being unpaid workers within the home. Susan Willis (1990) comments:

> This means that whatever notions of alterity that previously informed the bourgeois family and home as separate from production are now collapsed as the home, office, and highway merge into every woman's production/reproduction circuit. Then, too, because most women are brought into production as part-time or service workers, their wage labor is as devalued as their domestic labor was (and is) invisible. (p. 12)

Economic structures in society change the nature of women's work, but certain ideological underpinnings continue to have currency. The illusion is that women and women's work are of little consequence. This makes it seem natural that working women's salaries or wages, for example, average 75 cents to the working man's dollar (NPR, 1991). Women make significant economic contributions to society whether they work outside of the home or not; however, the hegemonic or mainstream discourse about women and work considers women's work peripheral. Thus it is not surprising that other aspects of women's lives are considered just as peripheral and are just as devalued.

The Ideology of Romance and Dependency

In the Western "conjugal" family, the belief is that people marry for love as well as for economic support. Hence the notion of romance is an important construct within the ideology of dependence, which involves both economic and emotional dependence for girls and women. Both aspects work together to attempt to position women and girls growing into womanhood within the patriarchal family as it is discursively constructed. Although there are class, race, and ethnic differences, the elements of the dominant model of the Western "conjugal" family (Scanzoni, 1986) conceptualized here are as follows:

1. The male head of the household, the father, is the sole economic provider.
2. The female head of the household, the mother, is the homemaker, and is responsible for domestic care and the socialization of the children. She is a helpmate to the husband, providing support for him in his struggle for the family's survival.
3. The children are helpless and dependent, vulnerable and malleable. They must be nurtured full-time by the mother (or mother-surrogate) only, as emotional stability is essential.
4. The family is a private institution and within it individuals can fulfill their most important needs. This fulfillment is based on the foundation of the economic income provided by the husband (where necessary, supplemented by the state). Only then will economic and material needs for love, esteem, self-expression, and fulfillment emerge within the family.
5. Healthy families produce healthy individuals, who adjust to social roles. (p. 349)

As women make sense of themselves within a broad cultural framework like the one outlined above, they are confronted with the ideological framework that supports such a family structure and that stresses romance and economic dependence. Although the ideological constructs that determine women's conflicts with these role expectations are present throughout a girl's life, they become particularly apparent during adolescence. As Carol Gilligan, Norma Lyons, and Trudy Hanmer (1990) point out, young girls in the United States frequently know more at 11 than they do at 16, at least in the upper middle class. Gilligan and her colleagues note that there is a crisis of knowledge in early adolescence in which many young women come to realize that what they value, primarily relationships, is at odds with what the dominant culture values, individuality.

Theorists and researchers in cultural studies have been similarly interested in how specific ideologies within a continuum dealing with romance and dependence are constructed and used by teenage girls. For example, Sandra Taylor (1987) has examined three sets of discourses that research on cultures of femininity have pointed to. These are the domesticity/paid work conflicts concerning girls' futures; sexuality, or the "politics of reputation" (what Cowie and Lees [1981] call the "slags" or "drags" conflict) and maturity issues, or the conflicting expectations for girls of their being rebellious and independent (like the boys) while they are also expected to be proper young ladies. The latter belief leads to confusion, according to Barbara Hudson (1984), to the extent that they sometimes feel that whatever they do is wrong. This is a good example of the double bind in which both adult and young women find themselves in the face of dominant constructions of "reality."

The first pattern that Taylor mentions is the conflict between filling an economic role and filling a role within the family. The maintenance of this first contradiction, which is built into the definition of the family given earlier, is important to the reproduction of gender relations in society. It perpetuates the notion of public and private spheres and places women and girls in the private sphere where domestic relations are expected to be their major concern. Here they can also remain economically dependent.

The second discursive strategy, one discussed by Taylor, which functions to keep girls within the constraints of their expected future marital role, is the labeling of young women as either bad or good, "slags" or "drags." These terms can be seen in several ways, "as friendly joking; as bitchy abuse; as a threat or as a label" (Cowie & Lees, 1981). They can also be seen to slide among the actual behaviors that merit particular labels. In any case, the discourse about the binary opposition between good and bad is powerful for women. It relates directly to a young women's marriageability, the assumption being that for teenage girls a future without marriage and the family situation described earlier is not only not desirable but also hardly conceivable.

The third set of Taylor's discourses has to do with age and maturity and is closely related to the second. The mature young woman does not cause trouble, is not a problem. She is silent as well as chaste. This, along with the other two, serves as a powerful force to regulate sexuality and put pressures on teenage girls to get and keep a boyfriend, an act that models family behavior and protects her "good" name. All three discourses feed into what Wendy Holloway (1984) has called the "to have and to hold" discourse that associates acceptable behavior with monogamous relationships. Together these form an ideology of romance. These three discourses can also embody the threat of sexual pollution. The politics of reputation, the need for proper (i.e., nonthreatening and nonsexual) behavior, and the discourse of domesticity (and thus financial dependence and controlled sexuality) ideologically can leave young women few options. Such discourse is important in the construction of a feminine subject in this culture.

Conversely, the ideology of romance can also be seen as a rational response to material and economic subordination (Cornell, Davis, McIntosh, & Root, 1981). When one's sources of power are limited, the ideology of romance can be particularly compelling both because it is socially rewarded and because there is sometimes little economic choice for women. Such romantic ideology positions young women is such a way that they can easily decide to buy into the system. As Michele Mattelart (1982) points out, as long ago as 1917, Alexandra Kollontai questioned the "innocence" of romantic love stories in terms of class political issues. Mattelart (1982) herself refers to "the order of the heart" (p. 140) as the order that organizes romantic discourses. According to Mattelart (1982):

> It invalidates any form of struggle against social inequalities (the existence of which is admitted) by means of this diffuse explanation: only love can cross class barriers. Not only is the solution individual—never collective—it is also linked to the miracle of love. Love comes to be a universal explanation which can resolve social contradictions through denying them. (p. 140)

The "miracle of love" of which Mattelart speaks is borne out in the *Harlequin Romance Editorial Guidelines* (1991). The guidelines tell authors who write for the Harlequin series the parameters of the current romantic formulas. Their business is the perpetuation of the romantic notions that sell their products. The guidelines state: "The plot should not be too grounded in harsh realities—Romance readers want to be uplifted, not depressed—but at the same time should make the reader feel that such a love is possible, if not probable" (p. 2). Specific guidelines for the Harlequin Presents series are similar. They emphasize "the shattering power of . . . love to change lives, to develop character, to transform perception" (p. 2). The Harlequin Temptation series, Harlequin's hottest series, "exemplifies the female experience of love, blending the decisions women must face in life with the questions only her heart can answer" (p. 2). These emotional strategies are at work in cultural texts dealing with the ideology of dependence. But women don't necessarily simply absorb these cultural texts and act accordingly; instead, many women talk about them. Consequently, we need to take a look at the context and parameters of women's talk.

Gossip and Women's Narratives

Gossip among women has been devalued in much the same way that other cultural forms valued by women are critiqued. Deborah Jones (1980) defines gossip in the context of women's oral culture as

> a way of talking between women in their roles as women, intimate in style, personal and domestic in topic and setting, a female cultural event which springs from and perpetuates the restrictions of the female role, but also gives the comfort of validation. (p. 194)

The form of gossip includes reciprocity and paralinguistic or nonverbal responses—the raised eyebrow, the sigh, the silence—forms that assume and articulate the shared experience of repression. The implications of such conversations, according to Jones, are contemplated, not argued, and each participant contributes her own experience to the pattern of conversation. Phyllis Chesler (1972) describes women's conversations similarly: "Their theme, method and goal are nonverbal and/or nonverbalized. Facial expressions, pauses, sighs and seemingly unrelated (or nonabstract) responses to statements are crucial to such dialogue" (p. 268).

Jones lists four functions of gossip—house-talk, scandal, bitching, and chatting. House-talk is basically women's talk about housework, husband, and children—training in the female role. Scandal involves judgment about domestic morality over which women, according to Jones, have been appointed guardians. Scandal reinforces moral codes that women enforce but have not created. Scandal, however, also serves a second function. It caters to women's interest in each other's lives. It provides a "cultural medium which reflects female reality, and a connection between the lives of women who have otherwise been isolated from each other" (Jones, 1980, p. 197). Likewise, Jones maintains, it has an entertainment value, "perhaps a kind of vicarious enjoyment of a range of experience beyond the small sphere to which the individual woman is restricted" (p. 197). Bitching, the third function of gossip, is an overt expression of women's anger at their restricted role and inferior social status. Consciousness-raising in the women's movement is a political form of bitching. Chatting, the fourth function, is mutual self-disclosure. It implies a trusting relationship between the participants and is nurturing. According to Sue Brower (1990):

Gossip promotes moral consensus, seeks to generate group esteem for the one imparting guarded information, and places the object of gossip in the dual position of ordinariness (identified with the group because they are discussing him or her) and specialness (possessing unique characteristics worth discussing). (p. 228)

Gossip appears to have specific functions in women's culture. It validates women's socially recognized area of expertise (the home). It points out contradictions in institutionally expected social behavior as opposed to actual social behavior. It provides entertainment in the form of storytelling. It provokes a sense of intimacy. According to Patricia Spacks (1985), gossip blurs "the boundaries between the personal and the widely known, it implicitly challenges the separation of realms ('home' as opposed to what lies outside it). . . . Gossip interprets public facts in private terms" (p. 262). In Spacks's opinion: "*Gossip will not be suppressed.* It thrives in secret, it speaks what needs to be said" (p. 263, italics in original). Brower, Jones, and Spacks all underline the importance of gossip for women and hint that it conveys information contrary to ideas validated in dominant or hegemonic culture. Such talk, it seems, produces, circulates, and validates feminine meanings and pleasures.

Narrative logic in gossip sometimes hinges on intensity. The uninteresting parts are simply left out in order to talk about the parts of the story that interest the audience. Susan Kalcik (1975) describes a type of story she encountered in women's rap groups, which she calls the kernel story. When she consulted the folklore literature, she discovered that this type of story was not officially classified as a story by folklore experts. She also notes the folk belief that women do not tell jokes or stories correctly, that they tell the punch line or the most important part first rather than last. This was the same way in which the stories she noticed in women's rap groups were told. Here is her description of the kernel story:

> Most often a kernel story is a brief reference to the subject, the central action, or an important piece of dialogue from a longer story. In this form one might say it is a kind of potential story, especially if the details are not known to the audience. It might be clearer to call this brief reference the kernel and what develops from it the kernel story, keeping in mind, however, that many of these kernels do not develop beyond the first stage into kernel stories. Kernel stories lack a specific length, structure, climax, or point, although a woman familiar with the genre or subject may predict fairly accurately where a particular story will go. The story developed from the kernel can take on a different size and shape depending on the context in which it is told. . . . Kernel stories may be developed by adding exposition and detail or by adding nonnarrative elements such as a rationale for telling the story; an apology; an analysis of the characters, events, or theme; or an emotional response to the story. A story also can be developed by stringing several kernels together to produce an elaborate story or a unit longer than a story, such as a serial. (p. 7)

When Kalcik notes that the discrepancy between what counts as a story and what counts as the proper way to tell one means that "women cannot tell stories and that what women do tell are not *real* stories" (p. 7, italics added), she points up the idea that official knowledge or public knowledge and women's knowledge sometimes are different from each other. But, as we have seen, the issue goes further than differences in what is considered valuable. Sometimes what women or other subordinated groups need to say is not sayable because there is not an existing paradigm or category or appropriate words in which to organize that speech in dominant knowledge structures, research structures, or language itself.

The Unspoken and the Power of Talk

The title of Susan Kalcik's article is "Like Ann's Gynecologist or the Time I Was Almost Raped . . .," which refers not to some overarching category with a consistent meaning to anyone within a culture but to shared oral experiences that have a rich meaning within the group of women in question. Even women not in the circle touched on by Kalcik's group, however, can come to some understanding about what is being discussed. Their similar positions in society as subordinated people make such a reference clear to many women. Such positions in society can be manifested in both language and the contexts of women's conversations.

Scholars (Spender, 1985; Thorne, Kramarae, & Henley, 1983) have pointed out that language often has no meaning equivalents for women (master, for example), that the supposed generic "he" is still in use, or that syntax, vocabulary, and diction often make language spoken by women "other" to the dominant form. Moreover, in certain contexts, women's speech is simply not taken seriously. In groups including men and women, women's comments are often ignored, women are interrupted more often than men, and women's ideas are often attributed to others (DeVault, 1990). Similarly, in *Man Made Language,* Dale Spender (1985) argues that women are a "muted" group, that women's speech is often limited both institutionally and individually by their lack of power and social control.

Other feminist scholars (DeVault, 1990; hooks, 1981) have pointed out that understanding "woman talk" is not guaranteed by gender alone. Different blends of power and oppression that come from class, race, or ethnic differences can leave women in different positions from which to learn to hear and speak different variations and versions of "woman talk" (DeVault, 1990; Riessman, 1987), but talk between women often traverses differences in age, race, class, or nationality in favor of a common ground. When women talk over class, race, or ethnic boundaries about their lives and interests with an awareness of their mutual oppression, then talk is mutually validating and therefore often pleasurable and potentially empowering. Because of the general societal devaluing of women's talk, a situation in which their talk is validated can produce confidence and the potential ability to speak again. In contrast, analyses of conversations between men and women are often conducted in ways not satisfactory to the women involved. Within the family, conversation between husband and wife has been analyzed in terms of who does the work in such speech acts. Pamela M. Fishman (1978) maintains that it is in the everyday conversations between partners that "much of the sustaining reality of the world goes on" (p. 398). Her analysis of interaction between couples indicates that there can be an unequal distribution of work and power within conversations between women and men within a family. Women ask more questions, apparently because it is possible that they won't be talked to if they don't ask questions. They use attention-getting strategies in attempts to get a conversation started; but in Fishman's study, more often than not, the women are not able to establish continuing conversation. In her study the only sustained conversations that took place were those introduced by the men and responded to by the women (which these women always did), and the conversations continued until the men decide not to participate.

Furthermore, her study points out why talk with men in the context of the home is often not pleasurable for women. Rather, it can often be classified as another form of women's work. Fishman (1978) concludes:

> Besides the problems women have generating interactions, they are almost always available to do the conversational work required by men and necessary for interactions. Appearances may differ by the case: sometimes women are required to sit and "be a good listener" because they are not otherwise needed. At other times, women are required to fill silences and keep conversation moving, to talk a lot. (p. 405)

Fishman postulates that women who do this interactional work do so to maintain their gender identity, and the notion that *work* is being done is obscured by the fact that this work is seen as a part of who women *are* rather than what they do. This study and others relating to conversational interactions between men and women (West & Zimmerman, 1983) point to other reasons that women's conversations with other women can be very pleasurable.

Although conversations with men can define the interaction and the reality constructed by the conversation in ways that cause women to be misunderstood and devalued (Oliker, 1989), conversations with women frequently not only give women a place and a time to speak, but they can also define their reality differently than men's reality. This reality is constructed from a women's point of view and takes women's concerns seriously. However, because the very language we speak structures power relations, it is necessary to understand that we have no categories for some of the things that many women do and sometimes no specific language to define women's concerns.

Marjorie DeVault (1990) has suggested that women can listen for the "translations" in other women's speech or the places where women's experience doesn't fit the language. At these places there are usually hesitations. DeVault calls this listening "as a woman" wherein women listen from their own experience, which helps them to understand things that are incompletely said. DeVault attempts to analyze the disjunctures that create these "translations." She is referring specifically to her research on women's work in preparing food for their families and to the way that, in feminist research, women can interview other women with an ear to understanding what is actually being said despite patriarchal language and language practices. However, we can extend her observations to other times when women talk to each other. Part of the pleasure that women experience in talking with each other is, for the listener, the pleasure of filling in these gaps and, for the speaker, being heard and understood. Women are often highly skilled listeners as are members of other subordinate groups.

Spender (1985) suggests that dominant groups who control the production of knowledge are more interested in expressing their views than listening to the views of others; hence nondominant groups like women have developed the more sophisticated listening skills. According to DeVault (1990), these skills involve listening for the unarticulated experience. In her view, the unsayable gets "translated" or said in a way that is "close enough," or becomes words that don't quite fit, which, by necessity, gives them more complex meanings. Other times, saying the unsayable involves saying part of what one has experienced and then searching for words indicating the inadequacy of the language to fit the situation. In the context of a similar women's experience, however, these statements make "perfect sense." To use an example from DeVault's interviews concerning the way that meals are served, the interviewee explains:

And the service is important. You know how the table is set and so forth. We probably, again when I was growing up we never had paper napkins except when my dad was out of town. We do now have paper napkins, although we have cloth napkins and I like it. What I would like—maybe I will but probably not—but at one point where we lived we had cloth napkins and everybody had their own napkin ring, and that way you didn't have to keep changing the napkins. (pp. 103-104)

Often the gaps will be signaled by hesitation, or the words "you know," or by an equivocal statement like "maybe I will but probably not" (DeVault, 1990, p. 104). The equivocal statements, DeVault feels, are a type of strategizing similar to planning, which, if the person talking were not being listened to by a woman, would be interpreted either as insignificant or as a sign of uncertainty. In the world of the middle-class household, women are often emotionally invested in how the daily rituals are performed. Many women have an understanding of these household rituals, so that when another woman talks to us about the meaning of small elements of a household ritual, we can identify with her position as a conductor of household rituals—events seldom talked about and little valued in public society. Thus our making sense of this account depends on our ability to identify or to be able to create meaning for ourselves rather than for this other person whom we happen to be interviewing. Our ability to identify with her is created by similar elements in our life experiences.

Feminine discourse relates to women's culture in a similar way. It enables its practitioners to insert themselves into the culture and at the same time to distance themselves from it. Within woman's culture, there is a tension between what we learn from ideologies of the family constructed in dominant discourse and what we learn from our mothers, sisters, and friends. It is sometimes the emotionally strengthening aspects of everyday family life (like the significance of the napkins we put on the table at mealtime) that make the work one does within the nuclear family meaningful. It is also the tensions between valuing our work and ourselves in a world where often neither is valued that enable women to participate in the conversations around stories and to understand the gaps in other women's conversations.

To understand the relationship of women's talk to oppression, however, subordinate groups must first recognize their submerged status. Second, the oppressive strategies used by the dominant group must be recognized and resisted, and, third, the submerged group needs to develop a discourse system out of their own experiences (Coyne, 1990). We can see that, when women deal with the irreconcilable contradictions in their lives, as evidenced by the strategies evident in women's oral discourse, they have taken the first step; they have recognized their submerged status and begun to develop a discourse out of their own experiences. To survive, subordinated groups must struggle to recognize themselves within a dominant culture's constructions of their roles and their lives. Women may do this in a number of ways:

1. They do so playfully (thereby making fun of dominant notions).
2. They do so with an intellectual militancy (thereby taking a political stand against these notions).
3. They do so by maintaining power over particular aspects of their lives (thereby refusing complete submission to dominant notions).
4. They do so by talking to other women (thereby questioning these notions).

Women's Friendship Networks

Even so, in our culture, most women are controlled in some way by the discursive constructions dealing with romance, dependence, the family, and sexuality. Representational systems also intersect significantly with these discourses. However, women negotiate their positions in society in a number of ways. One of these ways is by relating to other women in the context of oral networks. Networks based on orality seem to offer people in socially subordinated roles significant spaces in which to construct positions of identity for themselves. Informal oral networks, having no official rules, develop behavior based on consensus, and meanings developed within the group help to create subject positions for women based on their own discourse. Although women's friendship networks do not all operate in exactly the same manner, they seem to perform a similar function, providing a space for women to construct their world in their own terms.

Feminist historians have pointed out the intense bonds of friendship, love, and emotional support among women in the past. In the late eighteenth to the mid-nineteenth centuries, there existed, according to Carol Smith-Rosenberg (1975), "two cultures" resulting from the divergent upbringing of men and women in the middle class. The extent and nature of personal correspondence among these women delineates close female bonding not only in kinship networks but also in friendship networks. Such letters document discourse among women as a source of intense pleasure. The way that conventional history and ethnography have valued structures of power and government and ignored women's structures have made it difficult to confirm such a connection because so little of women's domestic culture has found its way into these writings. The dimensions of women's oral cultural networks in the past have been obscured by the emphasis in ethnographic studies on how oral traditions as texts relate to place, which is defined in terms of family and village structures. Such models of oral transmission have obscured women's connections and relationships to other women because the centering of the analysis in male-controlled property individualizes women's connections to the male-defined patriarchal family (Barwick, 1985). Women's structural problems with the system are thus seen as individual problems rather than problems with the system itself. Women's place in such a hierarchical model is indirect, defined by their relationship to the household head. The networks of women who generate and maintain women's oral culture often operate within and between households; therefore they surface in the gaps in traditional ethnographic analysis.

Social separation along gender lines is common, in one form or another, to most, if not all, European-based cultures. For example, in nineteenth-century Italy, the coming together of sisters, daughters-in-law, aunts, mothers, grandmothers, nieces, godmothers, and friends was commonplace to perform such women's work as sewing or weaving, and usually women from a number of neighboring communities would be represented in such a gathering because the women, upon marriage, would move to the homes of their husbands. The performance of songs, the telling of tales, the arrangement of marriages, discussion of health problems, kinship gossip, and work-related hints might all form part of women's talk on such occasions. Yet in terms of the hierarchical model of the family as a component of the village, and ultimately of the state, this confluence of women is hardly recognized. Even folklorists studying the variation of European ballads, surely known to both men and women, had recourse to the figure of the male traveling singer as the main source of innovation and change in the tradition. So it is not surprising that the peripherality of the concerns expressed in women's talk to the public issues of power, war, and commerce led to the characterization of women's culture as trivial and idle, if not actually evil in its distraction of thought from higher things (Barwick, 1985).

Like folk culture, women's oral culture is practiced informally outside of established institutions and is recognized, though differently characterized, by both insiders (women themselves) and outsiders (men, dominant institutions). Television viewing practices involving gossip among women, when conceptualized as part of women's oral culture, are not just individual or in-home experiences or only a part of women's discourse; they are also part of a preexisting social organization or social infrastructure of exchange offering an alternative construction of reality.

Thus we see that women, as a subordinated group, have responded to dominant constructions of their place in society; but many have also developed their own way of talking to each other, their own way of acknowledging and understanding the contradictions of their position in society. The way that, in some cases, women can accept their socialization while at the same time rejecting it is an example of how hegemony can be seen as leaky. Even though there are barriers within language, social situations, and even the construction of knowledge, women are still often able to communicate. Let us look again at R. F. Coyne's (1990) theory of the development of a resistive voice. It is clear that women speaking feminine discourse recognize their oppression and develop a discourse system out of their own experience. Whether the oppressive strategies used by the dominant group are recognized and resisted is still open to question. We shall return to this question; but first let us give our attention to the way that soap opera as a genre developed specifically to cultivate women, conceived of as socially and economically isolated in their homes, as consumers, not only for themselves but for their families as well.

3

Soap Opera and Hegemony

In tracing the development of soap opera in the 1930s, we can get a clearer idea of how hegemony can operate in terms of the development of a new genre of radio programming. To begin with, the people who own and run the networks, and thus have the power to create and air new forms of drama, sought to incorporate elements of women's culture, as they conceived it, into the new daytime dramas. Then as women in their suburban homes, at whom the soap operas were aimed, listened to the radio while they did their housework, they recognized some of their own identity in this product created by the media power brokers. Hegemony theory explains the formation of dominant culture by a shifting coalition of elites who make use of complex cultural elements to maintain a power base. The coalition first incorporates elements of a subordinated culture into a form of popular culture. The subordinated group then recognizes some of their identity in the very culture that exploits them, and it is the recognition of their own identity that draws the subordinates to use and experience pleasure from dominant mass culture. Theoretically, through this means, subordinate groups are said to participate in their own exploitation. In this chapter I would like to explain how this complex process may have taken place in the particular instance of the development of soap operas and, subsequently, suggest that modern soap opera audiences may begin to take up these very elements and put them to their own use.

The following elements would be operative in a media hegemony formation and are relevant to the establishment of a new media genre—all existing simultaneously. A new genre would need to attract a particular type of audience and build the loyalties of this audience. To do this, the new genre would first need to articulate the interests and aspirations of this audience; it would need to understand the context in which the media would be used by its audience; and it would need to respect the constantly changing conditions of this audience. For example, at a certain point, women's programming would need to bring in the "liberated woman" because the audience demands this. Also a new genre would be trying to sell the products that have justified the broadcasting industry in the first place. In addition to a commercial product, it would need to "sell" a national culture and an ideological system as well. Even though a new genre may incorporate resistive discourse, it must ultimately respect the broader cultural demands of dominant discourse. For example, contemporary women's daytime soap opera may incorporate feminine discourse by dealing with issues relevant to an aware audience such as rape or violence against women. However, if it ever came to *really* threatening many aspects of patriarchy or capitalism, like by concluding that the problem is systemic, the dominant system would win out and individual solutions would be sought to individual problems. In addition, a new genre must respect the overall limits of the medium and the demands of the production process. In the case of television soap operas, the production could be created cheaply because no other competition incorporated women's perspectives and was as accessible, cost as little, did not take the woman out of her home and away from her housework, and yet could be later shared with her friends. Ideally, if a new genre can make use of a genre tradition that is already popular with the audience in question, like women's magazines, it has a higher probability of success.

In the United States after World War I, housing patterns had begun to change. In 1919, when World War I ended, living and working conditions in the cities were so bad that 4 million people were on strike. At the same time, white, male veterans were returning from the war to find that blacks and women had taken over their jobs. Unions, which had concentrated their organizing efforts on skilled male workers, were demanding what they referred to as a "family wage" (Hayden, 1984, p. 33), which meant that wives and children would not have to work because a male "breadwinner" would earn enough to support the others in his household. Industrialists also saw workers' families as a source of consumption for manufactured goods. Hence both unions and employers agreed that the model of the Victorian patriarchal suburban house should be reproduced as a dwelling for white, male, skilled workers. It wasn't, however, until after World War II that this strategy became a reality (Hayden, 1984).

What this meant for women was pressure to get out of the wartime labor force in order to give (white male) veterans jobs. The domestic setup, into which soap opera was designed to fit, was intended to foster "a conservative point of view in the working man" (Hayden, 1984, p. 33). The structure of the living spaces for families into physically and communally isolated spaces meant that women within the home were similarly isolated.

The home became a mini-patriarchal model. As Dolores Hayden (1984) puts it:

> As men were to become homeowners responsible for regular mortgage payments, their wives were to become home managers taking care of the spouse and children. The male worker would return from his day in the factory to a private domestic world. In his house, he would find a retreat from the tense world of work, and his physical and emotional maintenance would be the duty of his wife. (pp. 33-34)

Single women were left with few avenues of economic support in this scheme. These historical changes, as well as the development of the advertising industry in the 1920s, contributed to the emphasis on consumption, and consumption centered on the home.[1]

In the case of soap opera, the starting point was the desire of broadcasters in the United States (Europeans, with their noncommercial broadcasting, rejected the idea totally) to reach women in the home during the otherwise "dead" hours when there was no other programming. However, there were two problems: What material would attract housewives and who would be a likely commercial sponsor? Because soap opera programming was not originally considered valuable, its origins are obscure. Hence there is much speculation as to the beginnings of the genre, its sources, and its early programs (MacDonald, 1979).

Soap Opera's Probable Origins and Development

The idea for content and material may have come from women's magazines. Soap operas are very much like magazines. Magazines come at regularly scheduled times and create anticipation. They can punctuate the week or month and create a feeling of security by their repetitiousness and continuity. Magazines often contain continuing serials and those that do not have features that continue from week to week or month to month. Readers can look to the features and stories in magazines for possible situations and emotional dilemmas that they may face at one time or another. Magazines are also peppered with advertisements spread liberally among the features and stories. In addition, some women's and girls' magazines (as well as some newspapers) contain a "problem page," sometimes derisively called "advice to the lovelorn." Angela McRobbie (1991) describes this type of feature:

It recognizes the conflicts and torments which are part of the human condition. It is, of course, a primarily feminine form since it is not only women's lot to suffer personal unhappiness in a particularly acute form; it is also their duty to alleviate the unhappiness of other people. Caring and nurturing and attending to the "affects" are still women's work. (p. 158)

Problems are seen as part of women's lot. The position of women in society in relation to role expectations means that women must constantly negotiate their cultural position. As Janet Winship (1987) suggests, attention is not drawn on problem pages to the fact that many of the problems brought up are the result of the structural subordination of women and girls; rather, they are seen as individual issues brought about by personal shortcomings. American daytime soap operas use the technique of problem solving as a structuring device. The constant repetition of problems on soap operas is one of the genre's more salient characteristics.

Earlier newspaper use of the serial form has also been suggested as a source of soap opera style and form. In the nineteenth century, serial novels appeared in newspapers as well as magazines and were distributed separately in small volumes in many countries. Prominent writers wrote for this genre. In France, Eugene Sue wrote *feuilletons,* or novels published in newspapers, and, in Britain, Charles Dickens published his early works as serialized novels. *The Pickwick Papers,* published in 1836, seems to have had a cult following with the characters developing into a sort of "communal property" (Frey-Vor, 1990) similar to the way soap opera and television characters do in a contemporary setting. Morin (1962, in Martin-Barbero, 1993) considers the *feuilletons* to have mediated between the bourgeois novel and the fantasy literature of popular culture. *Feuilletons*, while remaining novels, followed the conditions of production of the press. It was fiction, according to Morin, written in the discourse of information. In other words, the culture industry produced products in which "the extraordinary and enigmatic events of daily life play a central role and an imaginative fiction in which realism predominates" (Martin-Barbero, 1993, p. 55). This tension between melodrama and dominant narrative structures is very much like the position of fictional soap opera in relation to many hegemonic narrative forms (Jordan, 1981). Realism—that is, the dominant narrative construction of reality in written fiction, television, and film—is considered more authentic than the melodramatic view of life.

Latin American *telenovelas* still follow the novel form, and thus end at some point. They are written by prominent authors, as were the nineteenth-century *feuilleton* (France) and *folletin* (Spain). The Anglo-American soap opera's literary heritage is often attributed to another type of serialized fiction, the nineteenth-century American domestic novel by such authors as Mary Jane Holmes or Augusta Evans Wilson (Stedman, 1981). The domestic novel centered on women's lives in their homes and featured, among other things, problems and suffering. Another lively, early nineteenth-century serialized form in the United States was the story paper, some of which, like *The Hidden Hand* by E. D. E. N. Southworth, featured heroines who captured pirates and rescued other women in distress. According to one source, female bonding was among the most popular themes in women's fiction between 1820 and 1865 in the United States (Baym, 1993). Yet another influence suggested by another author is exemplified in a 1912 issue of *Ladies World* with a picture of a young woman on the cover of the magazine and the caption: "One hundred dollars if you can tell what happened to Mary" (Kissane, 1988).

Serialized stories and features in women's magazines probably provided the model for the first soap opera along with the problem pages in the same magazines. The problem page has a particular type of appeal in that problems for women are often secrets. To be privy to another person's problems is to be in a very intimate relationship with that person. Just as gossip implies intimacy, so does the revealing of problems. Voyeuristic pleasure has to do with looking when the person looked at is not aware of the voyeur's presence. Contrary to that perspective, the revealing of problems implies that the teller willfully allows the listener to know her secrets, which infers an intimacy based on trust. However, like the problem page, whose editors choose the problems to be presented, thereby keeping them from being too controversial, the sponsors or producers of soap operas exercised a great deal of control over the content of the problems brought up.

In addition, soap operas apparently did at one point stand out as undisguised soap advertisement. A 1923 Ivory campaign to sell soap used a comic strip format featuring the Jolly family, whose lives and interests revolved around soap. When Proctor & Gamble studies indicated that a broadcasting campaign using a similar family narrative would also be successful, Irna Phillips, often thought of as the mother of the genre (Nochimson, 1992), was hired to create a serial called *Painted Dreams* featuring a family called the Suddses. The daily 15-minute show had a brief run in 1930 (Allen, 1985). It and its successor, *Today's Children,* also written by Phillips, were what were known as "selling dramas"; that is, the sales pitch was written into the drama itself. Frank and Ann Hummert took the serial narrative in a different direction by writing stories about "how women feel" (Nochimson, 1992, p. 14) in their soap operas *The Romance of Helen Trent; Mary Noble, Backstage Wife;* and *Our Gal Sunday.* By 1936 Irna Phillips had begun to use the same approach in her new serial drama *The Guiding Light* (LaGuardia, 1983). At this point, the soap opera can be said to have become entrenched in the American broadcast world. As Mattelart (1986) puts it:

"Soap opera," the radio (and subsequently television) version of the "lonely hearts" press, was born. . . . At the same time, a whole *household* definition of broadcast literature reveals itself plainly, making unambiguously clear a twofold function: to promote the sale of household products and to subsume the housewife in her role by offering her romantic gratification. (p. 5, italics in original)

Radio had begun to develop a relationship with its female audiences, a relationship that was apparently intended to be a dependent one. Mattelart quotes a Radio Luxembourg (now Radio-Television Luxembourg) executive who explains European radio's relationship to women as consumers, a relationship that developed in Europe only after World War II: "Women's attitude toward radio is significant: what they fundamentally want is somebody there. . . . RL will therefore fill this space and accompany our listener with its voice, in her home, *in her everyday life*" (p. 7, italics in original). As this quotation indicates, the function of soap operas was fitted to the needs of the capitalist economy in which it was necessary for women to remain in the home and devote themselves to the "collective restoration of labor energy" (LaGuardia & Dumoulin, in Mattelart, 1986, p. 8). Women became the cement of class society by virtue of their gradual isolation from the world of production in the monogamous family with its links to the system of private property.

By the 1930s the radio networks had developed a system wherein they sold transmission time, rather than programming, to sponsors who hired advertising agencies to produce the serials surrounding their commercials. Thus an advertiser like Proctor & Gamble would sponsor an entire show rather than buy commercials within an already produced program. In 1939, for example, Proctor & Gamble was the sponsor of 22 serials (Buckman, 1984). The name "soap opera" (as well as "washboard weepers" and "sudsers") was originally developed to describe this radio production phenomenon (MacDonald, 1979). With sponsors actually producing the serial, they obviously also controlled the content of the program.

Although the practice is rarer today in American soap operas, Proctor & Gamble still sponsors several daytime television soap operas in the United States. Soap opera as a genre, then, grew up in radio, in response to the perceived isolation of women in the home and the subsequent attempt to colonize these women as consumers of domestic products.

In 1940 there were 64 radio soap operas broadcast in the United States each weekday (Cantor & Pingree, 1983). Radio soap operas were usually 15 minutes long and often featured a matriarch (in *Ma Perkins*) who gave advice about problems to other characters on the show. Additional favorite anchoring personages were the woman alone or the independent woman (in *Helen Trent*) and the woman who married into a strange or hostile environment or was a Gothic heroine (*Our Gal Sunday*). The first character type, the matriarch acting as surrogate mother, grandmother, or godmother, often gave advice on the best laundry detergent to use while she was counseling other characters on personal problems. The early radio soap opera combined the confessional form with the giving of advice, a device that fits well into the commercial sponsor's needs because both "problem" and "solution" are articulated. As mentioned earlier, the device also related the newly developed soap opera to an existing women's genre, the magazine problem page.

As soap operas evolved into television productions in the 1950s, the idea that one could reach an audience for longer periods of time for the advertisement of household products was strengthened and the programs stretched. By 1973 most television soap operas in the United States had adopted an hour-long format. With the hour format, multiple plots and large numbers of characters (around 40 per show) became the norm. This increase in characters meant more convoluted plots and more characters for fans to talk about. As increasing numbers of women joined the workforce, the female characters on the soaps changed with them. Women characters began to hold high-status jobs like surgeon, psychiatrist, research scientist, or business woman. In the early 1980s, when *General Hospital* added younger characters and more adventurous plot variations to attract a teenage audience of both sexes, the other daytime soap operas followed suit in response to the possibility of attracting younger audiences and therefore new consumers (Passalacqua, 1991). Coeducational dormitories on U.S. university campuses gave many young men access to some aspects of women's culture, like soap operas, thereby increasing male viewership. The 1970s women's movement also made it more acceptable for men to participate openly in women's culture.

American daytime soap operas have proved extremely profitable for broadcasters. Soap operas are inexpensive to produce because they are usually shot in broadcast studios, mostly in the sequence in which they are to be shown, thereby avoiding costly location shooting and extensive editing. In addition, the production practice wherein the main writers outline an episode in detail, making sure that it meets with the sponsor's approval, and then farm out the writing of the actual words the characters say to dialogists, decreases scripting expense. Some of the major writers or inventors of a particular soap opera like Frank and Ann Hummert or Irna Phillips in this way kept control of the serial and also of the rights to each serial. This also explains why a few writers could produce large numbers of soap operas all airing at the same time. Throughout their development, soap operas have attracted large audiences, an estimated 80 million in 1991 (Passalacqua, 1991).

The characteristics of American daytime soap opera audiences have changed in the late 1980s and 1990s. According to Mediamark Research of New York City (in Waldrop & Crispell, 1988, p. 30), 30% of the audience is now male; 45% is young (18 to 34 years old), as compared with less than 40% of the American population; and 44% of the female viewers work full or part time. The market for publications about soap operas is said to be 40 million. *Soap Opera Digest,* published since 1975, was joined by *Soap Opera Update* and *Daytime Confidential* in 1988; "Soap Opera Highlights," which updates fans on the plots of all 12 U.S. soap operas, is published in almost 100 newspapers. "Soap Talk," a 900 number where fans can get hints about upcoming episodes, claims to have received half a million calls in its first week (Waldrop & Crispell, 1988). Additionally, computer hot lines are abuzz with soap opera speculation. Viewers are clearly involved with the stories and characters. In the 1970s, when *Days of Our Lives* featured an interracial marriage, 90% of the letters registered disapproval, so the relationship ended. In 1988, when *General Hospital* featured an intimate portrayal of the same topic, only 65% of the mail was negative and the marriage took place (Waldrop & Crispell, 1988). All of this would lead one to believe that soap operas are neither so conservative nor out of touch with political reality as popular discourse would have us think. However, soap opera advertisers continue to direct much of their advertising toward stereotypical housewives.

According to Lauren Rabinovitz (1990), soap operas have also changed in response to shrinking daytime profits. In 1988, she points out, profits from daytime advertising on soap operas were about equal with prime-time profits, whereas in earlier years soap operas made more money than prime-time television. Although the numbers of network viewers in general have decreased because of competition from cable television, working daytime viewers often watch outside of the home or use videocassette recorders to view their programs at a later time, which makes accounting for this audience by current methods of measurement difficult. Because of concerns produced by lower profits, according to Rabinovitz, the narrative structure of American soap operas has undergone changes. Soap operas are now designed to peak during sweeps weeks that occur four times a year. They often do this by staging a wedding or other spectacle or by speeding plots up and offering dramatic plot resolutions during sweeps weeks. Sometimes these plot resolutions forsake the multiple plot format that soap operas as a genre are known for.

Despite changes over time in both soap operas and soap opera audiences, a lingering image of the soap opera fan remains. She is still conceptualized as "other," inferior to more prestigious audiences (themselves constructions), morally questionable, and an enthusiastic consumer of the laundry detergents, dish-washing liquids, bath soaps, sanitary napkins, douches, hair-coloring agents, denture cleansers, and bladder-control products advertised on daytime television (Waldrop & Crispell, 1988).

Soap Opera Characteristics

Even though there are variations in the genre, the term *soap opera* denotes in general a continuous program with open-ended episodes, set in the present, and containing a number of alternating story lines. The continuous serial or soap opera differs from series drama on television both in its narrative structure and in the psychological relationship of the viewers to the program. In general, daytime soap operas are notable for

    a. the centrality of female characters;
    b. the characterization of female characters as powerful, often in the world outside the home;
    c. multiple characters and plots as well as multiple points of view;
    d. the portrayal of many of the male characters as "sensitive" men;
    e. emphasis on problem solving, and intimate conversation in which dialogue carries the weight of the plot;
    f. plots that hinge on relationships between people, particularly family and romantic relationships;
    g. the home, or some other place that functions as a home (often a hospital), as the setting for the show;

h. concerns of nondominant groups being taken seriously;
i. use of time that parallels actual time and implies that the action continues to take place whether we watch it or not;
j. serial form that resists narrative closure (never-endingness);
k. abrupt segmentation between parts without cause-and-effect relationships between segments.

Each of these characteristics can be used to illustrate the hegemonic process working to incorporate cultural constructions of women into the program itself and thereby construct the genre as a feminine one.

The Centrality of Female Characters

The fact that female characters are central to the genre seems an obvious hegemonic move given that women are assumed to identify with female characters. Even though television itself is sometimes characterized as a feminine form of cultural production, a close look at the programming offered on nighttime television through the 1950s, 1960s, 1970s, and 1980s has convinced some writers that television merely caters to dominant conceptions of what should be there (Nightingale, 1990; Tuchman, Daniels, & Benet, 1978). Gaye Tuchman and her colleagues (1978) have gone so far as to call the treatment of women's issues on television "symbolic annihilation."

Content analysis studies (Lichter, Lichter, & Rothman, 1986; Tedesco, 1974) of prime-time television have given us evidence that female characters are outnumbered by males, that women are usually younger than men, more likely to be minor characters, more likely to be the victims of violent crimes, and more likely to be married and to hold less powerful positions than men. Hence soap operas, which not only show many women in multiple roles but also take their concerns seriously, have, by doing only these two things, made themselves more accessible to women's culture than prime-time television. It is difficult to generalize about characters on nighttime television, however, because there have been times and places where nighttime television has portrayed female characters in ways that relate to feminine discourse (Byars, 1988; Press, 1991).

The Characterization of Female Characters as Powerful

Andrea Press (1991), in looking at female characters on prime-time television, points out that prefeminist women characters, those who appeared before the second-wave feminist movement of the early 1970s, sometimes not only showed solidarity toward other women, but appeared on programs that featured a subtext which involved resistance to the conventional role of housewife. She cites the *I Love Lucy* show, in which Lucy (Lucille Ball) continually struggles to escape her prescribed housewife role in order to enter the show business world where her husband Ricky (Desi Arnaz) works (see also Mellencamp, 1986). She is aided in her schemes by her friend Ethel (Vivian Vance), and a strong bond of solidarity is shown between them. Lucy, however, even with the help of Ethel, never achieves her aim. On the *Jackie Gleason Show,* Ralph (Jackie Gleason) and Alice (Audrey Meadows), who are constructed as a working-class couple, experience various tensions, most of which are resolved by leaving Alice in a morally superior position. Press concludes that prefeminist fiction dramas did feature active and personally courageous women.

According to Press, during the feminist era (roughly 1969 to 1975), women characters on prime-time television began to be seen in public spaces rather than only in the domestic world. Programs like *Charlie's Angels* featured women who, at one and the same time, were sex objects and independent career women. According to Ella Taylor (1989), many shows in the early 1970s like *Hill Street Blues, Alice,* and *The Mary Tyler Moore Show* featured women in "work-families"; that is, workplace associates fill in as a substitute family. The women in these shows were reasonably independent and complex and supported by their work-families. However, according to Press, television's "flirtation with feminist representations" (p. 38) was brief. In postfeminist prime-time television, Press concludes, women's success is shown in terms of isolated individual achievement rather than as members of a collective group. Press (1991) sees these images as being first anti-women's movement (see also Baehr, 1980; Tuchman et al., 1978; van Zoonen, 1988); second, offering personalized and individualized solutions to collective problems; and, third, as being packaged along with commercial femininity so that feminism itself is lost in the process.

Much of what Press sees in prime-time television has its parallel in soap opera images of women. Changes in female characters pre-, during, and postfeminism show women as having jobs, but often we never see them pursuing their work. Feminists who are identified as such in a positive way are invisible. Individual solutions to structural, collective problems are systematically repeated, character by character. The class-based issues in the workplace are seldom brought to the surface, and commercial femininity abounds, particularly in the commercials. And yet, women relate to the women on soap operas just as they do to the women on prime-time television. Women relate to the responsive chord struck when middle-class Lucy tries to escape the restricted role of housewife or when working-class Audrey proves again that she has superior wisdom. Although television may not offer an unproblematic reading to feminist women, a program may offer a reading to which women can relate due to their common subordinated position. This aspect of identification is amplified by Rowland Barthes (1972) with his theory of inoculation. According to this theory, nondominant ideas do come up in dominant media only to be restructured into dominant conceptualizations. For example, in the early seasons of the television series *Murphy Brown,* the independent and assertive Murphy (Candice Bergen) was often left lonely and alone at the end of individual episodes. As John Fiske and John Hartley (1978) point out, television attempts to "claw back" any concessions that it makes to the people in favor of the system that creates and supports it. The inoculations of resistive ideas are always, to some extent, hegemonically reclaimed.

Still, powerful women are available in soap operas: The villainess is an often used example. As Tania Modleski (1982) points out, although the villainess may be bad, it can still be pleasurable to see her at work. For good or for evil, powerful women characters do exist on soap operas. Like the novels of Barbara Taylor Bradford (admired by many of the women in the present study), featuring powerful matriarchs, soap operas provide for women a fictional position only rarely available in the mass media.

Multiple Characters, Plots, and Points of View

Soap operas feature multiple characters as well as multiple points of view, which means that problems can be approached from many angles. Unlike the problem page, whose writer selects the letters to print and constructs a single hegemonically carved answer, soap operas repeat the problem from many perspectives. Most narrative forms in our culture, particularly Hollywood films, are constructed so that an audience member will identify with a particular character, usually a hero whose feelings and insights the audience shares.

This type of identification is achieved by structuring the narrative to include one or only a few main characters. Point-of-view shots then work to show the audience what the main character sees. For example, the eyeline match shows the main character looking offscreen. The next shot shows us what that character is looking at. The shot-countershot technique uses camera shots that picture first one and then another person talking or looking at each other. This style of camera work, perfected in Hollywood films of the 1930s and 1940s, is the predominant feature of film realism in Western cultures. It uses visualization style to suture the film spectator into the text in such a way that she or he is said to identify with the main character by virtue of the fact that everything in the film is seen from the perspective of that character. A similar technique is used in literature, although it is descriptive rather than visual.

The idea of identification as a way of partially establishing a sense of self has gained such credibility that it is taught in schools as virtually the only way to relate to a text. However, there are other ways of both constructing and reading character. John Davies (1984), for example, suggests about soap opera viewers that, once "hooked," they vacillate between their need to know, or the pleasure of anticipation, and an *implication* with characters, which is more complicated than identification. In an implicatory reading, rather than identifying with one character through thick and thin, the reader recognizes many possibilities in character types—the villainess, the ingenue, the good mother—but at the same time chooses to be involved with these characters. In this reading practice, an audience member will involve her- or himself with a character but will draw back if what happens to that character becomes uncomfortable. For example, if the character becomes involved in something the reader feels is impossible to identify with, perhaps battering, the audience member simply distances her- or himself from that character. In other words, the audience is not tied to an individual character, as theoretically happens in identification. Implication, as a reading strategy, is audience controlled and is therefore active pleasure. I would also suggest another reading strategy associated with soap operas in which a reader does not just view a soap but adopts it along with all of its characters, good and bad, and then treats that soap and its characters with a familial loyalty.

The use of multiple characters seems to refuse a single or fixed subject identification; at the same time it also prevents the hierarchy of characters present when there are only a few well-rounded main characters whose discourse is given more weight than that of minor or secondary characters. Because issues are seen from each character's perspective sequentially in soap operas, there is not the same preferred point of view as seen in narratives with a single protagonist.

Multiple characters fit women's culture. Because frequently in our culture women's moral decisions are based on relationships rather than distinctions between right and wrong (Gilligan, 1982; Gilligan et al., 1990), the nature of decision making is often different for women than it is for men. The rules for dominant culture make sense for most men but not always for women; thus things are often not black and white in women's culture. Modleski (1982) considers the use of multiple characters, each of whose faces is focused on intensely by the camera, to be training in the cultural construction of motherhood in which the viewer is constantly monitoring the feelings of others rather than taking care of herself. Multiple characters, however, also emphasize the group over the individual, an idea that fits with the notion of group solidarity among women as a profeminist reading.

The way schools teach the reading of character can be seen to put the individualistic notion of identifying with a single character in opposition to narratives like soap operas, which seem to demand another kind of reading. According to Fiske (1986, 1987), the reading that sees a character as an analogue of a real person, where the viewer projects him- or herself into the point of view of that character, is a practice of the ideology of individualism. Such a reading may be considered to be the only way of understanding character, because in our society the individual is considered the primary source, or definer, of experience (Fiske, 1987, p. 17). The idea of the well-rounded character, according to Fiske, is a product of individualistic or dominant discourse, a discourse that minimizes structural issues in society concerning class, gender, race, age, or more complex distinctions. If dominant ideology centers on the individual for whom the process of identification, with its "psychologistic reading" (Fiske, 1987), is culturally rewarded, then soap operas, with their multiple characters and lack of a specific heroine or hero, stand in opposition to that view. Because the ideology of the individual considers each person responsible (or to blame) for her or his own position in society, it denies gender and class politics, which are structural in nature. Such thinking does not consider social and structural organizations as definers of meaning but considers the individual's unique, personal characteristics as the elements responsible for defining experience.

Generating multiple characters for which the relationship of the audience to character is more ambiguous than identification with a specific character fosters for women what Fiske (1986, 1987) describes as a discursive reading strategy. This strategy involves the enactment by many characters of some of the social and personal discourses available to women. For example, the fact that there are many characters enables an issue to be settled by several characters in different ways, and leaves the text open to several meaning possibilities. In addition, the multiple points of view of the many characters make it easier for audiences to talk about soap operas, and talk can serve to integrate soap operas into women's lives.

Even though the concept of identification with specific characters may not be possible with soap operas, this is not to say that audiences are not intensely involved with soaps. As Davies (1984) aptly points out: "Soap opera audiences are not passive consumers of light entertainment, but active participants in negotiating complex role models and contradictory ideologies with definite, if unconscious motivation" (p. 33).

Male Characters as "Sensitive Men"

Along with the possibility of power for the female characters, the male characters on soap operas are often "sensitive" men. The sensitive man is one who embodies many of the cultural characteristics of the social construction of women. The sensitive man is empathic and caring. He likes to talk about the same things that women do, but, above all, he listens. Soap operas are essentially about women's talk, with its emphasis on problem solving and the affirmation of being listened to. The subsequent valuing of women's words, thoughts, and ideas by both male and female characters and the availability of women and men who listen is comforting to women in a culture where the silencing of women's voices seems natural.

Problem Solving, Intimate Conversations, and Dialogue

American daytime soap operas emphasize the process of decision making showing the plethora of details and nuances in the articulation of problems that ever so slowly advance the plot lines. Action is kept to a minimum. A 1-hour episode of *Days of Our Lives,* for example, often contains 90% dialogue and 10% action. If one is reading from a dominant perspective, one could simply say that women are only interested in the trivial details of everyday life, and soap operas therefore reinforce already problematic aspects of women's lives. Another way to negotiate this reading is that soap operas value, rather than put down, the fabric of women's lives.

Relationships Between People

Relationships between people are the essence of soap opera plots. This emphasis on relationships mirrors the construct of femininity in our culture. The public world of wars, morality, rules, money, and competition are constructed as masculine, whereas family and relational matters are assigned to the culture of women. Women's talk, although it may include politics, sports, and morality, may also place major importance on the decisions one makes within relational worlds (Gilligan et al., 1990). Relationships between women are important on soap operas, but relationships between women and men receive the greatest amount of attention. Soap operas emphasize heterosexual romance. Hegemonically, the producers of soap operas, interested in attracting audiences rather than delivering paternalistic messages (see Ang, 1991), have catered to something that dominant culture would rather leave invisible—female sexuality. Soap operas are a place where female sexuality and feminine desire are portrayed from a feminine point of view rather than from the masculine perspective commonly available, particularly in mainstream films.[2]

The Home as Setting

Often the home is the setting for soap opera plots. Culturally, domestic areas are familiar settings to women. Homes can limit (Hayden, 1984) as we saw earlier, but they also comfort. Women often compare their homes with others' homes and use homes to surround themselves with familiar objects and exercise creative freedom. The home is symbolic of comfort and safety for many women. Although, for battered women and abused children, the home may represent very real danger, culturally the home is constructed as a positive place for women, a place where women's expertise is valued. The home is also the place of rituals participated in and often controlled by women. In the construction of family traditions around holidays or birthdays, for example, women are often decision makers and planners. The construction and maintenance of family traditions and small events give important meaning to everyday life in cultures of the home where domestic production is valued. Women frequently orchestrate these events and pass on particular styles of creating them to their children. The home in dominant culture is seen as the arena of feminine expertise. According to Charlotte Brunsdon (1981), discussing the now defunct British soap opera *Crossroads* (which was similar to American daytime soap operas),

The ideological problematic of soap-opera—the frame of field in which meanings are made, in which significance is constructed narratively—is that of "personal life." More particularly, personal life in its everyday realization through personal relationships. This can be understood to be constituted primarily through the representations of romances, families and attendant rituals—births, engagements, marriages, divorces and deaths. In Marxist terms, this is the sphere of the individual outside waged labor. In feminist terms, it is the sphere of women's "intimate oppression." Ideologically constructed as the feminine sphere, it is within the realm of the domestic, the personal, the private, that feminine competence is recognized. However the action of soap-opera is not restricted to familial or quasi-familial institutions but, as it were, *colonizes* the public masculine sphere, representing it from the point of view of the personal. (p. 34, italics in the original)

Brunsdon's comment reverses the common notion that women in the home are being colonized by soap operas. As she points out, although events outside the domestic are represented, that representation happens from the point of view of women.

The domestic work that women are often expected to perform is repressed in the soap opera narrative but surfaces in the ads (Flitterman, 1983). Hegemonic control over the construction of women's work cannot quite mask this contradiction. The assumption that these unromantic jobs are not pleasurable to women, hence the invisibleness of household tasks in the main narrative, is yet another hegemonic use of knowledge of women's pleasures by the producers of soap operas, but the flow of the narratives through the mininarratives of housework in the commercials provides small points of closure within the viewing experience (Flitterman, 1983) where women characters are seen to find intense pleasure in a clean floor or shiny dishes. The ambivalence of women's role expectations is left exposed here. The ads not only bring us back to the constrictions of dominant narrative form with its resolution or climax at the end of the piece, but also return women to the role of the unpaid domestic.

Similarly in the American daytime soap operas, when the characters gather for an occasion like a charity ball or a wedding, the clothes worn by the female characters are notable. The genre almost caricatures this aspect of women's lives because women are socially constructed as excessively interested in clothes and the clothes worn on daytime soap operas are certainly excessive. But fashion and style have also been places where women can exert expertise or participate in an alternative economy by constructing style through secondhand clothes (McRobbie, 1992). Weddings, on American daytime soap operas, are given the same kind of emphasis. Socially, weddings are constructed as the high point of a woman's life after which she simply "lives happily ever after." Young women and girls are hegemonically expected to dream about what their own wedding will be like, to rehearse it in play, and to plan for it well in advance. Of course, commercially, weddings are big business. Thus each soap opera wedding dress not only reflects something of the character wearing it or has some thematic significance, but it is also usually very expensive. On *Days of Our Lives,* for example, wedding dresses have cost as much as $20,000. Soap opera, with its emphasis on romance tied in with weddings, serves capitalism by helping to create an industry based on women's fantasies of status and security built around marriage, symbolized in the wedding as a consumption practice (Rabinovitz, 1990). The messages in the narrative encourage viewers to consume expensive clothes and elaborate weddings while the women in the ads encourage the consumption of household products even though the characters in the narrative don't do housework and the weddings in the narrative do not symbolize a lasting relationship.

Concerns of Nondominant Groups

Despite their emphasis on consumption, soap operas also take the concerns of nondominant groups seriously. In the case of American daytime soap operas, the concerns of not only adult women are taken seriously. British soaps do the same for working-class men and women. Australian soap operas, particularly *A Country Practice,* often take the concerns of children seriously. For example, a child's desire to have her pet with her in the hospital is given serious attention on *A Country Practice* as is sexual harassment of children by teachers. But the major concerns are women's. Issues of concern to women are also brought up in soap operas in ways that may be ambivalent at first glance. Take, for example, the issue of paternity.

The attribution of paternity on daytime soap operas has become an obsession, according to Laura Stempel Mumford (1991). Mumford maintains that, if it were possible to describe soap operas as being about one thing, that thing would be paternity. A typical paternity plot involves a female character who becomes pregnant and will not reveal or does not know who the father is. The identity of the father is eventually proven and made public, although sometimes many years after the actual birth.

Mumford (1991) sees this as a powerful position for the female character. Contrasting with the real life male-dominated family, families on soap operas confer a "very real power on women: the power to name, or to misname the father" (p. 53). She believes that the paternity plot contributes significantly to women's pleasure in watching the soaps. However, the establishment of the identity of the one true father, usually through blood tests, she feels, restates and therefore reinforces dominant ideology.

As Mumford (1991) points out, at stake in establishing paternity is more than a simple biological factor. It means the inheritance of property and name. It defines kinship patterns and is a central axis of power. Women access this power by their relationship to a particular man as mother of his child. In addition, this relationship defines a person's family position, which is often supremely important in the soap opera world and to women. Thomas Schatz (1981), in his book on Hollywood genres, points out that one of the reasons that genres exist is to provide an opportunity for the audience to play and replay issues of salient importance to them. The issue of paternity is crucial to women's well-being in an oppressive society.

Time, Serial Form, and Segmentation

Structurally, the soap opera genre uses time, segmentation, and lack of closure to give its audience a sense of continuous pleasure. Time on serial dramas seems to continue even though the audience is not present (Geraghty, 1991). The illusion one gets in watching soap operas is that each group of characters continues to interact with each other even after the cameras and microphones are off. This is one of the reasons that it is so easy to pretend that the characters are actual people. This extended sense of time, combined with the genre's ability to move relentlessly from one group of characters and setting to another, makes it possible to keep up with each set of characters just as one keeps up with one's friends. These features match the cadence of everyday life. Pleasures for women in our culture include the pleasures of friendship, the pleasures of motherhood, the pleasures of community, the pleasures of work (Gilman, 1915/1979) as well as desire, or pleasure expressed in sexual terms. Within the genre of soap opera, women can vicariously experience multiple kinds and levels of pleasure. Additionally, talking about these aspects of life adds another level of pleasure for women.

Soap Operas and Orality

It is evident that soap operas wedge themselves nicely into the type of feminine culture that is constructed to support dominant or hegemonic notions of femininity. Soap opera's connection to orality also gives it a unique connection to women's oral culture. Two characteristics of soap opera style, its serial form and its abrupt segmentation within its narrative flow, fit with women's oral narratives; and, as we shall see, this is perhaps the most important type of pleasure that women experience when watching and discussing soap operas. It is incorporated into soap operas in the form of soap opera dialogue, which, in its style, replicates many of the characteristics of the oral subcultural discourse of women.

Although primary oral cultures with no knowledge of writing probably do not exist today, secondary orality is still prevalent. Written expression derives from a literate cultural set and possesses a narrative form that embodies a literate thought process. The narrative form and conventions of the soap opera embody the characteristics of orally based thought and expression listed by Walter Ong (1982):

1. Additive rather than subordinate [one segment or idea is just as important as another];
2. Aggregative rather than analytic [each episode or segment is concrete rather than abstract];
3. Redundant or copious [situations and formulas are repeated over and over again];
4. Conservative or traditionalist in forms and values [the values represented are societally approved];
5. Close to the human life-world [the stories are about everyday life];
6. Agnostically toned [conflict is apparent];
7. Emphatic and participatory rather than objectively distanced [conflicts are seen in individual characters rather than as social issues];
8. Homeostatic [they are about people];
9. Situational rather than abstract [they are about particular rather than symbolic events]. (pp. 37-49)

For people trained in evaluation techniques appropriate to literate thinking, these characteristics of orality are unacceptable. Because feminine culture and feminine discourse are primarily oral, part of the power of feminine narratives to generate alternative meanings has to do with their structuring of a type of realism that is not characteristic of literate realistic narrative convention but speaks to a different narrative code, one based on orality.

Michael Presnell (1989) describes oral narrative structures and specifically links them to women's narratives. According to Presnell,

> Oral narrative structures follow an episodic development rather than a beginning-middle-end development . . . oral structures follow pragmatic associations rather than an abstract schema of logical development. The climax or main point of a story might be told in the middle of the story. Episodes might be connected by their relative entertainment value to a perceived changeable audience rather than by a non-contextual, causal, temporal, or formal logical sequence. The stories might return to parts of the story already told to amplify points and fill in details which become significant only later in the story. Oral discourse presents us with a collection of episodes that circle back on one another depending on the context of interpretation. (pp. 125-126)

Presnell writes that the distinction of orality and literacy as gender differences stems from "(a) women's forced illiteracy and their consequent preservation of oral traditions, (b) gender specific socialization patterns within the traditional nuclear family, and (c) the subordination of women in interpersonal encounters" (p. 126). The foregrounding of the distinction between orality and literacy seems to mark oral forms of women's culture as different than dominant hegemony, which is based on literate hierarchies and structures of thinking.

One of the most striking features of soap operas in this regard is the openness of their narrative form. In many other television and most film narratives, even when characters and some plot elements are carried on from one episode to another, the episode tends to be defined by the presentation of one major story. Whereas television and film forms based on traditional literary narratives have a beginning, middle, and end, soap operas consist of the often quoted notion of their ever-expanding middle (Modleski, 1982). Their lack of a conventional introduction is compensated for by greater narrative redundancy, that is, the presentation of the same or similar situations in a number of different scenes and the characters' frequent retelling of their own and others' histories. The recent surge of talk-based daytime programming on U.S. television also indicates people's fascination with oral discourse and people's retelling of their own life histories and circumstances. Soap opera fans are adept at the logic of oral discourse.

Thus the casual viewer of soap opera will experience an episode of a soap opera very differently than the fan. The fan's long-term knowledge of the soap opera, its characters, their histories, and its narrative conventions bring a depth of significance to the action that is not available to the novice, who needs the interpretations and explanations of the knowledgeable viewer in order to make sense of what is going on. The same is often true of orally transmitted narratives. For example, interpretation of the narrative significance of one particular version of a story will be quite different when it is informed by the knowledge of previously heard versions of the same or similar stories. Often readings made by inexperienced listeners or those from outside the culture will be considered ludicrous by insiders or, in this case, fans.

Traditional literary narratives, which of course also include their own set of cultural preconceptions, attempt to make the narrative self-explanatory within the limits of the piece. They also rely much more on psychological motivations to explain the narrative development. Thus the characters' actions stem from the sort of person they are, and part of this construction of what, in dominant culture, is called a realistic character is consistency of behavior in different situations. By contrast, soap opera characters often behave quite inconsistently, depending on their past and present relationships with other characters, and also on the actor who plays the character. In traditional oral narratives, there is no direct way of comparing present and past versions of a character within the temporal process of the plot, although the use of video recorders is changing this for soap opera viewers (Cook, Gomery, & Lichty, 1989). However, part of the talk about soap operas by knowledgeable viewers turns on comparison or awareness of such contrasts between history and the present. History, in this case, is based on memory and relies on oral repetitions to keep it alive, similar to oral storytelling.

Whereas inconsistent characterization in literary narratives is usually considered to be a fault, inconsistency in soap operas is understood to be an inescapable consequence of their process of production. Similarly, in traditional oral narratives, there is little or no attempt to explain characters' actions in psychological terms; the actions are functions of the plot, which unfolds in accordance with generally accepted, if problematic, cultural possibilities. Such an approach to narrative construction is much like Vladimir Propp's (1968) analysis of Russian fairy tales. In his analysis, Propp found that all of the tales were based on 33 narrative possibilities and 13 characters. Soap opera narratives function similarly except that the narrative possibilities are not based on the hero-centered stories of the fairy tales but on women-centered possibilities.

Many of the characteristics commonly found in both soap operas and oral traditional narratives can be related to their process of production, which in each takes place in real time. Both oral narratives and soap opera narratives require that the audience's attention be held continuously from moment to moment, in contrast to a written narrative, which can be put down and taken up again and in which the reader can back up if necessary to retrieve forgotten or skipped information. As Robert Allen, writing about the early radio soap operas in *Speaking of Soap Operas* (1985), has pointed out: "In radio . . . the listener, not the narrative, was the commodity being sold; thus, closure became an obstacle to be overcome in the attempt to establish regular, habitual listenership" (p. 138). The same avoidance of total closure applies to contemporary television soap operas in which the producers and advertisers aim to reach the widest possible audience and keep them viewing for as long as possible.

In live performance the performer adapts the song or tale depending on the audience's receptiveness and responses. Soap operas have been and continue to be comparatively responsive to the interests of viewers. For example, Robert LaGuardia (1977) reports that, in the 1970s, "if a show had slipped half a point in the ratings shares, the poor writer would be given orders to make someone pregnant to get the numbers back up" (p. 41). Annie Gilbert (1976) reports that networks keep track of fan mail to monitor the popularity of particular story lines (the story is judged most successful if the fan mail is split 50/50, but possibly changed if the reaction is mostly one way) and of particular actors, whose parts in the show might be expanded if their popularity is increasing (p. 10). Conversely, viewers might exploit this responsiveness of the producers by organizing campaigns to rescue popular characters perceived to be in danger of being killed off (Soares, 1978, p. 23). Soap opera scripts are much more dependent on viewers' reactions than are many other television narratives. It must be pointed out that this phenomenon is most widely documented in American soaps. In Australia, where there is a much greater delay in screening, and where most daytime soap operas are of overseas origin, viewers do not generally perceive themselves as powerful in this way.

The managing of multiple story lines over long periods of time is another factor that affects narrative construction. Manuela Soares (1978) reports that writers favor ambiguity in their story lines because it leaves more options for future development of the story (p. 17). Irna Phillips, in writing and producing many of the early radio and television soaps in America, maintained an ideal of live performance in her production practices. For example, she describes her reasons for dictating all her scripts:

> It allows me to play the parts of all my characters and give them dialogue that sounds like real, colloquial speech. And I avoid tape recorders. I dictate to another person to get that essential human contact, that other person's reaction to my dialogue that tells me a word or phrase doesn't sound right. (Irna Phillips, quoted in Gilbert, 1976, p. 17)

Phillips also preferred live broadcasting of her television soap operas long after the technology was available for delayed broadcast, because she believed that taping "took the excitement out of the production" (Cantor & Pingree, 1983, p. 60).

As mentioned earlier, from the early days of radio soap operas, the scripts were produced by teams of writers. The producers or advertisers had some input into the content and general principles of suitable material, the head writer would make decisions about which story lines would be developed and how, and the dialogue would be written by teams of writers. Of course, story lines also would be potentially affected by contingent factors such as actors' illnesses or departures, viewers' responses as outlined above, and even by the stage of development of similar plots in other soap operas. The version of the script that finally goes to air is therefore constrained in quite different ways than a written literary narrative. In the lack of an individual author and in the responsiveness to a particular set of external conditions governing the final shape of the narrative, then, the conditions of production of a soap opera have much in common with the formulaic processes of oral composition, in which the broad outlines of a story passed down in oral tradition are realized in performance in different ways, depending on the performance context.

So far, we have seen that many of the similarities between soap opera and traditional oral forms are engendered by similar processes of production that differ in significant ways from the norms of written narratives. The perpetuation of many of these literary norms, such as narrative closure and psychological character formation in much television drama, has been the result of the historical evolution of these forms from literary novelistic and dramatic forms and the prevalence of a literary aesthetic in the producers and audiences. Soap operas, on the other hand, evolved in a more ad hoc fashion from radio programming that was deliberately

TABLE 3.1   Literacy, Orality, and Television Soap Operas

Literacy Books, newspapers, magazines, film	Oral	Orality TV
Masculine	bardic	news/sports/ action-dramas/ documentaries
Feminine	grandmotherly/domestic/ women speaking/singing	soap operas/"talk" shows/ quiz shows

designed to appeal to women's domestic culture. In these unofficial narratives unashamedly aimed at drawing and holding an audience for their sponsors' products, producers were less likely to consider that what they were making was "art" and were therefore relatively free from the constraints of literary definitions of narrative form. Furthermore, many popular radio entertainers had been drawn from the orally based tradition of popular theater. For example, the vaudeville characters Amos (Freeman Godsten) and Andy (Charles Corelle) moved from film to radio with the slump in film production caused by the Great Depression (Allen, 1985, p. 104). Thus radio programming drew on nonofficial orally based narrative forms in a number of different ways.

In *Reading Television,* John Fiske and John Hartley (1978) have described television as "bardic," referring to television's capacity for a

> metonymic "contact with others" in which all Lévi-Strauss' lost storytellers, priests, wisemen or elders are restored to cultural visibility and to oral primacy: often indeed in the convincing guise of highly literate specialists, from news-readers to scientific and artistic experts. (pp. 125-126)

These oral bards, however, are nearly always men speaking in the public domain (of nighttime television). Fiske and Hartley (1978) do not go on to explore the extension of their parallel in the relationship between women's oral lore of the domestic domain and the soap operas of daytime television. Daytime TV is just as sealed off by the (Australian and American) children's school hours of 9:00 to 3:30 from exposure to a "serious" audience as the domestic kitchen might have been isolated from the important business of the marketplace in a primarily oral culture; and, paradoxically, this time period is just as free from the constraints of formal public utterance. How soaps may be positioned in relation to literate culture is described by Fiske and Hartley (1978) and delineates an oral tradition within women's culture.

Fiske and Hartley (1978) equate oral modes with television, and literate modes with dominant modes in our culture. They list the following oppositions between television and dominant forms:

Oral (television)	Literate (dominant)
dramatic	narrative
episodic	sequential
mosaic	linear
dynamic	static
active	artifact
concrete	abstract
phemeral	permanent
social	individual
metaphorical	metonymic
rhetorical	logical
dialectical	univocal/consistent (p. 17)

They claim for television polysemic qualities that rest, in large part, on the characteristics of orality within the medium, to be found in such conventions as direct address and segmentation. It may, however, be too simple to invest literary discourses alone with dominant perspective, and indeed in some ways the tendency to place oral and televisual forms in opposition to a dominant literacy obscures the operation of different discursive strategies within television itself. Soap operas, more than most other forms of fictional television programming, parallel and replicate women's oral traditions.

On Balance

We can see that soap opera producers in the past and present acknowledge and address women's cultural practices, especially the characteristics of women's gossip and the general oral influences in women's culture. Soap opera, like most mass-produced popular texts designed to appeal to a subordinated group, is at best ambiguous in terms of the primary text. It is both patriarchal and capitalist and a place where women can identify with the discourse. In a sense, hegemony means ambiguity: complicity, seduction, getting drawn in, but also resistance and disidentification. In short, hegemony means a space of continual struggle and negotiation and the establishment of some areas of compromise and common identification. Women regain their space when the construction of meaning gets back into their own territory—the spoken text.

Notes

1. See Greschwender (1992) for a full discussion of the origin and evolution of the "cult of domesticity."

2. See Nochimson (1992) for a detailed elaboration of the theme of women's desire as evidenced in soap operas.

4

The Spoken Text

The attempts within television texts to control meanings, even while subordinated social groups create their own meanings, are evidence of the hegemonic struggle between subordinate and dominant groups that makes itself felt in what I am calling the spoken text, that is, the text that people create when they talk about television. The term *tertiary text* has been used by Fiske (1987) to designate such a spoken text as well as other modes of talking about the text—letters to fan magazines, for example. I prefer to use the term *spoken text* here because I am referring only to oral conversations. To understand the possible foreshadowing of the spoken text in television audience research, it seems relevant to follow the development, in the literature about soap opera and in related theory and research, of interest in how members of the audience construct meaning from a television text by talking both about the television program and about themselves. This chapter looks both at past research and at how people engage in the creation of the spoken text.

Soap Opera Research

A series of early soap opera studies conducted by W. L. Warner and S. E. Henry (1948) and Rudolph Arnheim (1944) give us a picture of the soap opera listener as isolated housewife. Warner and Henry (1948) conducted a study of the radio serial *Big Sister*, looking at both scripts and audiences. The audiences were composed of two groups: regular listeners and people who did not ordinarily listen to soap operas but who listened for the period of time in which the study was conducted. Both groups were given projective psychological tests to tap into their "deeper anxieties." Warner and Henry concluded that the regular listeners were threatened by women not of their own class (implying that listeners were working-class) who had professional status. The function of *Big Sister*, Warner and Henry concluded, was to resolve the conflict in favor of the traditional roles for women. According to Thelma McCormack's subsequent (1983) analysis of Warner and Henry (1948), these women were "lower-class women whose opportunities for upward mobility are so blocked that they retreat into moralistic and highly bizarre fantasy, a regressive process of projection without any ego strength that might lead to a more critical view of class realities" (p. 277). This characterization of the audience views women in the home listening to radio soap operas as lower-class, politically unaware, and lacking in a sense of their own identity. It is a characterization of soap opera viewers that many people employ, even today, and one that I would dispute.

Rudolph Arnheim's (1944) study looked at the content of 43 serials. He noted that all of the positive characters were middle-class and found the stories themselves to be too simple, with the single-classed world lacking the complexity of the real world. He concluded that the serials did not provide the listeners with a perquisite for autonomy or control over their own lives.

Herta Herzog's (1944) study, done at the Paul Lazarsfeld Bureau of Applied Social Research at Columbia University, along with the other two studies mentioned above, remained the definitive work on soap opera audiences for more than 30 years. Herzog and her colleagues (1944) found that women of all social classes watched soap operas but that a typical soap opera listener was married, between the ages of 18 and 35, living in a rural area, with a high school education or less. Herzog's (1944) findings characterized the listeners as active and strong, though not political. She concluded that there was social learning through identification with the strong women characters. Soap operas, according to Herzog, were thought of by many of these women as ways to learn social skills appropriate to middle-class status. McCormack (1983) interprets these initiatives as reflecting the isolation of the middle-class nuclear family (p. 279), and M. J. Matelski (1988), reinterpreting the data more than 40 years later, characterizes the "typical" listener as mostly interested in her home and having few hobbies or little other outside entertainment.

Herzog's uses and gratification study listed the three primary reasons for listening to soap operas: emotional release, fantasy fulfillment, and desire for information and advice. Research from a uses and gratification perspective, although it views audiences as motivated and selective viewers who listen to the radio, watch television or movies, or read newspapers to gratify specific social and/or psychological needs (Rosengren, Wenner, & Palmgreen, 1985), tends to characterize audience uses of media into only a few general possibilities. The data are gathered by questionnaire, and responses over the years have caused researchers to establish the following four categories (McQuail, 1987) as the reasons people use media:

1. Information: Learning about the world, practical knowledge
2. Personal identity: Understanding personal values and acquiring a sense of identity
3. Integration and social interaction: Learning how others live, reinforcing a sense of belonging, gaining conversational topics
4. Entertainment: Diversion from problems, aesthetic enjoyment, relaxation, and emotional release

The data for such studies rely on people reporting what they actually do, a factor that is problematic; however, if we take these studies at face value, they yield results worth thinking about. The designated categories, although seemingly divorced from political significance, are interesting in that the soap opera studies we have discussed match these characteristics in all but one dimension, the dimension of personal identity. This idea fits with the general characterization of soap opera fans that some researchers seem to favor. For example, Nathan Katzman in 1972 described the typical viewer of daytime serials as a "southern or midwestern woman from a large household with relatively low educational and income levels" (p. 205). His conclusions were drawn from the educational levels of heads of households, which, he felt, were closely related to household income. Thus, although the audience he was looking at was female, he drew his inferences from the Nielsen figures, which measured the, usually male, head of household's educational level.

By the 1980s soap opera audiences who were measured by uses and gratification research methods were at least thought to be more educated than they were considered earlier. A study done by R. J. Compesi (1980) looked at *All My Children* and some of its viewers. In his group, only 9% had less than a high school education. This research found its soap opera audience members to be relatively detached, independent, and self-sufficient. These women, he found, were not particularly emotionally involved with their soap opera. McCormack (1983) describes Compesi's (1980) audience member as "the detached woman who belongs nowhere" (p. 280) thus falling into a postmodern category every bit as depressing as McCormack's earlier categories. McCormack's interpretations of this research are included here because much of the negative evaluation of soap opera audiences seems to come from later interpretations of uses and gratifications research.

Each new researcher seems to burden the existing research with his or her own biases.

More recently, D. Lemish (1985) has referred to three sources of possible gratification for soap opera audiences. They are (a) content, (b) exposure, and (c) social context. These categories comprise three of the types of gratification listed earlier—information, entertainment, and social functions—again leaving out the fourth category of personal identity. Later studies of this type have been conducted addressing, among other things, college students' use of soap opera. A. W. Rubin (1985), for example, concludes that students with a high satisfaction with life watch fewer soap operas. Thus the less satisfied with their lives, the more they seem to be involved with soap opera characters and stories. As noted earlier, the missing ingredient for soap opera audiences seems to be personal identity. It is hard to tell if this lack is thought to be caused by the failure of soap operas to provide the "proper" example for building personal values, as might be implied from the conclusions of many of these studies, or, as I contend, by soap opera audiences having different reading practices than the audiences of many other radio or television narratives. They do not "identify" with characters in the way that other narrative and critical forms seem to expect.

As we have seen, most uses and gratification soap opera audience studies have pointed to a psychologically, if not physically, isolated viewer. The presumption of these studies is that women follow soap operas alone and in the home with virtually no social interaction with other women. Later uses and gratification studies about soap opera audiences like A. W. Rubin's (1985), although obviously aware that soap opera audiences talk to each other, still imply that soap opera watching may be a substitute for actual friendships, and hence by implication fans watch soap operas instead of talking to other people, although one recent uses and gratifications study of soap opera audiences seems to rate sharing of program information through talk as a highly significant source of gratification for soap opera viewers (Whetmore & Kielwasser, 1983).

Researchers who use the cultivation effects theory developed by George Gerbner and colleagues have likewise investigated soap opera audiences. Cultivation research looks at how television viewers perceive the actual world in relation to what they see on television (Gerbner, 1972; Gerbner & Gross, 1976; Gerbner, Gross, Morgan, & Signorielli, 1980). In other words, an aspect of characterization such as occupational membership can sometimes be exaggerated by viewers of certain types of television. According to Gerbner's (1972) study, for example, television viewers think larger numbers of people are employed as police than is statistically true in the United States. Studies of this type on soap opera audiences by Buerkel-Rothfuss with Mayes (1981) and Carveth and Alexander (1985) indicate that frequent viewers of soap operas have a tendency to overestimate the size of occupational groups often seen on soap operas, such as lawyers or doctors, and they also overestimate the incidence of illegitimate children and of divorce in the United States. Cultivation research, although concerned with people's perceptions of life, does not look at how they acquire these perceptions and virtually ignores people's tendency to talk to each other about television and thereby perhaps influence their perceptions about the world.

Content analysis studies of soap opera began emerging in the 1970s after an extended hiatus in academic research on soap opera. Content analysis research paints a picture of what life is like for the characters who populate the soap operas, the assumption being that soap opera characters are potential role models for audiences. In *Life on Daytime Television* (Cassata & Skill, 1983), female characters were found to be slightly under-represented on U.S. daytime television compared with the numbers of women in the actual population—49% versus 52%—however, compared with prime-time representation, where the female-to-male ratio was 1 to 3 at the time of the study, daytime television was more nearly accurate. In the case of black characters of both sexes on the soap operas, the representation was 4.8% as opposed to 9% during prime time and 11% in the U.S. population in general in 1980. Not surprising, sexual behavior on soap operas has also been a much studied phenomenon by content analysis researchers (Franzblau, Sprafkin, & Rubinstein, 1977; Greenberg, Abelman, & Neuendorf, 1981; Lowery, 1980; Lowry, Love, & Kirby, 1981; Lowry & Towles, 1989). These authors discovered that, despite the fact that soap operas are supposed to support an economic system that hinged on the nuclear family as the base for consumption, on American daytime soap operas, at the time, almost 70% of the characters were either single or divorced (Cassata & Skill, 1983).

A 1988 study of the characters on the top-ranked soap operas on each of the three major U.S. broadcasting networks—*The Young and the Restless* (CBS), *General Hospital* (ABC), and *Days of Our Lives* (NBC)—revealed that soap operas in many cases have picked up on the demographic characteristics of their audiences, but in other cases have not. The ratio of males to females on these soap operas was the same as that in the general population of the United States: 70% of the female soap opera characters between 16 and 64 worked outside of the home while 66% of the women in that age group in the general population at the time of the study did the same. The marriage and divorce ratio, however, was less on the soaps than it is in the general population. Although 20% of soap opera viewers were nonwhite, only 8% of the characters in these three soap operas were. There were fewer characters under the age of 20 than in the general population (20% versus 30%), fewer characters over 65, more characters aged 30 to 49, while the number of people aged 50 to 65 was proportional to the general population (Waldrop & Crispell, 1988, p. 30). As Robert Allen points out in *Speaking of Soap Operas* (1985), there is no simple, immediate relationship between reality and soap opera. Thus, while content analysis is certainly of interest and many theories of identification indicate that we identify with characters most like ourselves, ultimately content analysis by itself fails to tell us how audiences construct meaning from soap operas.

It should be noted that none of these studies finds actual physical depictions of sex on soap operas, hence what is coded is verbal and implied instances of erotic touching, heterosexual intercourse, prostitution, aggressive sexual contact, homosexuality, incest, and other sexual behaviors. Soap operas, like other televisual forms, have recently become more explicit. For example, a recent (March 8, 1993) episode of *Days of Our Lives* did show two characters making love, albeit fully clothed. One study compared a sampling of 1979 American afternoon soap operas with a similar sample taken in 1987 and found that there was no major increase in sexual behavior in that time period; however, there was an increase in the number of sexual interactions by unmarried partners as opposed to married partners (Lowry & Towles, 1989). Although not part of the research findings, the authors did note that there was some discussion of responsible sex on some of the soap operas they viewed, a practice that continues into the 1990s. Even though it may not have been explicitly shown, rape has played a major part in the story lines of several soap operas in recent years. The most famous of these is the 1979 rape of Laura (Genie Francis) by Luke (Anthony Geary) on ABC's *General Hospital*. Two years later, Laura married her assailant, a plot twist objected to by some critics on the grounds that it tended to minimize the seriousness of rape (Waggett, 1989). The plot lines on American daytime soap operas have reflected many issues of concern to women—abortion, rape, breast cancer, infertility, AIDS, child abuse, marital rape, wife beating, and the murder of prostitutes—which often bring these issues into the discourse of everyday life when viewers talk about the issues in the context of discussing the programs themselves. We shall discuss examples of this later in this chapter.

At this time, some of us may consider such discussions a useful effect of soap opera viewing, but until recently many researchers in communication seemed to hold low opinions of soap opera audiences, as did popular critics. According to Robert Allen (1985), researchers were "unable to fathom the appeal of soap operas" and thus regarded them as "unaesthetic (if not anti-aesthetic)" (p. 29). Therefore they constructed a "typical" soap opera fan who was intellectually, socially, economically, and sexually "one of them" (p. 29) as opposed to one of us. A major turning point in soap opera research has been the emergence of feminist perspectives on the audiences for women's genres on television, of which soap operas are a major representation (Allen, 1985; Ang, 1985, 1990; Brunsdon, 1981, 1983, 1984, 1986, 1987, 1989; Buckingham, 1987; Davies, 1984, 1986; Fiske, 1987; Geraghty, 1981, 1991; Hobson, 1982, 1989, 1990; Leal & Oliver, 1987; Modleski, 1982; Stern, 1978, 1982).

Ethnographic Research

Ethnographic research foregrounds the work of the audience in generating meaning. In the case of television, this type of audience research can be, to quote Ang's recent analysis (1989), "carried out in the form of in-depth interviews with a small number of people (and at times supplemented with some form of participant observation), [and] is now recognized by many as one of the most adequate ways to learn about the differentiated subtleties of people's engagements with television and other media" (p. 96). Although this trend exemplifies work that assumes audiences use and interact with television and other popular forms of entertainment in a variety of ways, depending on intercultural, social, class, gender, race, and age variables, there is still considerable discussion and controversy about the importance and methods of studying the audience.[1] Some recent research has given attention to the integration of the audience's experience, interpretation, and use of the text (Allor, 1988; Blumler, 1985; Budd, Entman, & Steinman, 1990; Carragee, 1990; Carveth & Alexander, 1985; Evans, 1990; Fiske, 1988; Gripsrud, 1990; Hartley, 1987, 1988; Jenkins, 1988a, 1988b, 1992; Jensen, 1987, 1990; Katz & Liebes, 1984, 1986a, 1986b; Lembo & Tucker, 1990; Levy & Windahl, 1985; Liebes, 1988; Liebes & Katz, 1986; Livingstone, 1989; Lull, 1988; Morley, 1980, 1981, 1986; Newman, 1988; Palmgreen, Wenner, & Rosengren, 1985;

Steiner, 1988). Some look at audiences as members of interpretive communities (Lindlof, 1988, 1991; Lindlof & Meyer, 1987; Steiner, 1988), while other audience research attempts to integrate interpretive studies of the audience with the economic, political, and cultural systems that influence the production and reception of media (Barnouw, 1970, 1975; Gitlin, 1985; Jenkins, 1992; Meehan, 1986, 1987). Here we highlight the relevant audience studies that use ethnographic methodology.

For example, Dorothy Hobson's *"Crossroads": The Drama of a Soap Opera* (1982), which looks at the production side of the British soap opera *Crossroads* using case study techniques, is also one of the first participant observation research studies to show how fans use soap opera to negotiate issues in their lives. She found that *Crossroads'* fans did not just view the program but "worked on" the text in relation to issues in their own lives or in their conceptions of the way life is to be lived. Fiske (1987) has pointed out that the tertiary text which people construct in their conversations about television can be public, such as letters to newspapers or fanzines or the results of opinion polls. Conversely, it can be private, such as the gossip among friends or conversations between family members (what I have referred to as the spoken text), or it can be somewhere in between these two poles, which is where the responses given to researchers in the process of ethnographic data collecting fall. Hobson's later piece, "Women Audiences and the Workplace" (1990), goes further in the acknowledgment of the importance of the spoken text than her early work. In this article she hypothesizes that "it is the discussion after television programs have been viewed which completes the process of communication" (p. 62).

In this later work, Hobson uses an interview with a young woman who works in the telephone sales office of a large pharmaceutical company as the basis for her article. She asks her informant, Jacqui, to describe how the women in her office spend the working day. Hobson illustrates from their conversation how women can "work on" television texts. According to Jacqui, there were some topics discussed that drew in the whole group of 17 women in the sales office. Television was one of these. Typically, a conversation about television would start out with someone asking something like, "Who saw *Coronation Street* last night?" Some would say they had and some would say they hadn't, whereupon a person who had would tell the story, sometimes complete with facial expressions, and others who had seen it the night before would let her know if she left out any parts.

From there, according to Hobson, the conversation would turn to speculation on what might happen next. The next phase would be for them to discuss what they would do if they were in similar circumstances. Or if the events on the soap opera were too close to home, a person might wait until someone else had said what she would do and then ask a question like, "But what if you loved him?" This way they were able to talk about very personal or painful topics without feeling they were revealing too much of themselves. It is clear in Hobson's analysis and her use of Jacqui's conversation that these women at work sometimes negotiated their views of their place in the world in relation to television by the creation of the tertiary text. In this way, they also created their own culture within the workplace.

Ien Ang's 1985 study, *Watching "Dallas": Soap Opera and the Melodramatic Imagination*, investigates what happens in the process of watching *Dallas* that makes it pleasurable or unpleasurable for its viewers. Her data are in the form of letters from fans. The letters are seen as the discourses people produce when they account for their preferences. Ang viewed the letters as a form of social discourse much like talk. According to Ang, the accounting for their preferences

> will have to call on socially available ideologies and images which channel the way in which such a television serial attains its meanings. It is by tracing these ideologies and images in the letters that we can get to know something about what experiencing pleasure (or otherwise) from *Dallas* implies for these writers—what textual characteristics of *Dallas* organize that experience and in which ideological context it acquires social and cultural meanings. (p. 11)

She concludes that, while pleasure eludes rational consciousness, in the case of these *Dallas* viewers, it was the series' emotional realism in relation to tragic structures of feelings having to do with the (gendered) pain of ordinary living that generates the pleasure of recognition for women. Although some of the letters mention the way fans talk about *Dallas,* Ang's research model itself invites talk in the form of letters and in the process creates a type of tertiary text similar to the letters found in fan magazines analyzed by other researchers (Fiske, 1987; Whittenberger-Keith, 1992).

Among the theorists and researchers who have acknowledged soap opera's unique form and have attempted to describe and/or theorize soap opera reading, it seems to be evident that the tertiary text forms at least part of the data out of which the theorizing takes place.

David Morley's 1980 study, *The "Nationwide" Audience: Structure and Decoding,* which he calls an "ethnography of reading," is credited as being the first attempt to develop an ethnographic system of "decoding" television audience responses that takes into consideration differences in interpretive activity and attempts to correlate them with economic, social, and cultural categories. Using Stuart Hall's (1980) adaptation of Frank Parkin's (1979) idea of negotiated meaning generation involving dominant, negotiated, and oppositional interpretation of the same program by varied audience groups, he showed tapes of the BBC news magazine show *Nationwide* to groups of viewers drawn from various social and economic strata, noting similarities and differences in the responses among the groups. He found the interactions to be much more complicated than had been previously assumed. Not only were the three categories of responses not adequate for encompassing the responses, but also the responses from the groups of viewers were more complex than he had anticipated. Later works by Morley (1981, 1986, 1989; Silverstone, Hirsch, & Morley, 1991) have further refined and changed his approach to ethnographic research.

This strand of research in cultural studies not only attempts to investigate the theoretical areas that merge when meaning is made, but it also foregrounds the notion that watching television can be related to social power. This latter move means that the interaction among the audience members and their interpretation of the text are primary research concerns, a step that leads us closer to the concept of integrating interpretation with discourse (see Morley, 1993).

According to John Fiske (1987), although many ethnographic studies contain numerous examples of tertiary texts, they tend to read such texts as the result of viewing rather than as material that can be, and is, read back into the text, thereby activating the meanings available in specific discourses. Even so, many ethnographic studies seem to show evidence that the tertiary text is used to activate television texts. Fiske points out that Robert Hodge and David Tripp's (1986) study of schoolchildren's interpretations of the Australian soap opera *Prisoner* seems to indicate that gossip among these children would have been used to feed back into the text to help create meanings related to their school experiences.

David Buckingham's volume, *Public Secrets: "EastEnders" and Its Audience* (1987), looks at Britain's *EastEnders* in order to specify its audience's multiple relations with this particular text. According to Buckingham, in the process of watching *EastEnders,* viewers are invited [by the program] to engage in many different types of activity: recollecting past events which they have seen; imagining ones which they have not; hypothesizing about future events; testing and adapting these hypotheses in the light of new information; drawing inferences, particularly about the characters' unstated emotions and desires; and learning new facts, both about the characters and their fictional world, and about the world at large. In all these respects, the viewer is positioned as an active participant in the process of "making sense" of the text, as a partner in an ongoing debate about how it will be understood. (p. 49)

Buckingham analyzes the institutional and intertextual contexts of *East-Enders'* ongoing production. He used group interviews with 60 school-children between the ages of 7 and 18, all of them *EastEnders* fans, to discuss viewing patterns, secret-telling or gossip, prediction, text construction variables both inside and outside the text, moral and ideological judgment, realism, identification with characters, and characters as they represent social groups. His study clearly documents the importance of the tertiary text in constructing meanings. In a later work, Buckingham (1991) specifies that much of the meaning that evolves from television reading takes place in verbal language. He views meaning generation from television as "a participatory, social activity: the meanings which circulate within everyday discussion of television are 'read back' into individual responses to the medium, thereby generating a dynamic interplay between 'social' and 'individual' readings" (p. 229).

Elihu Katz and Tamar Liebes's (1984, 1986a, 1986b) cross-cultural research comparing interpretations of *Dallas* by American viewers and Israeli viewers shows evidence that gossip among the participants in the study, who were interviewed in their own friendship groups, must have created the activation of certain meanings over others. While Katz and Liebes's *Dallas* research focuses on social experience and does not mention the notion of the tertiary text, the written account of the study shows evidence of the use and existence of such a text. For example, Katz and Liebes (1986a) conclude: "What seems clear from the analysis, even at this stage, is that non-Americans consider the story more real than the Americans. The non-Americans have little doubt that the story is about 'America'; the Americans are less sure and are altogether more playful in their attitudes toward the program" (p. 197). The idea that these viewers exhibit what the authors call "playful" behavior indicates that there is plenty of interaction on the spoken level.

This interactive aspect of the process of watching is also clearly illustrated by Cassandra Amesley in "How to Read *Star Trek*" (1989). The tertiary text created while watching *Star Trek* is ritualized through familiarity. It involves the repetition and reenactment of parts of the program in a kind of distancing and parodic pleasure. The rules of this interaction, known to fans, consist of not making comments that bring into question the "realness" of the characters or revealing or predicting the plots, which, in this fanship group, have been seen many times. Amesley suggests that the meaning of the tertiary text not be considered to be generated only between text and audience, seen as an isolated individual act between a person and a television set, but generated "among audience members and the text" (p. 37).

Reading Reception/Reader Response Criticism

An emerging category of research about television audiences is often called reception-response or reading reception criticism. Reception and/ or response criticism comes from a type of literary criticism theorized by the German critics Wolfgang Iser (1974, 1978) and Hans Robert Jauss (1982a, 1982b) as a new paradigm in literary scholarship. Reader response criticism is opposed to the notion of criticism in which the reader is expected "to hunt for a truth tucked away in the folds of the textual fabric" (Holub, 1984, p. 155). Instead, meaning is thought to be reached as part of an interpretive process taking place between the reader and the text. Interpretation, then, does not entail the "discovery" of the meaning in the text but the experiencing of meaning as the process of reading happens. The work of Iser and Jauss, translated into English in the 1970s and 1980s, has recently entered the critical discourse on television, particularly in the work of Robert Allen (1985) and David Buckingham (1987). Thus a whole range of reception studies acknowledge the existence of and bring into the discourse of media analysis the concept of the tertiary text (Corner, 1988; Fiske, 1987; Gray, 1987; Hobson, 1989; Jenkins, 1988; Morley, 1986, 1989; Palmer, 1986a, 1986b; Reid, 1989; Richardson & Corner, 1986; Seiter, Kreutzner, Warth, & Borchers, 1989; Silverstone, Hirsch, & Morley, 1991; Tulloch & Moran, 1986; Whittenberger-Keith, 1992; Whittenberger-Keith & Lutfiyya, 1992).

It is Robert Allen, in *Speaking of Soap Operas* (1985), who articulates that soap opera's position in discourse determines its meaning. According to Allen, the way that soap operas are constructed in the discourse both of aesthetics and of social science circumscribes the range of questions to be asked and the methods likely to be used in answering them. Allen also suggests that soap operas are open texts in which the effect of an act or emotion is seen on a large number of characters whose actions do not necessarily advance the plot. According to Allen, the function of the soap opera character *in* the community is more important than what the character does; hence, to the experienced reader, soap operas' networks of relationships among characters open up major potential meaning unavailable to the naive reader. During various gaps in the narrative, commercials, for example, or the time between programs,

> the reader inserts himself or herself into the text through these necessary gaps, filling them in part—but only in part—according to his or her own frames of reference. . . . But just as the text does not merely take over "real-life" conventions in the construction of its world, the reader cannot simply impose his or her referential system upon the text. The process of a "gap-filling" is regulated by the text itself. (p. 78)

Although Allen's analysis, like much reader response criticism, gives the balance of power to the text, he has succeeded in describing the functioning of the text as it interacts with the audience. Acknowledgment of this aspect of the tertiary and spoken text at the empirical or research level in television studies is essential to understanding how soap operas function in women's culture.

With the gradual emergence of feminist researchers, the research done on soap operas and their audiences has begun to change the discourse on soap operas; and theorization of feminist and other egalitarian perspectives has begun to give weight to the argument that we can take soap opera viewers, as well as their talk, seriously. Thus the social climate both for women and for research paradigms has changed to accommodate recent studies of female audiences and women's genres (Ang, 1987; Longhurst, 1987; Modleski, 1982; Radway, 1984; Seiter, 1982).

Soap Opera and Friendship Networks

The present research takes these issues further and attempts to see how discursive networks constructed around soap operas actually work as spoken text. Thus the spoken text is an integral part of the experience of the text. Talk is the necessary first level required if the text is to be an influence in people's lives. It seems clear that, even though the watching of soap operas can be a solitary experience, most often the experience is discussed with others who form a community of viewers of particular soap operas.

The soap opera fans in this study are often not members of specific fan clubs. They call themselves fans, but their fanship networks are less formal than groups with membership lists. They consist of social networks that operate on two levels. First, there are usually a small number of close friends or family members who are regular viewers of the same soap or soaps. A second level of fanship is considered to be all people who watch the soap in question. One meets second-order people in buses, at work, at school, or somewhere else in passing, finds that they watch such-and-such a soap opera, and discusses the current issues on that soap opera with them. Sometimes these people are never seen again, but often they are acquaintances whose major connection is their soap opera fanship.

Soap opera fans of the first type stay in close touch by telephone or in person. When one of them goes out of town, the others keep up with the soap opera for her. This may consist of writing letters, using a videotape recorder to tape episodes missed, or simply remembering the story while the person is gone and catching her up when she returns. The phenomenon is most common among women and girls but sometimes men are let into a fanship group of the first type, and men often are part of a second-level soap opera network. In Australia, where soaps are produced with teenagers in mind and programmed in early evening and prime time, a great number of girls and boys watch them, although there is some evidence to support the idea that television plays a larger part in the lives of girls than boys in Australia (Palmer, 1986a).

The American and Australian adult fanship groups of the American daytime soap *Days of Our Lives* observed for this study operated similarly to each other. In both countries, videotape recorders are relied on heavily to keep fans up with the soap, a practice that has been documented in several countries as the heaviest nonseasonal use of videotape recorders (Cook et al., 1989; Rabinovitz, 1990; Stoessl, 1987). Although those women who are regularly at home during the day often watch their soap opera at the time it is broadcast, integrating the soap into their daily activities, women who work outside the home often tape their soaps to be played back at another time. Working-, middle- and owning-class women seem equally likely to be fans. Most of the fans in this study considered themselves middle class at the time of the interviews, but a number originally came from working-class families. (See the Appendix for specific data on these fans.)

Adult fanship groups have varying degrees of formality or informality. Often they are not conceived of as a group per se, but other members may be referred to simply as someone else who watches one's soap. In other cases, group boundaries are distinct. For example, one group in a remote section of Western Australia meets for a wedding breakfast every time there is a wedding on *Days of Our Lives.* In the Australian outback, women are particularly isolated from other women and sometimes use their soap network as an important social network in which they can be in regular contact with other women. In addition, mothers and daughters are often fans of the same soap opera, although they may also be a part of separate gossip networks.

Teenage fanship groups in this study tended to be large and to consist of friends rather than family. The Australian-produced early-evening soap operas seemed to be watched by virtually all young teenagers (13-16 years old) of European decent in Australia. For example, when *Sons and Daughters* was on the air (from 1981 to 1987), it was programmed from 7:00 p.m. to 7:30 p.m. Monday through Thursday for most of its run. This meant that most high school-age teenagers were either home or at friends' houses where they could watch television when *Sons and Daughters* was broadcast and hence could watch it at the time it was aired. There was no other soap opera in competition during that time slot in Western Australia, where these fans lived. In the case of *Sons and Daughters,* then, a fanship network would consist of all the friends with whom one regularly discussed the soap.

On the other hand, if one is a teenage fan of *Days of Our Lives,* the process is a little more complicated. Most teenage fans in the present study reported becoming interested in the serial, broadcast at noon in Western Australia, when they were home from school during an illness. In addition, some fans reported that *The Young and the Restless* was once broadcast in the afternoon at a time when they could watch it if they rushed home immediately after school. Because it is station policy that the American daytime soap operas are taken off the air during school holidays in Western Australia, it is college-age teenagers who are more likely to be fans of *Days of Our Lives,* both because their schedules are more flexible and because they are often affluent enough to have access to a videotape recorder. It is common in Western Australia for college students to live at home, and all of the college students in this study did.

Among U.S. university students, both women and men watch soap operas regularly in coeducational dormitories and in the public common areas of student unions. In Britain, where the U.S.-produced daytime soap operas are not shown, the Australian *Neighbours* is a great favorite in university common areas. Australian teenage *Days of Our Lives (DOOL)* fans who participated in this study had more clearly defined fanship groups, that is, groups that actually got together to watch the soap on a regular basis, than did the fans of *Sons and Daughters*. On the other hand, they also listed the people they knew who watched *DOOL* as in the hundreds, which, although perhaps an exaggeration, indicates its popularity among university students. These young women listed none of their family as those with whom they talked about *DOOL* but considered most of their female classmates to be fans. Only sometimes did they talk to their male friends about *DOOL*. Those older teenagers seemed more inclined to view soap operas as funny than the adults or younger teenagers and also were more likely to watch them in groups, chatting about them as they watched. The same was true of the British university-age fans of *Neighbours*.

Soap opera fanship groups vary in their makeup from first-level groups, with elaborate means of keeping up and consistent interaction concerning the soap opera in question, to large groups of people with whom ongoing conversations about the soap operas are routine, even if these conversations are not necessarily with the same people. The close-knit groups exist among both adults and teenagers, but second-order soap opera fan relationships are more prevalent with teenagers. In Australia, if one is a teenager, one can expect virtually all of one's friends to keep up with *Neighbours, Home and Away,* or *Sons and Daughters,* all soap operas produced for teenage consumption. If the soap is moved to another time slot, as *Sons and Daughters* was (to 3:30 p.m. weekdays from early evening), it is possible that teenagers will not watch. None of the adults in this study watched the early-evening Australian teenage soap operas, but some watched other daytime soap operas or British soap operas also broadcast in the early evening. British college-age fans of *Neighbours* assumed that almost all of their friends and acquaintances kept up with *Neighbours*, which is broadcast at noon and repeated in the early evening. Many watched the soap as part of a group audience at their university and watched it again at home that evening.

With the exception of teenage and younger fans of Australian and British soap operas, fanship often seems to have been handed down among women and most of these women discussed soap operas primarily with other women. Thus soap opera fanship functions for these groups within women's culture, although some fans also discuss soap operas with men and seem to admire men who watch and keep up with soap operas. Teenagers' viewing practices also differed from adults' in that teens frequently parodied scenes from soap operas and/or enjoyed imitating the voices of certain characters. We shall look more at this aspect in Chapter 7.

We shall look now at one group of American fans of the American daytime soap opera *Days of Our Lives* to illustrate how soap opera fans incorporate the text of women's oral culture with the soap opera text, thereby constructing the spoken text. Let us begin at this level to look at how a group of soap opera fans talks about viewing a soap opera. This group of fans, all from a city in the southern part of the United States, is the first group gathered for this study. The networks, of which these fans are a part, preexist the groups that I gathered for the purposes of this study; but in a sense, the groups I constructed also became networks (more on this later). This group is mixed in age and contains seven women and two young men. In the group are two mother-daughter pairs and a pair of cousins. They are middle- and working-class. Four members are in high school, and one is almost 80 at the time of the interview. This group brings together three already established *DOOL* gossip networks. One network consists of Sue, a former teacher, now an accountant, and her daughter Karen, a high school senior, and Karen's boyfriend Carl. They tape *DOOL* and watch it together in the early evening. Another network is represented by two cousins, Fern and Laura, as well as Fern's daughter Melanie. Their extended family, particularly their mothers and grandmothers, have discussed *DOOL* as long as they can remember. This network, consisting of a real estate agent, an interior design student, and a high school student who also works as a horse groomer, rarely watches together but frequently discusses the soap among themselves and with other women in the family. Emma, a retired nurse, discusses *DOOL* with several friends and her daughter, who seldom watches but is part of the oral network.

In the context of friendship and family relations, soap opera discourse networks are facilitated by the conventions of soap operas and the familiar pleasures of women's lives together that invite conversation. The process of being a soap opera fan, as implied in the previous paragraph, is not always just the process of watching. For long periods at a time, some fans miss watching their soap but "keep up" with it through conversations with other fans. A person who has been a fan of a particular show over a long period of time does not simply stop watching and erase the show from memory. Sometimes fans report having not seen a show for years only to catch up for the missed years by watching an episode or two. Elaborate telephone chains exist in which a person can be caught up on a missed episode. Sometimes friends will refrain from discussing a soap opera episode until everyone in the group has seen it because some people, particularly working fans, record the program and watch it later than its broadcast time.

Once a soap opera is chosen, fans usually remain loyal until there is a substantial change in the show, but switching can also be brought about by a new set of friends who watch a different soap opera. Friends of a viewer often switch to the same soap or, if a person moves, she may switch to the soap opera viewed by her new friends. This suggests that viewers are not just loyal to a particular soap but are also loyal to the community of viewers with whom they are affiliated. Fans can reconstruct a soap's plot by what Timberg (1987) calls "backstory," which is the recounting of past events and relationships so that a new viewer or a returning viewer can catch up quickly. The viewer in need of updating can also rely on conversations with friends. For some fans, fanship is almost all talk. As one group member recounts:

Karen (to Laura): How many years have you been watching?
Laura: Seven or eight years, but only off and on, I've never had a television set.
    I just sort of keep up off and on.

The pleasure here is in the kinship with other fans, not in the text itself. The use of the text is the real point for her in that it enables her to participate in the feminine cultural community of fans.

Although daytime soap operas are similar in construction and appearance, viewers often choose a particular soap opera to watch, which is usually referred to as "my soap." Such nomination gives a soap opera a privileged position in that person's cultural experience. The time slots in which particular soap operas are programmed are important in the choice of which soap to watch. They are often associated with breaks in the day's activities and form part of the structuring devices of a woman's day if she is working in the house.

Emma: Well I watch them during lunchtime. That's how I got to watching *Loving.*
    Loving comes on at 11:30 and by that time I'm just fooling around. And I
    started watching it and I got interested in it. It's about a very wealthy family
    and how they are dressed to the peak, to the nines. It's real interesting. And
    then I have lunch and watch *Days of Our Lives.*

Often a fan's close friends know which soap opera (or soap operas) she watches and refrain from telephoning or otherwise disturbing her during that time.

Soap Opera and Women's Culture Within the Family

Daughters are often raised with a particular soap and continue to watch it after they leave home. The progress of the story is then a topic of conversation when mothers and daughters converse. Because of a soap opera's longevity, mother and daughter can discuss over generations what has happened and what is likely to happen. Consequently, longevity is one of the ways that soap opera works to hegemonically insert itself into women's lives. Women, often the bearers of family traditions and the preservers of the details of everyday life, appreciate knowing that soap operas will be there every day at the same time for years and years. A particular soap opera becomes a part of a family's shared history, handed down in the same way that mothers and daughters share recipes and, with both recipes and soap operas, the memories of shared hours in the kitchen or near the television set.

The community of fans provides a women's oral culture that bridges geographic distance, a bridge that is vital for oral culture in a mass, mobile society. For example, a mother and daughter in one soap opera group discuss the mother's introduction to the soap opera network in a new town and the daughter's first memories of watching soap operas:

Sue: In 1976 I moved to Knoxville and I went to bridge and they were talking about people just like this. Back then it was 1:30. No, it was the 2 o'clock soap opera back then. They stopped lunch, bridge. Anything. If I was going to be their friend, I had to watch it if I was going to carry on a conversation, and when Karen was born I would make her sleep during that time [the time the soap opera was broadcast].
Karen (Sue's daughter): No, I would sit next to you.
Sue: Oh yes, later on. Not early.

The power of the soap opera stimulates conversation among friends as well as giving new friends a common community to talk about. The daughter's emotional involvement in their time spent watching together is also clear in the above segment. Sons less often share in these feminine cultural practices. The 12-year-old boy in the group told me that after the summer he planned to stop watching *Days of Our Lives* because he had now outgrown the soap opera, an act that seems to parallel the male child's need to reject that which is female by pulling away from his mother. Although the girl child may feel comfortable in the culture of women of which soaps are a part, the boy child has to reject it. Nancy Chodorow (1978) points out that a girl's female gender identity is learned in everyday life and is "exemplified by the person (or kind of people—women) with whom she has been most involved" (p. 51). Soap operas can be a part of women's culture within which girls are socialized and women construct pleasures and meanings for themselves. A good part of this pleasure seems to come from talking with other women.

Soap Opera Conventions and the Invitation to Conversation

Soap opera production values stimulate discussion. The audience often debates the limitations of soap opera realism. This is evident in the following discussion:

MEB: Do they ever show outside scenes?
Sue: Yeah, occasionally. That was a highlight to show things outdoors.
MEB: You mean they didn't show things outside at all?
Sue: When they did show things outside it was the park bench, 15 years ago.
Karen: But that was a studio park bench, Mother.
Sue: But there were trees behind the park bench.
Laura: There were birds twittering.
Karen: People would walk back and forth behind them and pretend.
Sue: No, Bill and Laura sat on the park bench and talked. That was the only outside scene.
Karen: It wasn't a park. The park was fake.

Although it is clear that the park is fake, that fact does not, for some viewers, interfere with the enjoyment of the program. In fact, whether or not the set is realistic is yet another prompt to conversation. Soap opera style has a form that enables it to intersect easily with the culture of everyday life. Because daytime soaps are "cheap" productions, they have a look and feel that is different than classic realistic television drama and they evidence an ordinariness that evokes the unassuming look of the everyday (Hobson, 1982, pp. 117-120).

An additional way that soap operas' production values stimulate discussion is the actors' conventions on soap operas. For example, the actors can change in the middle of a scene. If, for example, an actor gets sick and is replaced, the beginning scenes with the first actor are often not reshot. Thus a character becomes transformed to the new actor. When such a change takes place, the character can change also.

Karen: Remember Mary Anderson? She really changed. They had the blond Mary Anderson who was sweet and then they had the redhead for a while who turned into a real witch.

MEB: You mean they don't keep the same characteristics when a new actress or actor comes in?

Sue: The first Laura would never have done anything evil, but the third Laura, you were ready for her to go.

It is not that the viewers of soap operas do not know that literate conventions of representation are being broken but that they accept the conventions of soaps operas in the light of the constraints imposed by practical considerations such as the show's budget and oral storytelling traditions in which the characters may vary with each telling (or in this case each new actor). These characteristics of oral storytelling existing in the genre promote discussion both by their differences from other norms, particularly film and prime-time television, and by the differences in one actor's portrayal of a character from that of another. For soap opera fans, norms and expectations are governed by the conventions of the genre. For example, when characters have gone through a number of the formulaic changes that are available to them, like changing characteristics a number of times or being involved in too many plot variations, then characters are said to be "fizzling out," and it is expected that they will be written out of the show. These are variations in what might be considered "real," "true," or "believable" in a soap opera and, in addition, make up the gaps that promote conversation among the fans.

Entering into the world of soap opera viewing also involves the knowledge of the constraints imposed on soap operas by dominant culture or the real world and often involves a vast amount of intertextual material gleaned from sources outside of the program. This conversation illustrates an aspect of audience reading practices (or play) that involves the playful crossing over of the boundary between fiction and reality. "Real life" is, of course, that contained and articulated by dominant discursive practices, and viewers' talking about the characters as though they were real defies the dominant conception of what constitutes reality.

Sue: There's a new bad person on the scene.

Laura: What if he's Stefano? (laughter)

Sue: Stefano's dead!

Emma: We don't know Stefano's dead. We just think he is.

Carl: No one ever found his body.

Karen: Some people think that Roman is still alive.

MEB: Why do you think that Roman is still alive?

Sue: Because they didn't find his body, and, I'd swear, on one soap opera they said Stefano's dead, but they put his body on ice.

Emma: Roman left the program. He wasn't pleased with something—his money or his part. Before he was killed, there was an article in *TV Guide* or one of the books that he was going to leave, that he wasn't pleased. I don't know whether it was—I think it was over his part, the way it was developed.

Knowledge about the characters, actors, or plots from an external source contributes to the need for discussion. Is Stefano really dead? Is Roman? Even if those questions are settled, there is still the issue of whether Roman or Stefano will "come back," that is, return from the dead. If the actor is not pleased with her or his contract, will she or he resolve the differences and return to the show? The conventions of soap opera "truth" leave almost everything open—what I earlier called lack of closure—inviting fans to speculate.

Among soap viewers, there is also amusement at the complications of soap opera plots and the complex interrelations among their characters. For example:

Sue: Oh, Alex and Marie. They weren't married. Marie was a nun. Before she was a nun, she lived in New York. Even before that there was Tom Horton Jr. who had amnesia and who somehow or another had plastic surgery and somehow or another he wandered back to Salem with plastic surgery and nobody knew him and he didn't know anybody.

MEB: You mean Tom has a son?

Sue: Yeah. He fell in love with his sister, Marie. And they did their thing and they were going to get married and all of a sudden Tom Horton Jr. remembered. So Marie got sick, and she fled, and nobody knew where she was for a while, and then later on she went in a convent and became a nun. But meanwhile, when nobody knew where she was, she went to New York and had an affair with Alex and had a baby.

MEB: Who's Alex?

Sue: Alex is the really bad one.

Karen: The consummate evil one.

Sue: He did Stefano's dirty work.

MEB: So he and Marie had a daughter?

Sue: I'd forgotten about her. She got married. Who did she get married to?

Karen: She married Joshua, she was engaged to Jake, the Salem Strangler.

Emma: Oh yeah.

In the group discussion noted above, everyone laughed when it was mentioned that Jessica, Marie's daughter, was once engaged to the Salem Strangler. The humor takes in not only the discordance of the specific situation but also the character's history.

If one has followed Marie's story over the years, one knows that she has been subjected to the most absurdly terrible (and, because of the excess, humorous) series of tragedies that one can imagine. These events, nevertheless, only differ in kind and degree from those that might beset another character, Marlena, for example. Marlena's litany of problems would also elicit laughter. It is the cumulative effect emerging when one is talking about them that makes them funny. The same viewers who at the moment of viewing enter wholeheartedly into the pathos of a particular situation, are, when they look at the plot over time, quite capable of laughing at the same event (Brown, 1990b). This invitation to laughter and play provokes talking and joking. Some research suggests that this is more true of middle-class women than working-class women (Press, 1991), but both American and Australian audiences found *Days of Our Lives* equally amusing.

Location offers another level of interest and speculation among soap opera viewers in relation to realism. The following quote from the discussion transcript concerns where the soap opera takes place.

MEB: Does anyone know where Salem is?
Karen: We've been trying to figure that out for years. They mention Chicago a lot and they mention New York a lot.
Sue: I think it's closer to New York City.
Laura: I think it's closer to Chicago.
Carl: I think it's in Ohio . . .
MEB: So we can't figure out where it is?
Karen: Some of the soaps like *General Hospital.* You know where that is.
MEB: Where is it?
Sue: Port Charles, New York.
MEB: And where is Port Charles?
Laura: It's upstate New York, isn't it?
Sue: It's a real place.
Karen: They make allusions to places that you know.
Carl: Like it's only a couple of hours to New York.

Salem (like Port Charles) is not a real place, but it seems real. The above speculation stimulates gossip because it values the pleasure of direct comparison with the audience's different experiences of America—it can be, and it is, close to New York, Chicago, and Ohio—and its factual indeterminacy makes it a recurrent source of pleasure: "We've been trying to figure it out for years"; which is so different than New York—*Kojak*'s New York—or *The Streets of San Francisco* or *Miami Vice*'s Miami. Classic (masculine) realism depends on reference to external reality, a closed or completed notion; soap opera realism is internal and thus more open to possibility. Because we do not know where Salem is, it can become ours. Salem can be anywhere we want it to be. The same type of speculation about place exists for *Hill Street Blues,* a program that, in its early days, evidenced many of the characteristics of daytime soap opera. Place is thus, at least in American daytime soap operas, yet another invitation to conversation. However, as Christine Geraghty (1991) points out, the sense of place in British soap operas is quite distinct and important to British audiences.

Incongruities of time are also tolerated (and enjoyed) by soap opera viewers. Time is not necessarily altered to make cause-and-effect relationships clearer or more logical but to emphasize those moments of heightened emotional intensity.

MEB: Time goes faster?

Karen: They can warp it however they want. Time can go really slowly or it can go fast, you know. It just depends on what they want. They can make one evening last for three days and then a year can go by like that (snaps fingers). But it's funny the way they slip it in. Like just the other day Marlena was saying Roman's been dead all this time. They're making it sound like Roman's been dead for years when in real time it's only been about six months.

Soaps allow the audience to speed through story details that are without much emotional appeal, and like memories or gossip, they sometimes allow us to linger over moments of pleasure. On the other hand, viewers often assume that actual time and soap opera time are the same. This is because, as mentioned earlier, soap operas are designed to treat time as if it goes on while the viewers are not there, just as our time does. Time, after all, is constructed. Oral culture and the culture of the home does not always treat time in the way that public culture does. Time on soap operas is ambiguous enough to provoke conversation. In fact, common to all these points is the ambiguity between the actual and the fictional, which viewers navigate very well because they understand which is which and yet, at various times, are ready to suspend disbelief.

Soap Opera and Familiar Pleasures

Because of the longevity of the viewers' association with the characters and content of soap operas, there is also the pleasure involved in familiarity and regularity. Brunsdon (1984) refers to this as "ritual pleasure." Over a long period of time, the viewer goes through the day-to-day issues with soap characters as well as the celebration of holidays and special events like weddings, births, and other gatherings of the soap "family."

Sue: I'll tell you what I like is Christmas. When they put those ornaments on the tree.
Emma: Each one has their own name on it. Each one that comes in the family has a Christmas ball with their own name on it. And each one puts their own name on the tree.

The way things are traditionally done is often a point of conversation and concern for women (DeVault, 1990). Family rituals that are repeated year after year are particularly pleasurable to women who value and preserve rituals in the home. During the television rituals, women often discuss their own rituals. They may mark the growth of children on the soaps as well as compare how old a particular child of their own was when something significant happened on their soap opera. Ritual, longevity, the need to work out plots from the past together—all of these things present the possibility of discourse, readily taken up in the groups we discuss here.

When dealing with the problems presented on the soaps, the viewer is aware of both the content of the show and the problem as it relates to her own social experience. As Brunsdon (1984) notes:

For the soap fan, one of the moments of pleasure is when you can say "Oh, I *knew* that was going to happen!" But this is not the same feeling as the attendant fascination of *how* it is going to happen. At the moment, I really don't think that Sheila Grant [of Brookside] is going to have the baby she is pregnant with. My reasons are partly generic—I know that a very high proportion of soap opera pregnancies come to little more than a few months' story. They (her reasons) are partly what I experience as "intuitive"—she is in her forties, she has already got three children, the house isn't big enough. (p. 83)

Soap opera "reality" and social reality converge here in Brunsdon's recounting of the pleasure of solving, or attempting to solve, the problems that soap operas constantly present to the audience. Rather than experiencing as frustrations the constant postponement of the resolution to problems in soaps, Brunsdon and the viewers quoted here in this study experience them in the nature of story problems much like puzzles to be worked on for pleasure, as suggested in the quotation below.

Sue: And you always know, if something doesn't work out, it will with somebody else later on. You always know that.

The ongoing puzzles, then, offer tests of viewers' ability to outguess the writing and production considerations inherent in the genre or to will something into being. The social implications for viewers often involve social role expectations of women and also of the viewer. All of this encourages talk and discussion in which women, so often silent, find pleasure.

The Power of the Spoken Text

Thus we can see that talk creates the spoken text. Although the very early work on soap operas seems to have acknowledged the existence of the spoken text, there was no attempt to analyze what went on among audience members when they talked to each other. Although the cultivation research described earlier in the chapter has pointed to some interesting assumptions among individual audience members, it too has failed to tap the seemingly obvious resource of what people tell each other. Content analyses, in turn, tell us what people would be talking about were they talking about the text.

It is ethnographic researchers who have begun to look closely at what people reveal in the course of their conversations in the context of fanship. Through these conversations, we can see the beginning of the emergence of a theory of sociocultural empowerment in the field of hegemony centering on the political economy of the patriarchal family. Soap operas are not the cause of this process of change or of empowerment as such. Rather, myriad structural changes are introducing structural strains in the traditional family roles and women are renegotiating at the level of family structure the relationships of power and the institutional definition of their roles. The tension that such struggles generate can be dealt with within the boundaries of soap opera networks, something that we shall explore in the next chapter.

Note

1. Susan R. Suleiman (1980), in her introduction to *The Reader in the Text: Essays on Audience and Interpretation,* lists six approaches to audience-oriented literary criticism: rhetorical, semiotic and structuralist, phenomenological, subjective and psychoanalytic, sociological and historical, and hermeneutic. Referring specifically to media research, Robert White (1991) delineates four approaches: (a) an Anglo-American critical cultural studies approach, (b) an American symbolic interactionist tradition, (c) a consensual cultural studies tradition, and (d) a tradition primarily concerned with theories of hegemony and mediating social contexts developed particularly in Latin America. Here White's categories are narrowed to those critical cultural studies approaches (in general from the Anglo-American tradition) that use ethnographic methods, particularly interviews and participant observation.

5

The Boundaries of Pleasure

Although the theory of hegemony seems to argue that ultimately the discourse of women, or any other subordinated group, supports the dominant group, I have found that, in specific situations, subordinated groups may speak in contrary ways. As I have pointed out elsewhere (Brown, 1990a), such contextual pleasure can be looked at in terms of genres of discourse. Feminine discourse is such a genre. Genres of discourse are the possible ways of speaking within specific situations. When specific situations involve groups of other women, often one is able to speak differently than one might speak in a more public speaking situation.

Several pieces of research support this idea. For example, Elizabeth Frazer (1987) comments on the fact that hegemonic discourses are supported in some situations where, for example, young women's conceptions of their own reality tell them a different story than the one conceptualized in dominant discourse. She cites as an example Angela McRobbie's (1977, in Frazer, 1987) study in which the young women speaking seemed to say that women do not go out to paid work, but instead do child care and domestic work in their homes. The statement was made even though most of the members of the group had mothers who did go out to work (p. 413). Thus the young women were stating what they knew dominant notions to be rather than the actual situation. In a similar vein, Shirley Pendergast and Alan Prout (1980) interviewed 15-year-old girls about motherhood and marriage. When they were talking informally with the girls, a body of knowledge concerning the tedium, exhaustion, loneliness, and depression exhibited by mothers of young children was evident. Such knowledge was usually firsthand, gathered from sisters with young children and the girl's own experiences baby-sitting and/or with primary child care of younger sisters and brothers. Yet when these young women were asked in the formal interview to agree or disagree with the statement: "It is a good life for a mother at home with a young child," they almost all agreed in accordance with the hegemonic or sentimental notion of motherhood (Oakley, 1979). When returned, then, to the public discourse on motherhood by the formality of the questionnaire, the girls in general accepted the socially rewarded idea that motherhood is unproblematic.

Pendergast and Prout distinguish between these two distinct but contradictory bodies of knowledge as "illegitimate" and "legitimate." In their analysis, "illegitimate" knowledge is not generalizable while legitimate knowledge is. The young women in Pendergast and Prout's study were interviewed alone and some indicated that illegitimate knowledge was also private knowledge; that is, they kept it to themselves. However, in Elizabeth Frazer's (1987) study, in which girls were analyzing a story from *Jackie,* a British magazine marketed to teenage girls, the girls talked quite frankly (or illegitimately) in groups. Such private, illegitimate knowledge is what, in this volume, has been noted as feminine discourse. According to Frazer (1987), "such knowledge was shared among them, as it is among sociologists of the family, women in women's studies classes, consciousness raising groups and the like" (p. 421). Her conclusion is that "ways of talking, or knowledges, or discourse registers will be dropped in contexts where they are not supported" (p. 421). Women, in groups where such knowledges are accepted, can talk from their own experience rather than from a position constructed in dominant discourse. The soap opera groups involved in this study supported Frazer's (1987) and Pendergast and Prout's (1980) conclusions that in some groups "illegitimate" knowledges are openly discussed, valued, and accepted while the knowledge of "legitimate" ways of talking is also acknowledged as prevalent but different than the ways these women chose to construct themselves in discourse within the boundaries of their groups. Part of the pleasure women experience in groups of other women who share a knowledge of mutual subordination is in having clear boundaries—in having a cultural space from which to speak.

Let us now look at some of the ways women's networks are constructed. Such networks may be the one place where women can assert what limited power is available within patriarchal structures. As Michel de Certeau (1986) points out, the powerless are not able to operate from institutional places but must make use of the spaces afforded them in the culture in which they exist. Whereas dominant institutions employ strategies of containment, nondominant groups must use their own tactics to resist such containment.

Women's Reading Practices

A continuum of women's reading practices stretches from formally organized reading groups to informal fanship networks. Elizabeth Long (1986, 1987) has studied organized reading groups, looking at the ways they interpret their reading and the manner in which they choose the books they read and discuss. She found that women's, men's, and mixed sex reading groups "use their readership to mark a boundary between themselves and their neighbors, and the elite among such reading groups distinguish themselves from people who 'only read trash' " (Long, 1987, p. 306). Even the exclusively women's book groups she investigated (1986) defer to established authorities and traditional hierarchies when picking what books to read. Their choices range from the classics, at the top of the hierarchy, to other "serious" works but never include formula novels. However, even though cultural authorities such as academics are consulted for the selection of books, once read, the books are analyzed in decidedly nonscholarly ways. According to Long, the discussants give a wide variety of interpretations, many of them linked to personal experiences. Discussants often view the characters as though they were real and are generally "playful" in their discussions of a particular text.

In the public world of the book club, middle-class women appear to adhere to established, and preferably academic, criteria for choosing books; but because they are participating in reading groups for their own pleasure, they turn to chatting within their groups possibly because talking and sharing their own lives and experiences is a very real pleasure in the experience. Long (1986) concludes that these book groups, while not questioning the values of a "middle-class American world-view" (p. 610), evidence a supportive atmosphere that values women's opinions. Although the well-educated middle-class women in her study had been taught the "proper" ways of reading and evaluating books, they integrate literature into their lives quite differently than do literary scholars. At the same time, the boundary-setting functions of cultural authorities are strictly adhered to in their choice of books. But, like the Australian teenage girls whom we shall look at, they also use their own discussion groups, at least partially, to defy the literate educational values they have been taught.

Debra Grodin (1991), in a study of the readers of a largely feminine genre of books, self-help books, found that her readers sought a commonality and connectedness from their reading experience in order to assure themselves that what they were thinking and feeling fell within the boundaries of the "normal." The readers' concerns seem to mark the uncertainties women feel in adjusting to hegemonic power relationships. These, largely middle-class and college-educated, self-help readers did sometimes regularly connect with other readers in the form of self-help groups, but the books rather than the groups seemed to be their primary interest. According to Grodin (1991), although self-help books claim to foster liberation, these readers complained about the ways that some self-help books position women as victims. These sophisticated readers also object to the therapeutic ideal of individuality embodied in the books (p. 416). The group's rejection of the notion of individuality in self-help books may be the beginning of a political perspective, one in which it is hypothesized that institutional structures are responsible for the fact that women are most often the people that self-help books view as needing help.

These women may have come to the realization that there is not necessarily anything wrong with people who do not fit into the system, that there may be something wrong with the system. Another possibility is that the therapeutic ideal of individuality may be inappropriate for women who, in our society, prefer connectedness, as Gilligan and her colleagues (1990) have argued. The notion of such an ideal of individuality, which is preferred in dominant discourse, denies many women's preference for connectedness, which, in women's networks, is affirmed. Feminine friendship practices are often counterhegemonic to dominant notions that women cannot get along with each other because of rivalries over men. Both book reading groups and the reading of self-help books are acceptable and sometimes laudatory practices within dominant culture. The reading groups maintain dominant literary hierarchies, and they function formally as clubs that offer the legitimation of either self-improvement or higher ideals that fit with what Joan Rubin (1992) calls middlebrow culture. Self-help book reading sometimes pushes the boundaries of dominant culture a little further in that self-help books are sometimes critical of societal structures. Books for incest survivors, for example, are implicitly critical of a society that allows incest to exist. However, some self-help books label women as problems (e.g., *Women Who Love Too Much,* Norwood, 1985). In this they are similar to the problem page letters and answers discussed in Chapter 3 in that many of the answers offer individual solutions to structural issues. They are therefore counter to a nondominant political reading, which would critique dominant structures rather than blame problems on the isolated behavior of individuals.

On the other hand, cultural texts such as "female address" rock music videos have been documented to sometimes encourage fanship, with its active pleasures, to push against some definitions of femininity offered as cultural norms. Lisa Lewis (1990) points out that female fans of rock stars sometimes create visible signs of female significance and formulate new responses to gender inequality. Lewis studied fans of female rock stars, such as Cindy Lauper and Madonna, and these stars' productions of what she calls female address videos. According to Lewis (1990), when female address videos, those made by women rock artists specifically to appeal to women, particularly teenage women, appeared on MTV (Music Television) in the early 1980s, young women appropriated them as representations of their own cultural experience. Girls' lack of power, then, no longer had to be dealt with by the adoration of male power and independence manifested by male rock stars but could be centered on women with power. Angela McRobbie's (1984) theorization of dance as social power for young women falls into a similar category. McRobbie notes that dance allows girls to experience power through the use of their bodies, a power that is in their control and is female centered despite the fact that dance is often seen as existing for masculine pleasure in voyeuristic looking at the dancer. Women and girls often use forms of popular culture either to assert themselves or to struggle against their ideological positioning as passive or against their looked-at-ness. Recent work (Butcher, 1993) has suggested that the audience for country music videos is largely female and that the videos are thus designed to appeal to women, eliciting the female gaze at the male performers. Some even feature female bonding.

Women Within the Family: Uninterested Reading

David Morley (1986, 1993) finds that, in the context of some British families, men and women watch television in ways that are fundamentally different than each other—that women seem uninterested. The men in Morley's study describe having a clear preference for viewing in silence, attentively, and without interruption. The women describe television viewing as a social activity that involves ongoing conversation and sometimes the performance of some other domestic activity such as ironing. Although these viewing practices make the women described seem uninterested, among the 18 lower-middle- and working-class white British families that Morley (1986) interviewed, the power differential between men and women within the home was particularly acute. Not only did the men and boys watch more television than the women and girls, but the men usually checked the newspaper or teletext to plan their television viewing, operated the video recorders, sat in possession of the remote control switcher when they watched, and in general watched what they preferred to watch when they wanted to watch it. As Ann Gray (1987) points out, there is also often not-so-subtle intimidation going on in terms of which programs are valued within the family and which ones are watched. One of Morley's (1986) male subjects puts it succinctly: "We discuss what we all want to watch and the biggest wins. That's me. I'm the biggest" (p. 148). Given situations like these, women's uninterested watching of television may be a resistive act in itself.

Women may not be watching attentively because they are not interested in what their husbands have chosen to watch. Depending on the culture, sons' preferences may be put before that of adult women and girls. In addition, Morley and several other researchers (Brunsdon, 1986; Lee & Cho, 1990) attribute women's inattentiveness to the fact that, for women, home is not considered a place of leisure but of work, hence it is difficult for women to concentrate on and enjoy television viewing without complication. For example, in the case of a group of Korean families living in the United States: "Women rarely do what they want to do for themselves [in the home], and this is most evident in television watching" (Lee & Cho, 1990, p. 32). In Korean families, the status of each family member is based on gender and age. In the households looked at by Lee and Cho (1990), it was not uncommon for the husband to discourage his wife from watching soap operas or other women's genres by comparing her viewing choice with that of a housemaid, someone at the bottom of the social order. This tactic generates shame because the wife is considered to have damaged the family image.

In both the Korean families in the United States (Lee & Cho, 1990) and the British families looked at by Morley (1986) and Gray (1987), the wives formed what the Korean women call "video clubs" in order not only to watch what they wanted to watch but to watch it in an atmosphere where they could talk and do as they pleased. Usually they met when the men and children were out of the house. Such viewing groups set clear boundaries for these women. Within these groups, they can say what they want to say and do what they want to do. Here they are free to experience pleasure.

Clearly women's oral culture plays an influential part in how these women construct meanings and pleasures in their everyday lives. As Lee and Cho (1990) conclude: "The pleasure women find comes not from absorbing the dominant ideology but from their conscious resistance to the political power their husbands exercise" (p. 33). In both Morley's

(1986) and Lee and Cho's (1990) studies, women will often watch a tape a second time when they are alone, often after everyone else in the family is asleep, because when the women's video groups are together the talk is more important than watching the program. Thus we can see that women's television viewing varies with the circumstance. When the occasion is such that talk with other women is a possibility, then the pleasure of talking may be more important than watching the program.

In the Korean group (Lee & Cho, 1990), the women often use their time together for the category of gossip, which Jones (1980) describes as bitching, mostly in the form of complaining about their husbands, the tone of which seems reasonably powerful and the content of which indicates solidarity among the wives: "You learn a lot of things [about] how to get your husbands by just chatting with more experienced wives" (p. 33). Pleasure, power, and knowledge are easily combined here. These women use the skills they have to mount a limited challenge against the patriarchal traditions that dominant culture struggles to enforce. The tactics that they discuss in their video groups include gossiping about their husbands, an act that challenges the power of their husbands' private rule by making it public; refusing to cook their husbands' favorite dishes; and excluding their husbands from their attention while watching videotapes the husbands consider to be trash. It can be seen that these women regularly question their husbands' position of power.

Women's Isolated Reading: The Romance Novel

Although women's reading practices have been the subject of a number of recent inquiries into women's genres, one of the most notable studies of this type is Janice Radway's (1984) work with readers of romance novels. Although romance novels bear many similarities to soap operas, there are also significant differences in both the construction of the narratives and the reading practices associated with each. The romances favored by Radway's readers are exemplified by Kathleen E. Woodiwiss's *The Flame and the Flower* (1972). This type of romance usually features a happy ending, a heroine who shows some assertive, independent behavior, and a hero who is cruel but not extremely so. On the whole, these novels deal with the seduction myth of the innocent young woman who meets her true love and at the end of the novel marries him, expecting to live happily ever after. Soaps also deal with a seduction myth, but the characters are not necessarily innocent; the love is not usually the woman's first love (or the man's); marriages don't last forever; and there are many protagonists, not definable heroes and heroines.

In addition, romance plots deal with potential danger and violence toward women from men. Male aggression is tamed in the hero at the same time that the heroine comes to accept the patriarchal construction of her sexuality. The form that "victory" takes is modified in this feminized version of the traditional narrative. The hero has to be turned into a nurturing male before he is fit to marry. At the end of a masculine adventure/ romance (e.g., the James Bond narrative), the masculinity of the hero is untouched by the feminine influence of the woman, which is symbolized by the narrative closure, which always leaves the male hero single, free, and uncomplicatedly masculine. Romances, like soap operas, appeal to a feminine wish to have nurturing relationships. Radway (1984) uses Nancy Chodorow's idea of nurturance in *The Reproduction of Mothering* (1978) to explain her subjects' need for nurturing:

> As a social institution, the contemporary family contains no role whose principal task is the reproduction and emotional support of the wife and mother. "There is a fundamental asymmetry in daily reproduction," Chodorow concludes, "men are socially and psychologically reproduced by women, but women are reproduced (or not) largely by themselves." (Radway, 1984, p. 94)

Romances encourage women to take up this reproductive process in the context of a male/female relationship. In preindustrial societies, women had readily available female networks in the form of extended families in which they were supported and reconstituted. The effect of the suburbanization of women in urban societies has been their isolation within the domestic environment. Organized in traditional narrative style, the romances preferred by Radway's group achieve narrative closure when the hero finally understands that the heroine is different than other women and "the heroine is gathered into the arms of the hero who declares his intention to protect her forever because of his desperate love and need for her" (Radway, 1984, p. 97), thus reproducing the isolation of the nuclear family.

Romances of the type described by Radway are also about the containment of female sexuality. In them, female sexuality is constructed as the complement to the discourse on pornography. Andy Metcalf and Martin Humphries (1985) describe the need for the complicity of women in masculinized desire:

Woman's complicity is a conceit fundamental to the workings of soft-core pornography. Without it the whole project would collapse, a tendency which is apparent in the narrative of certain hard core pornography. The assertion of masculine authority—in the sense of power legitimated by the desire of the governed—has given way in hard porn to the symbolic exercise of naked power. (pp. 38-39)

Power is evidenced in romance novels by violence (often in the form of rape), the threat of violence, or implied violence just as it is in pornography, but in romances the perspective is the point of view of the victim. Such plots are pleasurable to women only if the hero changes and accepts a female value system, becomes gentle, and uses his power to protect her. The anger of the heroine at her own powerlessness and her victimization because of her lack of knowledge (sexual innocence) is satisfied only in that she learns of herself in male terms. As Radway (1984) puts it:

It is . . . a figurative journey to a utopian state of total receptiveness where the reader, as a result of her identification with the heroine, feels herself the object of someone else's attention and solicitude. Ultimately the romance permits the reader the experience of feeling cared for and the sense of having been reconstructed effectively, even if both are lived only vicariously. (p. 97)

Romances are thus seen by Radway to position women as relatively powerless.

The power involved in role-identified masculinity is power maintained by force, a power requiring surveillance lest those without that power transgress. It also connotes danger for those not in power. Both soap operas and romances evidence an awareness of this danger. In romances, the danger comes from the hero, who is eventually converted to domesticity—a safe mate for the heroine. On the other hand, in soap operas, the danger is to the family and to happiness, which is found within the family and its close relationships among people of both sexes. Both romances and soaps, then, key into aspects of women's lives that are socially and psychologically understood by women. Hence both popular forms take femininity as the norm.

Radway points out one way in which reading romance novels can be looked at as resistive. Individual women in Radway's study defy their husbands' wishes in order to gain the private psychological space and mental separation from their families provided by reading romances. The resistive aspect of this act is that the women feel and believe that they are resisting male authority. According to Radway, the feeling of resistance seems to come both from identification with an assertive heroine and from the act of claiming uninterrupted time and space for oneself within patriarchal marriage, which often allows women little psychological or real space for themselves. The pleasure, then, is in claiming the right to solitude. Although romance readers do set up boundaries in this way, their solitary reading practices prevent them from establishing solidarity with other women; however, romance reading does attempt to set its own limits within patriarchal society. Recent conferences of romance readers and writers seem to indicate that the fans of this genre are beginning to form social networks, which may strengthen their solidarity with other women.

Cultural Space: Women's Fanzine Culture

Although the science fiction fanship community is predominantly male, one part of this community is made up almost entirely of women. The women's fanzine community edits and writes stories, poems, songs, vignettes and produces artwork, photographs, and videotapes about the characters who populate *Star Trek, Blake's 7, Star Trek: The Next Generation, Doctor Who,* and other television and film source products. Between 1977 and 1988 more than 34,000 items had been produced by 10,000 community members from both English-speaking and non-English-speaking countries. Women make up more than 90% of this group (Bacon-Smith, 1992). The fanzine community, in addition to its literary output, also supports close-knit friendship circles assembled to produce and distribute the fanzines and gather the work produced by other circles. Although there are large-scale conventions of all types of *Star Trek* and science fiction fans, the core groups are the circles, usually of not more than 15 women who range in age from the late teens to women in their seventies.

These women write several types of stories. Among the stories about women, are what are called Mary Sue stories, tales about strong young women who join the heroes on the bridge of the starship, resolve the conflict, save the protagonists, and die at the end. These narratives are currently considered negatively. The second type are Lay-Spock or Lay-Kirk stories in which the heroine is sexually involved with the named party. Hurt-comfort stories feature one of the heroes as injured and tended by another protagonist. Narratives concerning males are about nonsexual relationships (also known as ampersand stories), hurt-comfort stories, and K/S stories in which Captain Kirk and Mr. Spock engage in a sexual relationship. Some of these writers also seek to reclaim female experience from within certain male-centered texts by taking a minor female character from one of the source texts and placing her in, for example, an all-female landing crew on its way to a lesbian separatist space colony (as in Jane Land's *Demeter*, 1987).

This huge, alternative literary network not only signals a vast community of women taking part in a nonvertical network in which there is no head, focus, or center, but the network is also outside of the consumer economy. Their work is produced on 8 ½" × 11" paper, photocopied, and distributed to the circle for free or exchanged for the work of other circles (see Bacon-Smith, 1992; Jenkins, 1992; Pendley, 1991). The fans discuss their work in terms of universes, or realities, that exist side by side, and several types of stories and products can fall into what Camille Bacon-Smith (1992) calls a story tree. In a story tree, stories, novels, and pieces of artwork, often by different people, will fall together because of their relationship to a particular universe or group of characters. Among these stories, there are many unresolved situations. Writers will then pick up on a dropped subplot, or bring back a dead or thought-to-be dead character, or tell the same story from another point of view. The tree itself, or a particular novel or short story within the tree, is of necessity open ended.

Obviously the story tree has many similarities with the structure of soap operas discussed earlier, and the particular type of literature that these women have created, while it is written, certainly has many connections to oral culture. Similarly, the way the circles are organized, with membership based, in large part, on knowledge about the conventions of the genre, brings to mind the way that soap opera fans relate to each other. Although people who write for science fiction fanzines are not usually soap opera fans (Bacon-Smith, 1992), the stories they create relate to women's culture in much the same way that soap opera fanship does. Bacon-Smith (1992) describes the stories of fan writers in the following way:

> Linear narrative cannot convey a story with any illusion of reality for women who perceive their lives as part of an ongoing multifaceted and simultaneous web that connects them to each other. The story must back up and leap forward, the past with its memories must explain present actions in flashbacks and embedded narratives. Stories may begin with the ending and work back to uncover the forces that led to that particular conclusion. The same events may be repeated from many points of view, and conjunctive stories may add the separate activities of secondary characters influenced by the main action or unwittingly influencing the given outcome. Nor is any story

ever completely finished; writers re-create the endings of their favorite stories and source products with bewildering regularity. (pp. 66-67)

According to Bacon-Smith (1992), fanzine writers know that they are engaged in a subversive activity, and thus their boundary setting is more purposeful than that of soap opera fans.

Subtle Pleasures:
Soap Opera and Boundary Setting

In the case of soap opera fans, the boundary setting occurs in the context of people's everyday lives. It is a subtle integration of dominant cultural expectations and the women's own use of them. To understand how such boundary construction might be negotiated among soap opera fans, let us look at the following conversation between Doris and Rita, two women who have known each other since high school. Both are in their late thirties. Rita lives on a remote station (or ranch) in northern Western Australia. Doris, who lives in Perth, records episodes of *Days of Our Lives* and sends them to Rita, who is married to the station owner and is thus the only woman at the station. The motor to which they refer is the electrical generator that is usually turned on only in the evenings, hence television is watched only in the evenings. All of the television sets on the station, which also consists of a bunkhouse and foreman's quarters, are set up so that they must be tuned to what the television set in the main house is playing. Doris and Rita have been fans of *Days of Our Lives* since their boarding school days. The conversation is tape-recorded by Doris, who is visiting the station, as they ride together in the station's four-wheel drive utility vehicle.

Rita: I suspect we'll have those flashbacks when Liz starts getting her memory back.
Doris: You know, I was annoyed that I missed that one.
Rita: The other one that I was very annoyed that we missed was Rene's pronouncements to everybody as to why she hated them.
Doris: I only had that on in sound—I didn't have any vision on that.
Rita: I also missed it, and I would have loved to have seen Rene getting stuck into them all. I saw it in flashbacks, at the party, but after she'd done that—just before she was murdered and after she was murdered, and the reason I liked that was you should have seen the beautiful gowns they had on. And that was the other thing about Hope's 18th birthday—
Doris: Clothes.

Rita: They were having a party at a restaurant in those magnificent gowns. They were all dressed in gowns. They weren't dresses; they were gowns.

Doris: They always wear magnificent clothes.

Rita: Yeah, but, usually they're within the realms of the—

Doris: Everyday rational. You can't believe that they're wearing those beautiful gowns.

Rita: But I don't believe an 18-year-old girl would be dressed up in that outfit that she had on.

The specific sources of pleasure annotated by this passage from the interview are obvious. The pleasure in seeing a favorite character "getting stuck into," or telling the others off, is one aspect. Another is the piecing together of what had happened from flashbacks, and another admiring the clothes.

The context in which these two women speak allows them to show their pleasure in watching a display of emotions that they obviously think Rene is justified in having, or watching a display of opulence in clothing while judging the propriety of 18-year-olds wearing such clothes. The relationship of women to clothes, although culture and consumer based, is one of great significance to women and is taken up in the soaps.

Knowledge of clothing and its appropriateness and significance is one of the areas of women's expertise. It is often the regimen of dress codes, hairstyle, and makeup restrictions that first exposes young women to gender contradictions. Young girls' desire to dress like boys is often an early form of resistance to the restrictions of female gender roles and expectations, and the relationship of clothes to bodily display and social response takes on pivotal importance in defining a young woman's social image. In addition, style imitation is a favorite form of fanship for adolescent women fans of female rock stars (Lewis, 1990, p. 166). Significantly, the myth that women buy clothes indiscriminately without relation to cost makes clothes and their acquisition a point of contention outside of women's culture. Doris and Rita's mutual pleasure in admiring the clothes on *Days of Our Lives* is taken by neither as necessarily a particular desire to buy them. It is like the pleasure of window-shopping when women enjoy the display without necessarily buying the goods, and as Ang (1985) and McRobbie (1984) point out, one's fantasies sometimes merge with hegemonic notions like those of consumption.

Because of the way that station life is set up around what can be done when the generator is on, Rita's husband has been let into the viewing network, but he has more difficulty with the discursive network than the two women. The following excerpt from another section of the interview illustrates this:

Doris: How did you get Gerard [Rita's husband] to start watching?

Rita: Well, he had to watch it because I wanted to watch it. I wanted to watch it. If I watch it, he's got to watch it, and I can't watch it when he's not there and I can't watch it when he comes in because that's when the news is on. The only time is after 8 o'clock at night.

Doris: So in effect, you could put the video recorder on your TV in the bedroom.

Rita: Yeah, then we'd have to be in separate rooms.

Doris: Yeah, I mean, it is possible—

Rita: Yeah, but he wouldn't like that. He'd rather watch *Days of Our Lives* than have me in a separate room, and then, that was how it began, and then because we wanted to find out about the murderer—he watches it now.

Doris: Does he like it or does he make fun of it?

Rita: I reckon it's fun—especially the romance thing.

Doris: But he keeps following it anyway?

Rita: Oh, yeah, he wants to find out who the murderer is. There's a couple of times we had—do you remember those scenes when they were showing us who the murderer was and they were showing you the hand—

Doris: —and they were crossing out the—

Rita: Yeah, we were pausing on it and having guesses as to who it was and what that was—that's the only reason. But as I said, he'll become hooked. Gerard got into it fairly quickly—he's got his pet hate on the program. I didn't think he'd be able to follow what's going on.

Doris: I reckon all the women are the same.

Rita: It was so annoying when he first started watching—every five minutes, he'd ask, "Who's that? What's she doing?"—and you can't possibly explain who she is. Like Kate and Julie. This is your stepmother, and then you just say, "No, it's a stepmother," then something comes up about Addie—and you say well, "In fact, her father was married—Julie's mother was her husband's wife as well—right?" and it's all ridiculous. Because it's all over by the—it took Gerard a long time. Every time a woman came on, he'd say, "That's the one that . . ." and I'd say, "No, no, that's Gwen Davy," and this is such and such.

This conversation between Doris and Rita labels them as insiders or possessors of knowledge in the discursive situation in which they are participating. They are the possessors of knowledge about soaps' conventions, which vary from narrative conventions common in other types of stories. However, Gerard has trouble with both the genealogies and some of the conventions of soap opera like the complicated plots or the fact that there are so many female characters and that they all look very similar.

Those soap opera conventions, which are the same in television programs intended for both men and women (Fiske, 1987), like the mystery convention of giving a few clues at a time in order for the audience to gradually discover who the murderer is, are easy for Gerard to relate to, but the subtleties of the differences between the female characters or the complexities of the genealogies and plots are simply left unexplained to Gerard.

The process of negotiating both power and pleasure is evident in the system Rita and her husband have worked out to decide when they will watch the taped episodes of *Days of Our Lives*:

Doris: Do you usually watch it at one sitting, all the tapes, or do you try to save a bit for each day?

Rita: We work it out by what's on television. If nothing's on, we watch *DOOL*. If there's something we can't quite make up our minds what we particularly want to watch, we work out how much *DOOL* we've got left. If we've got lots of *DOOL*, we'll watch *DOOL*. If we haven't then we'll watch the TV.

Doris: Save your last program?

Rita: Yeah.

Doris: How much have you got left now from what I brought up.

Rita: Oh a lot, about—oh, not a lot actually. Probably watched two hours.

Doris: You've only got two more then.

Rita: But that means we've been watching less television. Sometimes they last, you know, a long time, because of different programs on. It also depends on—you know, like one Saturday morning, we took the day off. We put the motor on and stayed in bed and watched *DOOL*—two tapes or something, an overdose on *DOOL*.

Doris: Even went to the extremes of putting the motor on?

Rita: Absolutely. I feel a bit embarrassed about them. I just hope that if the others put on their video (they can watch)—I keep hoping that they don't realize that we're watching *DOOL*.

The somewhat illegitimate pleasure that Rita and her husband experience by turning on the generator on a Saturday morning and staying in bed to watch 2 hours of soaps is a source of some embarrassment to her because anyone else watching television on the station will also tune in to *Days of Our Lives*. However, because the workers on the station are overwhelmingly male, it is possible, she feels, that they will not know what they are watching because it is, after all, outside of masculine culture in general but in particular in the Australian outback.

Although the boundaries of soap opera networks give women a cultural space from which to speak, and they allow women's concerns to be valued and validated, in the above example a man is let into the network. However his understanding of what is going on is limited, and the other men on the station, who have not been admitted to the private culture of the station's women (or often lone woman), are possibly at such a distance from women's culture that they may have no idea of what a soap opera even looks like. Thus the very devaluation of soap opera in dominant culture can protect the boundaries of women's culture.

This excerpt gives a much less stratified view of male and female culture within the family than do either Morley's (1986) or Gray's (1987) studies, both of which indicate that women do not control the television set within the home when men are present. This may be a class issue. Both Morley and Gray used working-class audiences and, obviously, station owners are not working but owning class. In addition, the circumstances of living on a remote station can change role relations between men and women. However, in terms of gender-class issues, some women deal with role-defined behavior in unexpected ways, regardless of their class, either by their relationship to a broad feminist ideology or by circumstances that give them more chances to be assertive.

Nevertheless, separate discursive traditions are often present between men and women, and separate (and empowering) knowledges exist in each. It is the recontextualizing of these knowledges that makes women's knowledges, in this case about soap opera, gain in importance. This shifting discursive position of women, which occurs when women assume a position of knowledge by setting up their own value system, places them in a more powerful position than when they accept the values imposed by masculine discursive positions.

For some teenagers, the very fact of their fanhood sets up a boundary against hegemonic expectations. Their refusal to take seriously many aspects of dominant culture distances them from conventional cultural positioning. Social boundaries for women often center on what is considered "normal" in terms of behavior. When one of the Australian university-age fans of *Days of Our Lives* picks Bo and Hope as her favorite characters, carries their picture around in her wallet, and shows it to her friends, she is actually setting herself off in two ways. Her upper-middle-class parents may well be disturbed that she admires American soap opera characters that much, but she may also be making fun of the characters, of U.S. culture, and of American daytime soap opera. British college-age teenagers deal with the Australian soap opera *Neighbours* in similar ways. Whereas they watch regularly and they consider themselves fans, they often do so in order to make fun of the show. Indigenous British soap operas are taken much more seriously.

In contrast, the concept of addiction implies that one is acting outside the boundaries of normalcy but at the same time establishing a boundary between oneself and those in the normal world. Addiction implies that people are sucked in and once enthralled perhaps can never return to the world of the "normal citizen," where narratives have endings and life is stable. A fan puts the idea this way:

MEB: Why do people say "addicting"?
Ellen: Because it is. It's like a pleasure, I think—a soap. It's like chocolates or something. It's like a treat. It's like a bowl of corn flakes. It's something really nice. It's not necessarily terribly good for you. It's easy spoon feeding. It doesn't demand very much of you. You enjoy it. On a certain level, it raises issues a little bit. You enjoy the jokes and the gossip and the fun.
MEB: The idea of addiction then has that little twist that it's somehow not good for you?
Ellen: The only bad thing about it is that kind of moral censure that you get for watching them. And because you watch them rather than doing virtuous things, like listening to classical music or educating yourself.

Underlying this comment is the idea that women should be acting in certain societally approved ways. For the middle-class woman, what she should be doing has to do with the value of education and high art. This fan gets more specific:

MEB: Is it mostly women who watch, or what?
Ellen: Oh, yes, I would think so—I think it's probably most women who would say, "Yes, I'm a *Coronation Street* fan." But I should think there's a high proportion of men who watch it because the women in the house are watching it. It's like Colin [her husband] would watch it because I was watching it because you are in the same room.
MEB: It's early—
Ellen: They are watching it, they are equally involved in the plots, probably but um—perhaps they'd never admit to the same kind of sympathetic—
MEB: What do you mean, sympathetic?
Ellen: Well, because of this about soaps being despised, generally. It's not something that you admit to watching much of. In England there is a certain kind of pride. Yes, I mean it is despised, but then everyone watches it, and everyone has a reason for why they watch it, and so it can also be fashionable for you to be a fan of *Coronation Street*.

Theoretically, one is set apart by claiming to be addicted. However, few people are actually addicted to soap operas. Intense pleasure for women has been reframed into a negatively valued social condition—addiction. Additionally, the dominant notion of addiction in some ways excuses the soap opera viewer from the stigma of having actually made an informed choice to watch a soap opera. The concept of addiction may also have its own boundary-setting function in this way.

One's knowledge about the soap opera can set a public boundary as well. People sometimes watch soap operas in order to participate in the public discourse about the soap opera; however, there is an uncomfortableness in watching soap operas for pleasure, which highlights the social condemnation connected with the genre. Ellen elaborates further:

Ellen: The gravest thing in Britain is watching telly during the day. That's really bad. I mean, you might admit to watching soaps in the evening, but if you sit around watching them during the day, like we are at the moment, that's really wasting your life.

In public discourse, then, daytime television is the ghetto of bad television. This notion appears to coincide with the idea that women (presumed home during the day) should be kept busy. The expectations of what women in the home should be doing might be called the ideology of busyness. It stems from other general categories of control over women through restriction of various kinds. Social expectations can demand unending hand sewing or elaborate food preparation or in other ways can organize every waking moment in a woman's life, all of which keeps women in a contained place, in most cases in the home (Lesko, 1988).

To watch television during the day violates the rule that women in the home should be kept busy. We have seen that the home is not always considered a space of leisure for women as it is for men. The categories of work and leisure were brought into tension by the industrial revolution, when manual work began to be considered alienating. Work in the house, though it is not leisure, is not considered either as alienating or as valuable as work outside of the home. Television, as a leisure activity within the house, occupies a contradictory and ambivalent position with women, particularly in a traditional family.

Text, Context, and Illegitimate Pleasure

Although soap opera fans do not rewrite the text, they do reconceptualize it and relate it to their own lives. Bacon-Smith (1992) recounts that fanzine writers enjoy what she calls "talking story" as a way of orally enjoying the process of imparting knowledge and creating new stories. Soap opera fans do something similar when they discuss their soaps. Just as the genre of science fiction provides a fantasy space for women's stories, concretized into fiction and other genres for fanzines, soap opera provides another cultural space for women that fuels oral instead of written networks. The text or program involved often sets the tone for any cultural challenge to dominant culture that might take place. As John Fiske (1987) points out:

> Television, with its already politicized pictures of the world, enters a context that is formed by, and subjected to, similar political lines of power and resistance. The intersection of its textual politics and the politics of its reception is a crucial point in its effectiveness and functions in our culture. (p. 77)

The pleasure that women experience while watching soap operas can have to do simply with the enjoyment of the activity, that is, active pleasure. However, the pleasure that women experience when talking about soap operas and constructing their own spoken text is often resistive pleasure. They use it not only to set boundaries for themselves where they can discuss their own cultural concerns but also to resist aesthetic hierarchies concerned with knowledge, accepted cultural capital, and domination by men. Although there are many potential sites of such activity, soap opera gossip networks are a particularly salient one.

What soap opera provides, in the context of discussion networks, is the imaginative-emotional material out of which, in the process of the construction of meaning that constitutes the spoken text, women reimagine their roles and feel again what it is to be a woman, particularly in the family context. The anger, for example, that is felt when a wife and mother returns home from work, tired after shopping for the groceries for the evening meal, and sees her husband sitting watching sports, complacent in the midst of dirty kids and the messy house while she faces preparing a meal, can be either negotiated or politicized in the context of the latest soap opera episode. The full contextual meaning of soap opera is not realized until one expressively discusses it with other women. Here one's feelings are responded to and there is a sorting out of the symbols most relevant to the situation—whether Bet the barmaid in *Coronation Street,* who puts down ineffectual men, or the complex plot or emotional relationships in the American daytime soaps. As Dorothy Hobson (1990) recounts in her conversation with Jacqui about how television is discussed in the workplace, women often negotiate their place in the world in relation to their discussions about soap operas and other television shows. This negotiation often takes place in the support groups that exist around soap opera fanship.

It is accurate to some extent to say that women could gather under any pretext to discuss the politics of their lives, but the examples that we have from research on female audiences seem to indicate that not only the specific medium but also its content and context does make a difference in its reception. Soap opera networks are a popular form of resistance partly because of the way women use them and partly because the form of soap opera itself defies hierarchies of cultural dominance.

In specific group situations, women or other subordinate groups may speak in a contrary way by speaking illegitimately. Within a social context, such talk can begin the process of awareness that must precede change. In women's discursive networks, many women experience this type of illegitimate pleasure based on the contradictions of living in a society in which dominant notions of reality are different than the women's. Within their networks, there is the freedom from the constraints of dominant constructions of feminine experience. Often these pleasures involve the ironic use of existing ideological restraints that are constructed out of the public discourses on women and the way that women react to them.

Women may internalize much of the hegemonic ideology having to do with their dependence, inferiority, and social roles, but not completely. They may instead establish boundaries in the form of fanship discourse networks, and create a space for their own pleasure. Within these boundaries, they may adopt their own kind of defiant cultural capital and their own strategic knowledges. In the next chapter we shall look at the context and significance of such a move.

6

Cultural Capital and Strategic Knowledge

Pierre Bourdieu (1984) has used the term *cultural capital* to describe how a person's class and social status are reflected in bodies of acquired knowledge. Cultural capital can come from schools, but most often it is a result of being brought up in a family or social group that already possesses it and therefore teaches and values it. Aesthetics, appreciation of classical music, history, or philosophy, and other forms of high art are examples of valued knowledges. Often referred to as reflections of "taste," such valued knowledge functions as a marker of class status. Bourdieu (1984) refers to this class marker as "an economy of cultural goods" (p. 1). It has a specific logic that places high culture at the top of the list while popular and mass culture remain at the bottom. In such a hierarchy of class and social status governed by taste, one's understanding of soap opera conventions is not a mark of high status, but the opposite. As we have seen, soap opera's position in discourse marks its audience as having low social status. Yet, many people, particularly women, continue to value the knowledge of soap opera and its conventions. This chapter discusses how certain strategic knowledges operate to enable those in soap opera networks to use their cultural capital defiantly if they so desire.

Oppositional Decoding

One might call the valuing of soap operas despite their low social status an instance of oppositional decoding, which happens whenever a group constructs meaning from a cultural product that varies from the accepted or dominant notion of the meaning of that product or expression. For example, Linda Steiner (1988) has noted a case of oppositional decoding in the responses to advertisements and clippings printed in the "No Comment" feature of *Ms.* magazine. During the 10-year period that Steiner analyzed, women sent in pieces to *Ms.* magazine's "No Comment" section, pieces that indicated that the senders were defining reality differently than the examples they sent in. These materials ranged from photographs of billboards to newspaper clippings, or texts from classified ads, defining women as men's property, implying that women enjoyed sexual abuse or violence, considering women silly or stupid, trivializing women's work or accomplishments, highlighting male privilege, or using the generic form of the masculine pronoun *he* in cases where its object was obviously a woman. These were then published in the "No Comment" column of the magazine. According to Steiner, this group activity served to demarcate the group's view of the world from that of dominant culture. This is one of the ways that readers, even geographically separated readers who do not know each other, sustain what Steiner calls "communities of sentiment" (see also Steiner, 1983). In this case, the community of sentiment is dispersed in what Stanley Fish (1980) has called an "interpretive community," or a community in which readers construct and employ similar meanings, assumptions, and strategies even though they do not necessarily talk to each other. The newly produced text printed in *Ms.* magazine challenged the dominant code and its value system as well as affirmed the alternative codes and values specified by the readers' critique.

The words used in popular discourse to describe soap operas can be appropriated for an oppositional reading in much the same way that the *Ms.* magazine readers used the "No Comment" feature for oppositional decoding. The word *trash,* for example, is frequently used to refer to women's genres such as soap operas or romance novels. It has a number of connotations in our culture.

First, *trash* connotes that which ought to be discarded, a sort of instant garbage; second, it connotes cheapness, shoddiness, the overflow of the capitalist commodity system. Third, it connotes a superficial glitter designed to appeal to those whose tastes are ill-formed according to the dominant perspective, or at the very least whose tastes are different than those whose use of the dominant value system allows them to dismiss popular art forms. Fourth, *trash* is excessive; it has more vulgarity, more tastelessness, more offensiveness than is necessary for its function as a cheap commodity. All of these connotations point to its uncomfortably contradictory nature: In the dominant value system, trash is the disparaged way of exploiting the subordinate, of appealing cynically to their vulgar tastes.

In the discourse of the subordinate, however, trash can be used defiantly. The devalued commodity may be detached from its devaluation and used positively in the subordinated culture as a source of meanings and pleasure that are formed partly in the knowledge that they are devalued by the dominant value system. For Hobson's (1982, pp. 109-110) soap opera fans, as for Radway's (1984, pp. 90-91) fans of romance, part of the viewer's/reader's pleasure lies in the knowledge that men disapprove of their taste and in their defiant assertion of their right to pleasure in the face of masculine disapproval. The insistence on their right to their own pleasure is not only an act of cultural resistance within the politics of the family in that it defies masculine power within the patriarchal family, but such insistence is also a recognition that the differences between masculine and feminine tastes can be understood in terms of a power relationship of domination and resistance. The term *trash* is so rich because it contains within it the social struggle for power articulated in terms of cultural taste and preference.

Women who use soap operas as a part of their cultural capital are thus not necessarily accepting the dominant notions attributed to soap opera and its audience. Instead, they may be pushing these notions to extremes in order to make fun of them. And the way that soap opera audiences do this is different than the way that fans of more literate cultural products express oppositional decoding.

By selecting soap operas as their cultural capital and speaking about them openly and with unabashed pleasure, soap opera fans reverse the meanings of this activity. They challenge the linguistic meaning codes associated with their cultural capital.

Literate and Nonliterate Knowledge

The gossip networks surrounding soap operas depend on knowledge based in orality that operates, to an extent, in defiance of literate-based school systems and institutions of knowledge. As Patricia Palmer (1986a) recounts about the teenage girls in her study *Girls and Television*: "Those who expressed enjoyment of school went on to talk about lunchtime or being with friends" (p. 50). Girls often enjoy school because it is where they meet their friends and talk. They frequently pay little attention to the regulatory systems in place at school and create countersystems in the form of gossip networks. These, in turn, are usually discounted or ignored in dominant structures. But it is these gossip networks that can give young women (and sometimes young men) training in understanding oral-based thought processes rather than the literate thought processes supported by schools and the hierarchies of cultural products taught by educational systems. Schools usually exclude soap operas from the cannon of hegemonically approved (or "quality") media because they do not represent what the dominant system considers to be "truth."

Dominant meanings concerning mass media gain credibility within a culture, and people in nondominant groups often outwardly accept these meanings because all of us are trained in the same institutions that determine and repeat dominant concepts. Often we all accept those values even though they may be inconsistent with the way that the members of our particular subcultural group understand the world.[1] As pointed out in Chapter 5, in the case of the concept of feminine discourse, a seemingly inconsistent double perspective is held by many women. At one level, dominant constructions of social knowledge are accepted and practiced; at another, they are questioned. The politics of who does the housework is a good example. Social conventions may be practiced, and hierarchies may be adhered to, but when women and girls are free to talk among themselves, ways of deconstructing such hierarchies sometimes emerge. Talk in this context can be critical of social practices adhered to in public. Similarly, even while acknowledging literate theories of evaluating art, literature, and, by extension, the media, fans of soap opera sometimes choose to apply other criteria to their evaluation of soap operas. As in all fanship groups, there is a kind of insider knowledge in evidence (Amesley, 1989; Jenkins, 1988b; Lewis, 1992). In the case of soap opera groups, the knowledge works to preserve the conventions of orality in the face of socially approved literate conventions.

Soap operas derive many of their conventions from oral culture. As I have already noted in Chapter 3, oral culture can stand in resistance to literate culture and knowledge. The most common educational training and experience in our society is in literate culture and thought processes; hence one needs to learn how to read soap operas. Such knowledge is essential to soap opera fanship and fans integrate an awareness of the production constraints of soap opera into their conversation about soap opera and understand these as parameters of predicting and speculating. In addition, fans possess intertextual knowledges about soap operas and their stars gleaned from other television and print media sources. In turn, these aspects affect how a viewer uses and understands the characters, plots, themes, and values conveyed by the soap opera text.

Soap opera fans develop a reading strategy that entails the ability to slip back and forth between several different layers of meaning generation. To start, if one considers the narrative like any other narrative, one may look at common ways in dominant culture of analyzing and/or evaluating the narrative—aspects such as plot, story, characterization, conflict, or setting. Right away one tends to have trouble with conventional analysis, for none of these aspects alone tells us much about soap opera. In fact, it is the failure of critics to move beyond these traditional ways of looking at literate or written narrative, that often involve the study of the text in isolation, that accounts in large part for the derisive accounts of soap opera that we often encounter.

The reversal of dominant conventions is not an innocent act. To understand how this reversal can be accomplished, we should explore Foucault's questioning of the Western will to truth. Foucault's analysis posits a relationship between power, knowledge, and discourse. Although *discourse* is a common term, Foucault uses it in a very specific way. Traditionally, there has been a distinction between discursive and nondiscursive practices. Discursive practices have been thought of as texts, ideas, theories, and the use of language while nondiscursive practices are considered to be economic systems, social and class divisions, and institutions (Welch, 1985). Foucault (1975) sees discourse as a combination of these distinctions. For example, he discusses a shift in medical discourse from 1770 to 1815. This discursive shift dictates as well a shift in the primary focus of health care from the family to the hospital, which also governed the design of hospital buildings and the shift to clinics as modes of teaching about medicine (pp. 196-197). Foucault's (1975) study of medical discourse indicates one way that he analyzes the power dimensions of discourse. He calls this method *archeology.* With it he analyzes institutions, systems of order, and types of exclusion and appropriation. But in addition to this, he also analyzes resistance to dominant forms of knowledge and power. He calls this second method of analysis *genealogy,* and with it he analyzes resistance to established discourses, describing these as "an insurrection of subjugated knowledges" (Foucault, 1980b, p. 81).

By *subjugated knowledges,* Foucault refers to the history of conflict and domination lost to the subjugated. Such knowledges are lost because of their erasure from the history of ideas or because of theoretical frameworks in which they cannot be tolerated. In addition, some knowledges are unacceptable to dominant culture because they are not sufficiently scientific. These are "naive knowledges, located low down on the hierarchy" (Foucault, 1980b, pp. 81-82). The question concerns whose knowledge is taken as real. Hence knowledge itself is tied to politics and power. The full force of genealogy entails the memory of conflict, the expression of alternate knowledges, and the struggle of such knowledges against dominant discourse. Foucault describes this task as "the attempt to emancipate historical knowledges from that subjection, to render them, that is, capable of apposition and of struggle against the coercion of a theoretical, unitary, formal and scientific discourse" (p. 85). Although the structuring of soap opera knowledges may not immediately appear radical, let us suspend judgment in light of Foucault's notion of strategic knowledge while we address some of these knowledges specifically.

Production Constraints

Whereas literate conventions seek to make the process of construction of the program invisible, soap opera fans are constantly aware of the production constraints at work in soap operas when they evaluate them. For example, the producers of soap operas are acknowledged and talked about. In addition, the suspension of disbelief, which is theorized as a major viewing practice in dominant culture, may not take place in soap opera viewing. The following conversation among *Days of Our Lives* fans may shed some light on these aspects:

Emma: I don't like it [*Days of Our Lives*] as well. There are too many characters and they're not following through on them.
Carl: Yeah.
Emma: Just like Marlena. She's had the twins and Roman died, then you don't hear a word about the twins. They're just dropped.
(Laughter)
Karen: They can't find babies, I think, to get on the soap operas so they have to, like, pretend they are out all the time.
Emma: Well, they just sort of faded them out suddenly rather than gradually.
Sue: But probably, OK, next year they are going to suddenly appear as teenagers.
Emma: Yes, they probably will.
MEB: How come they never have real babies? Do you think that's just a technical difficulty they don't want to deal with?
Emma: Well, Marlena had the twins, but you don't see them carrying them.
Sue: Well you know Liz's baby. We've seen her. For a year it's been the same baby.
Emma: Yes, she's getting bigger and you're sort of seeing her grow. And Cary, isn't that the little girl [Roman and Anna's daughter]? You see her once in a while.
Sue: Like I said, she's going to disappear for a year and then, just like Hope. Remember when Hope came? We saw Hope three or four years ago when she was a little baby and then she's—

Several aspects of the way soap operas can be viewed are illustrated in this conversation; however, throughout it is clear that the narrative is constructed. The producers of the show are thus mentioned frequently (known as "they" to most audiences). According to this audience, when the producers can't find babies for the show, they simply "pretend they are out all the time." This seems to be an acknowledgment that such production shortcuts are expected in soap operas. The message one might get is that the audience for soap operas—women—is not worth the investment of expensive, high production values. Perhaps these women are simply too dumb to notice. However, it is clear that this audience does not believe the soap opera conventions (any more than other people believe the literary ones). Nevertheless, these conventions can still be enjoyed. Similarly, there is no attempt to camouflage the fact that characters grow up too fast on the American daytime soap operas. These are merely conventions of the genre. In literate narratives the rapid passing of time is indicated by various conventions—the clock on the wall, the sequence of seasons, segments of dialogue, or superimposed dates—which take care of such lapses in linear time. Soap opera narrative logic, however, is more abbreviated and hinges on intensity. As pointed out in Chapter 2, this is like the way people gossip. The uninteresting parts are simply left out in order to talk about the parts of the story that interest the speakers and the listeners, and the conversation will circle back to perhaps add another aspect to the kernel of information that started the narrative.

Another convention of the genre that outsiders find difficult to deal with is the fact that dead characters often come back to life. Sometimes the character who returns from the dead is played by the same actor or sometimes an entirely different one who bears no resemblance to the original character. In the following excerpt from the interviews, we see the intersection of several of these production aspects at once, including the fact that the actors who play soap opera characters frequently make appearances in other genres of television, what Fiske (1987) has called horizontal intertextuality. In the following quotation, Anna (the character) is spoken of as if she (the actor) were still the character Anna, simply leaving Salem (the *Days of Our Lives* setting) to do a car commercial.

Karen: It's fun because you really can predict what is going to happen.
Sue: Emma [another member of the group] is positive that Stefano is alive.
Laura: Oh?
Sue: I think Stefano is dead.
Laura: It's funny how these people turn up. You see Anna? Anna is doing a car commercial.

Much has been made of the fact that soaps audiences talk within fanship networks as if an actor were actually a character, as is evident in the above conversation. The hypothesis is that soaps fans simply don't know the difference; in other words, they don't realize that the characters aren't "real." However, it is clear with these groups of fans that talking about soaps characters as if they were real is actually a manner of speaking that adds to the fun of speculating about soaps and is also a kind of shorthand sparing one the trouble of mentioning actor as well as character.

As mentioned earlier, one frequently knows when a character is going to die by articles in the newspapers or popular magazines about contract negotiations, a part of vertical intertextuality according to Fiske (1987). Other signs are the fact that the actor appears as a character on another television show or that she or he has started a singing career, a part of the circuit of popular culture where a star in one genre uses the familiarity generated in that genre to become more involved in another career aspect like singing (McRobbie, 1991). Thus judgments about characters are made from a much larger field of information than the text alone.

The logic of many of these practices is not to be found within the narrative but in the economics of actors' labor practices. American daytime soaps, for example, are not taped in batches of a season at a time the way that most prime-time narratives are, but are taped continuously about 2 weeks before they are broadcast in the United States. Hence, in the daytime soap operas, an actor can get sick and be replaced anytime. Audiences notice these things and sometimes see these practices as evidence that the producers are talking down to them. Other segments of the audience are amused by the same practices, but everyone who watches regularly seems to understand these negotiations as a soap opera convention. The process of predicting who is leaving (or not) is a major topic of soap opera gossip, and of course, as previously mentioned, characterizations may change with each new actor, not just in appearance but in personality as well.

So character consistency is affected by elements beyond the scope of the story line. Consider this conversation between college-age Australian teenagers, fans of *Days of Our Lives* and *Neighbours*:

Mary: Yeah, I used to like the old Jill. I don't like the new Jill.
Corie: Who?
Ada: Jill.
Mary: She's unreal.
Corie: No, the new Jill is the very, very old Jill. She was on before the previous one.
Mary: Really?
Corie: Mm. She's been on *Another World.* We've had—what's that girl's name? Sounds like?

Mary: Oh, yeah, they keep changing her—
Ada: I love Jill.
Mary: —back. She just had a baby, and she didn't lose weight, so they wouldn't let her come back on. So they kept on with the replacement.

Actors come and go while characters on the soaps go on indefinitely. The rigid separation between text and life, fiction and reality, intellect and body is not present in orality in the way that it exists in literate cultures. Hence character consistency is an issue only in literate cultures, which value unity and in which one can go back to read what a character was supposed to be like. In oral narratives, as in the daytime soap operas, characters change with the telling and with the teller/actor. Obviously, the character of Jill is somewhat inconsistent and, in literate value systems, unacceptable, but in subcultural value systems, Jill may even gain currency by her inconsistency.

In addition, soap opera characters, or rather the actors playing those characters, frequently make appearances at places such as shopping centers. Hence their acceptance or rejection by fans in these personal appearances is also figured into the speculation about whether a particular actor or actors will stay with the program and consequently what happens in terms of the plot. The following conversation concerns *Days of Our Lives'* Bo and Hope.

Sue: I thought they were going to die [Bo and Hope] in a plane crash or drown when a large ship will sink.
Karen: I think they're going to come back.
Sue: Their producers—They didn't hire them back.
Karen: Really?
Sue: Uh huh.
MEB: They were supposed to be such a hot thing.
Emma: Well I heard they weren't very well accepted when they were in St. Pete [Florida]. They said that people mobbed them. I don't know whether they were putting on airs or what or expected too much.

We see again that the world of soap opera fanship and its oral networks is much larger than just the text (the soap opera program) itself. In these three examples, we have seen how the appearance of a soap opera actor in a television commercial, magazine gossip about the actor's weight gain, or a shopping center appearance can affect the story line or enter into the process of speculation in general and hence the creation of the spoken and other forms of the tertiary text. In addition, actors will float from soap opera to soap opera, either becoming a new character or, in some cases, the same actor and her or his character will cross the boundary and enter a new soap opera carrying his or her emotional and historic baggage to the new program.

Because of the daily breaks in the story lines, much time is available for fans to speculate on what comes next, and a large part of soap opera gossip is taken up in this way. Needless to say, this is a pleasurable activity, much like the mystery fan's need to solve the story problem of the mystery. A similar evocation of Barthes's (1975b) hermeneutic code, the search for truth, is embodied in such soap opera speculation. But soap opera speculation has wide-ranging fields of inquiry much as women's knowledge does. Like circular or peasant knowledge, women's traditional knowledge, includes everyday life in its scope. Rather than categorizing what can be considered appropriate for a particular field, folk knowledge takes in everything in its speculations (Martin-Barbero, 1992).

Control

The issue of control is a strong one for women in general. Women often live their lives by someone else's rules. Soap opera producers seem to strive for tension on the part of the audience, while audiences maintain a skeptical attitude toward the producers. Audiences consider the soap operas to be their stories, yet their stories are controlled by a broadcast hierarchy only vaguely familiar to them. Like official bureaucracies whose workings are mysterious, the production operatives of television soap operas are also removed from the workings of everyday life. Thus these fans watch with some interest to see if soap opera producers, the frequently referred to "they," will come up with a successful variation on the formula. The producers of soap opera are not folk, and are at some distance from the fans. Although fans write them and tell them what should be done on the show, there is a great deal of tension between the two camps.

Although soap opera viewers do seem to feel they have a stake in the plot or the stars' comings and goings, they are often also somewhat dispassionate about the process. Here is a *Coronation Street* fan discussing an attempt to rejuvenate the show's declining popularity.

Ellen: They have brought in a whole series of new families and characters which they might run for a couple of months; and it doesn't work terribly well, so they get rid of them, and they are just at the stage where they are beginning to panic a bit.

Panic on the part of producers is viewed with some distance by this viewer. She has little personal investment at the time of the interview in the show's success or failure in the producer's terms, but continues to watch with interest as the soap opera producers struggle. There seems to be a reversal of power here, wherein the viewer becomes the one in power, in that she is able to disassociate herself from the producers' problems.

There is often also an issue of control of information, particularly about the actors on soap operas. Soap opera actors have only recently, with the publication of several new commercially produced soap opera magazines, entered the economy of the public display of actors constructed in their own right as stars (Dyer, 1982, 1992; Waldrop & Crispell, 1988). Actors who play parts in soap operas are most often thought of as "one of us" rather than "one of them." Soap opera actors then are just as much outsiders to the more privileged world of film production and its stars as women are to the world of dominant institutions. The real politics of soap opera actors are also under the control of the producers. The same viewer quoted above looks at these constraints:

Ellen: . . . Although she wasn't Elsie Tanner at the time, she actually left *Coronation Street* to try and do something—theater acting—she left just at the point when it [*Coronation Street*] began to go downhill, and her leaving it contributed.

MEB: Was her reputation based on her youth? In the past? Or was it based on her image in *Coronation Street*? I mean her reputation as such a glamorous middle-aged woman.

Ellen: Both, I think. Both. She was also a supporter of the Labor party and was quite vocal about that.

MEB: In the show or outside?

Ellen: Oh no, in the show. Not outside. They are very strict on *Coronation Street* about what the cast say. There was another sacking—one of the cast was sacked, Len. One of the main characters was sacked and he was sacked because he gave out all this scandal to the Sunday papers about the cast of the show, etc., about the behind-the-scenes stories.

The actor, then, was fired for giving out information that suited the quest of the audience for more information or gossip concerning the inside workings of the show and the real lives of the actors. The structure of gossip networks thrives on the release and flow of information whereas the structure of official information is based on constraint and control. These issues of control seem to be played out in the relationship of soap opera producers to soap opera fanship networks.

The problem that "they" have in keeping all of the elements of the show under control is evident, according to older teenage fans in this study, even with the slick (i.e., high production values and elaborate sets) soaps like the American evening soaps.

Vicki: Remember they did that with the year, when the whole past year was a dream. I think that's unparalleled, and to have a whole year of a soap [consist] of someone's dream—in *Dallas.*
Jackie: It was pretty pathetic. I reckon it was because they stuffed up the story line.
Vicki: Yeah, but that was such a blow, a case of the script not being written ahead, wasn't it?
Jackie: Yeah, it was just because they wanted to get Bobby back into the show. It was such a disgrace. I don't reckon it was revolutionary: I reckon it was disgusting.
Jackie: Oh, they could have done it some other way. It was weak.
Vicki: Oh yeah, they could have, but it just amazed me that they thought the audiences were stupid enough to accept it.
MEB: How could they have done it? I mean, they killed him off.
Jackie: Say that he had died or something.
Vicki: Say he was away in some place in Switzerland getting his whole body reconstructed or something stupid.
(Laughter)

Daytime soap opera logic is here applied to nighttime soap operas, which operate partially in the realm of dominant production conventions and partly in the realm of soap opera conventions. Although U.S. nighttime soap operas are not produced with the same kind of ongoing flexibility as the daytime soap operas, these viewers talk as if they were, which means that they can assume that perhaps a mistake was made in the story as is possible on a daytime soap opera. The producers are thought to have misjudged how important Bobby was to the show and, indeed, one might assume that such judgments by the producers could be made between seasons on a show produced in 13-week blocks. This group of fans would apparently have accepted the soap opera convention of bringing dead characters back to life but were unable to accept the dream sequence explanation.

Absurdity

Similar conventional issues crop up among other soap opera fans. These young Australian teenage fans of the Australian soap opera *Sons and Daughters,* for example, are extremely analytical about plot construction.

Jan: Most of what happens is based on revenge for what someone's done to them or working around greed for money, I think, and someone else's wife. (Laughter)

Sara: Or husband, as Alison.

Jan: Love or money and revenge. I think it is going to be pretty, um, shall we say dramatic for a while anyway, seeing as Alison is in such a critical condition at the moment in hospital.

In addition to general ideas about plot structure, in the same interview there is much specific speculation concerning how or whether the character played by Rowena Wallace, widely known as Pat-the-Rat, who had been killed off the previous year, would return to the show. The character of Alison is believed to be Pat-the-Rat in disguise, having had plastic surgery before returning to Australia from South America. At the time of the interview, it was becoming clearer that she would at some point reveal herself to be the original character. Here is the conversation:

Sara: Actually I think Alison being in the program is a good way of bringing Rowena Wallace back into it because Alison could either come back to life (she doesn't want anybody to know what she did beforehand overseas) made up to look how she was beforehand or she could die, and you know, someone looking the spitting image of Rowena Wallace could come back on the set.

Jan: But it is the only way they are going to be able to do it because there is no way they are going to get Alison and Rowena to play the same character. It's going to be a bit monotonous. It's like having two devils. You know how you usually have a devil in the episode? It's like having two of them, so they'll probably compete against each other for the limelight in the series.

These teenage viewers seem clear that there are specific formulas that have to be adhered to. It is evident that their calculations in terms of the plot are particularly technical. It is the variations in the telling that make it interesting.

The other side of plot construction in soap operas is their absurdity. Soap opera plots are often excessive. Although formulas may prevent soap operas from "having two devils," formulas don't prevent them from having plot twists that "try men's minds" (but apparently not women's). Some adult *Days of Our Lives* fans discuss plot in the following excerpt:

Jenny: James [Judith's husband] comes home sometimes and you try to explain it.
Doris: You try to explain it?
Jenny: Absolutely.
Judith: If you try to explain it, it really does sound absolutely ridiculous.
Doris: It does.
Sharon: You've got to say, well, Marie fell in love with this fellow who turned out to be her brother (laughter) with plastic surgery, and the one brother shot another brother.
Jenny: And Julie was married to Doug, who was married to her mother. (Laughter)
Sharon: Doug's daughter was really Julie's sister and—(Laughter)
Vicki: Can you remember when Marie and Alex were fiddling around with each other, you know, and she was one of those ladies that love him to hit her, what do you call them? You know, sado—
Doris: Sadomasochistic?
Vicki: She loved that.
Jackie: And then she became a nun and then she had a baby. (Background conversation/laughter)
Judith: And then fell in love with this guy who turned out to be her brother, but she didn't know because he'd lost his memory and had plastic surgery, and that wasn't all. She started to commit suicide and that didn't work, and she joined a nunnery, and that didn't work.
Vicki: They're all prostitutes on this soapie!
Sharon: That's what I'm saying.
Doris: Loose morals.
Sharon: When we're watching it, because it's developed so slowly, it doesn't seem so weird.

The tension here has to do with trying to justify one's pleasure in terms of dominant aesthetic notions of reality (Barbatis & Guy, 1991). Judith's husband, James (these are real people), refuses to give up his investment in the cultural capital that places him in the dominant stratum of society, while the women who have accepted soap opera conventions have no trouble discussing and enjoying a plot that they clearly recognize as excessive.

Specific plots become more amusing in relation to the long-range view of them, in relation to other plot twists, and in relation to external judgments. The above conversation concerning Marie's tragicomic life story is almost an exact repeat of the same story told by the American fans of *Days of Our Lives*. In each group, there was laughter and a general acknowledgment of the absurdity of the plot line; but at the same time, in each group, there was an apparent willingness to engage in the fun of talking about it without condemning the genre itself. The strategic information that these women possess makes it not only possible but pleasurable to enjoy the absurdity of some soap opera plots.

Sexuality

We also see sexuality talked about in a tongue-in-cheek manner in the preceding conversation. The judgment that these fans make does not seem to be moralistic. Vicki (who is in her eighties) jokes about prostitution and sadomasochism as the group notes matter-of-factly that the nunnery "didn't work." The irreverence seems to be, at least in part, about the absurdity of the limitations of viewing women either as whores or nuns. It is a characteristic of subordinated groups that belief in stable, rule-governed behavior is not strong, possibly because the rules are so often violated for nondominant groups and because subordinate groups have different sorts of rules. The contradictions in the lives of women are similar to the contradictions in the construction and content of soap opera plots. Morality and marital stability are often at issue. Marital stability is rule-governed behavior. As seen in the discussion about paternity in soap operas in Chapter 3, women are connected to these rules only through their relationship to men. The constant breaking of these rules in the American daytime soap operas is one of the reasons soaps are seen as a problem in dominant discourse.

At issue in soap opera viewing in terms of dominant discourse is not only what one does with one's time but also what one does with one's body. According to Nancy Lesko (1988), when a woman deviates from norms of any type, sexual deviance is imputed to her. Women who leave their place—that is, the position of having their lives laid down for them, of being deferential—are perceived as dirty, and their uncleanliness is often spoken of in terms of sexual pollution. This discourse concerning sexual pollution is a part of the discourse that functions to control women and that, in fact, attempts to control anything that threatens dominant hegemony. As John Hartley (1984) points out, television itself is a somewhat dirty category in terms of the unified categories preferred by dominant culture.

Soap operas are generally constructed in dominant discourse as sexually deviant. Sex on soap operas is commonly perceived to be a corrupting force in terms of the purity attributed to women. This kind of protective reasoning supports the idea that some women are bad and others are good—the whore/virgin dichotomy. In fact, sex on the soaps is different than sex in dominant media. Whereas in dominant representational systems, sex is often shown for its titillation value, on soap operas the symbolic representations of romance are just as prevalent—an engagement ring, for example—symbols offered not for arousal but for the sense of security they offer. As mentioned in Chapter 4, sex (as of this writing) is not often shown on soap operas. In fact, among regular fans, there are frequent disputes concerning whether a sexual act has actually taken place. Take, for example, the following conversation:

Corie: How about on her 18th when they made love. That was the best.
June: They did not.
Corie: They did make love.
June: No, her dad walked in.
Corie: Yeah, but after they'd made love.
Mary: No.
  (Laughter)
Ada: It was after, wasn't it?
Mary: No, it was before. . . .
Corie: Cuz, I've seen so many reruns of it, you know—how she remembers it?
  And they are honestly making love. I can guarantee you.
Ada: That must have been another time.
Mary: No, they only did it just before her dad walked in.
Ada: You know, Hope's still a virgin.
Mary: No, she's not.
June: She is, she is!

It is evident from this quote that these fans are having fun with the issue. They are in fact parodying the assumption that sex is everywhere on the soaps and also, in the process, the importance (in dominant culture) of virginity for women. Issues relating to the control of sexuality seem to be frequently made fun of by these fans, particularly the teenage fans. Sexuality, lack of order, and trashiness are linked concepts.

  The Australian soap opera *Sons and Daughters,* for example, was taken off of the air in August 1987 and replaced after a 6-year run by *Neighbours,* a different (and less trashy) kind of soap, one that some fans felt to be more "realistic," more down to earth, quieter, less likely to take in all the highs and lows of emotional possibilities in rapid succession or to display virtue and nonvirtue with simplicity. In other words, *Neighbours* is less melodramatic than was *Sons and Daughters.* This is subject to change, however, given that soap operas are never static.

Identification

The nicer or cleaner and less sexual a soap opera is, the less likely, it appears, that there will be either a villain or a villainess who represents pure evil—the villain we can "love to hate." In general the characters become more "rounded," more like us and sometimes, it appears from these interview conversations, less distant and less fun. Pleasure begins to hinge on fewer characters; we become fans of Kylie Minogue or Peter O'Brien (the actors themselves) rather than *Neighbours* or *Days of Our Lives,* or even Bo and Hope (of *Days of Our Lives*) or Scott and Charlene (of *Neighbours*). The following conversation seems to support such a claim:

MEB: But now *Neighbours*—do you think it's less risqué?
Ada: Yeah, I think it's less. I think it's a lot less.
Corie: But it's also families, you know, like old people, young people.
Ada: Yeah, it might change.
Corie: When the ratings get down, they try and get more sensationalized.
Ada: I mean nothing much happens. There's a marriage and birth and a car accident and some guy getting a job in a pub, I mean it's not very—
Corie: But the idea keeping a lot of people watching it is Charlene and Scott, I reckon.
Ada: And Peter O'Brien.

The closer the show comes to a literate formula, the more we relate to it in the way that literate ways of thinking lead us—the more, in this case, we think in terms of individuals or couples than groups and the more we begin to think of actors as embodiments of ourselves and hence begin to identify with a single character.

The audiences of the more melodramatic soap operas seem to evaluate characters both as constructs and as actors who are subject to the various constraints of their trade and their genre, rather than to identify with a designated hero or heroine as one is expected to do in many literate narratives. Thus, soap operas appear to be very disunified. There are too many characters and too many plots to give a unified account of, for example, what the soap is about. This is so much the case that sometimes, according to some fans, the soaps have to be brought back in line. This may be perceived by the audience as a mistake; perhaps the producers didn't realize how popular a person was. Then again, perhaps the show just got away from the writers and acquired a life of its own.

Women's strategic knowledge about soap operas centers on the fact that soap opera narratives are not expected to be real. Thus the attempt on the part of dominant narratives to convince us that characters are real is not the same kind of issue on soap operas, where such expectations are often negated. This aspect also functions as a negation of narrative form that naturalizes dominant constructions of reality.

To return to Foucault's notion of power and knowledge, Foucault resists a strictly ideological critique of power in relation to class interests. His notion of genealogy criticizes technologies of power, which in their formation control not simply class interests but whole structures of being. According to Foucault (1980b): "One can understand nothing about economic science if one does not know how power and economic power are exercised in everyday life. The exercise of power perpetually creates knowledge and, conversely, knowledge constantly induces effects of power" (pp. 51-52).

Taking Pleasure

The everyday practice of taking pleasure into one's own hands is a political act for women. Women usually function in our society as givers, not takers, of pleasure. Taking pleasure despite negative social construction of the activity means standing up to established norms and claiming one's space. Because women are silenced in many aspects of interaction, claiming one's space is tantamount to gaining one's voice. Thus choosing soap opera as cultural capital and acquiring a set of strategic knowledges that are counter to dominant constructions of reality can be seen as political.

Although, on the surface, it appears that women are consuming both soap operas and the products they advertise, if they use their own soap opera networks to question their status rather than confirm their status, then they are restructuring ideological norms for themselves. The social and cultural constructions of romance and family, in the case of women, are central for the control of meaning for woman in society. When patriarchal meanings are left unquestioned, women's position in society remains unchanged. It is only through the questioning of such meanings that hegemonic control can change.

The foundations of a theory of pleasure for women are in the social relations among women and the knowledge they accrue within them.

Women can and do talk to each other from a unique position—one of mutual subordination. Control of knowledge is a major form of social power and networks activate latent knowledge—things that women know by virtue of the fact that they both know what it is like to be a woman within dominant culture and also have access to women's underground networks. And, as Foucault (1980b) reminds us, knowledge is also strategic. Strategic knowledge puts us in touch with the conflicts that spark resistance.

Knowledge, pleasure, and power are equally important here. Several kinds of knowledge are at stake. There is knowledge of the complexity of restraints on women, which enables women to empathize with soap opera situations or reject them. There is knowledge of the conventions of orality, as opposed to literacy, which enables people to see soap opera as oppositional. There is knowledge about the actual soap opera story, which allows them to talk about their soap opera with other fans, thereby establishing boundaries of solidarity. Such knowledges, like secret codes, can establish intimate relations with people instantly. Knowledge of soap operas can activate women's strategic knowledge when women have a network in which to share that knowledge. Underground oral networks have kept alternative types of medicine and religion alive, for example, despite elaborate systems of denial from establishment institutions. Women also use soap opera networks to play with the rules—sometimes breaking them. These three dimensions—pleasure, knowledge, and the power to break rules—build on each other and are interdependent.

Social rules, as well as official rules, govern the behavior of women. Soap opera consumption and the oral networks created by soap opera viewers are places where women can break rules—particularly the rules of literate society and dominant hierarchies. Such situations are potentially political for women in that in the process women take pleasure into their own hands. They nominate, value, and regulate their own pleasure. In a more political context, these are the tools for recognizing one's own oppression. Such a political context can begin in the liminality occasioned when women give themselves permission in groups of their choosing to partake in the power of laughter.

Note

1. W. E. B. DuBois describes a similar position for American Negroes in *The Souls of Black Folk* (1961), which he calls a "double consciousness." Dates and Barlow (1990) relate this to mass media.

7

The Power of Laughter

Within the group of soap opera fans I interviewed for this study, there was a great sense of play. Although teenagers often imitated scenes from soap operas with great pleasure, adult women were just as jovial in other ways. This study was not the first to note a sense of play: Palmer (1986a) noticed it among teenage fans when describing their television viewing experiences and networks, and Davies (1986) describes the conversations held by one of his groups of what he calls "self defined 'housewives' " as "earthy and raucous" (p. 89) and more concerned with *Days of Our Lives* as a means of jogging memories to allow a space for the telling of anecdotes than making judgments about the quality or effectiveness of the drama itself. Although the adult fans of *Days of Our Lives* described in the present study never mentioned imitating the characters on soaps, teenage fans of *Days of Our Lives* and *Neighbours* and an adult fan of *Coronation Street* recited lines or imitated accents and voice qualities of soaps characters with great regularity. The younger teenage fans of *Sons and Daughters* never mentioned acting the part of a character, although they were aware and appreciative of voice nuances.

The data from this study were coded for laughter because from the beginning of the interviews it was clear how much fun everyone had talking about soap operas. It was a very different picture than the one produced in dominant discourse in which soap opera audiences simply accepted the medium in dreary silence. Instead, women (and some men) were acting in defiance of that stereotype. Not only were many things about the soaps absurd to these audiences, but often what was laughed at involved a complex acknowledgment of the audiences' own subordination and their devalued and often defiant cultural position as soap opera fans. To look at how these active instances of parody and play can be understood in the context of resistance, it is useful to look at the theoretical notion of the carnivalesque.

The Carnivalesque

The concept of carnival has been used by Mikhail Bakhtin (1965) and Victor Turner (1969, 1977a) to suggest that the making fun of role hierarchies and the status reversal that the pre-Lenten carnival involves can lead to a kind of empowerment for the people. Carnival involved role reversal in which the established hierarchies of life were ignored as people dressed and acted in unconventional ways, as fools or unruly lords, for instance. Turner (1977a) has gone on to state that the public manifestation of carnival is also concerned with liminality. By *liminality,* he means "a state or process which is betwixt-and-between the normal, day-to-day cultural states and processes of getting and spending, preserving law and order, and registering social status" (p. 33). The adolescent stage of life, for example, represents one of those betwixt-and-between times. Like carnival, liminality suggests what might happen. According to Turner (1977a): "Liminality is full of potency and potentiality. It may also be full of experiment and play. There may be a play of ideas, a play of words, a play of symbols, a play of metaphors" (p. 33). It is such a liminal state between reality and fantasy that can be created by the boundaries of soap opera gossip networks. There is a sense, in this unruly world, in which pleasure can transgress boundaries, and that transgression is brought about by laughter. In this chapter I will explore the possibilities of the carnivalesque available in soap opera networks.

Social practices for subordinated groups can be a mass of contradictions. Soap opera fanship networks acknowledge these contradictions, and in turn such contradictions have the capacity to provoke carnivalesque laughter. Carnivalesque forms, ranging from ritual spectacles to verbal expressions, have a number of common attributes; two of these are particularly pertinent here: First, they exist outside of dominant cultural practices, and, second, they are based in laughter. According to Mikhail Bakhtin (1965), the experience of carnival is opposed to everything ready-made and completed. The symbols of the carnival idiom are filled with a kind of "pathos" of change and renewal—a sense of the "gay relativity of prevailing truths and authorities" (p. 11). This consciousness produces what Bakhtin calls a "second life," a sort of parody of extracarnival life, "a world inside out" (p. 11). He stresses that this parodic mode is "far distant from the negative and formal parody of modern times" (p. 11) because "folk humor denies, but it revives and renews at the same time. Bare negation is completely alien to folk culture" (p. 11). In the case of soap opera audiences, such world-inside-out logic can be seen in the play between the audience's knowledge of the fictional world of the soap opera and that same audience's knowledge of the world outside the soaps. Entering into the "second world" of soap opera viewing thus involves the knowledge of the constraints imposed on soap operas in the "first world" of dominant culture. Further, soap opera fans also use their soap opera network to allude to constraints on women.

One way they enter this second world is by speaking of characters as if they were real. In conversations about characters, soaps audiences often speak as if these characters existed in "real life." "Real life" is, of course, contained and articulated by dominant discursive practices, and the audience's talking about the characters as though they were real defies that dominant conception of what constitutes reality. Kinship in soap operas serves as another evocation of Bakhtin's second world. Soap operas' complex kinship networks serve to question the hegemonic notion of kinship situations operating in our culture and constitutes a kind of in-joke on the subject. The number of characters who marry, remarry, divorce, have children together, and are relatives by "blood" or marriage cause the relationship patterns to border on incest. By contrast, more conventional narratives do not question or problematize kinship systems. The importance of genealogies in the soaps and in women's culture in general denies the status of the official histories promulgated in dominant discourse. Whereas history emphasizes orderly and unified cause-and-effect relationships, according to Foucault (1977) genealogies have an inherently uncontrollable disorder through the randomness of their development. Although Foucault goes on to develop the broader definition of *genealogy,* described in Chapter 6, not confined to kinship relations, it is easy to see that the genealogies (in the more restricted sense) are very disorderly indeed in soap operas. Knowledge of the former relationships and parentage of characters is an important element in gossip and discussions between fans and in the understanding of narrative developments.

A striking element in these carnivalesque reading practices is laughter. Bakhtin (1965) characterizes carnival laughter as festive, nonspecific, and ambivalent:

> It is, first of all, a festive laughter. Therefore it is not an individual reaction to some isolated "comic" event. Carnival laughter is the laughter of all of the people. Second, it is universal in scope; it is directed at all and everyone including the carnival's participants. The entire world is seen in its droll aspect, in its gay relativity. Third, this laughter is ambivalent: it is gay, triumphant

and at the same time mocking, dividing. It asserts and denies, it buries and revives. Such is the laughter of carnival. (pp. 11-12)

The laughter involved in soap opera fanship groups has similar characteristics, particularly its ambivalence. The ability to see things both ways, as both humorous and serious, characterizes both Bakhtin's hypothetical carnival participants and soap opera fans. The act of parody itself has a tendency to invert social hierarchies. As Robert Stram (1988) has pointed out: "By appropriating an existing discourse for its own ends, parody is especially well suited to the needs of the powerless, precisely because it assumes the force of the dominant discourse only to deploy that force, through a kind of artistic jujitsu, against domination" (p. 139). This inversion of social hierarchy also uses the power of speech in ways that are particularly cogent to women and other subordinated groups. According to Bakhtin (1971), in parody

> the author employs the speech of another. He introduces into that other speech an intention which is directly opposed to the original one. The second voice, having lodged in the other speech, clashes antagonistically with the original, host voice and forces it to serve directly opposite aims. Speech becomes a battlefield for opposing intentions. (pp. 185-186)

The types of play mentioned above often parody social situations for women. Thus they take the speech of characters produced by dominant institutions, in this case the television/advertising apparatus, and use it to serve opposite aims, their own version of making fun of the dominant system.

Laughter often marks the points in these conversations where soap opera fans break rules. The melodramatic aesthetic itself breaks most of the rules of literate culture. As Jesus Martin-Barbero (1992) has put it: "The melodramatic aesthetic dared violate the rational division between 'serious' and frivolous, treat political events as dramatic events, and break with 'objectivity' by observing the situation from the angle that appealed to the subjectivity of the reader" (p. 228). The excesses of the form (complicated plots, inconsistent characters, endless dialogue, lack of dramatic climax) and the subjective point of view (a subject position forever enthralled with relationships) put soap operas, in general, outside of the boundaries of legitimate drama and in contradiction with the rules of dominant cultural narratives (see also Mattelart & Mattelart, 1990).

Fanship networks, by taking as their object of fanship such a devalued form, are already breaking rules. They value something that society finds unacceptable, but they break many unwritten rules as well. They break the rule that devalues women's talk, women's storytelling ability, women's concerns, women's everyday lives, women's ways of knowing, women's traditions. Let us look at how the times these fans laughed construct into their spoken text not only an awareness of contradictions in the soap opera text but also an awareness of contradictions in their own lives.

The Pleasures and Follies of Fanship

One contradiction is that these programs, constructed especially for women, have such low production values, a fact that many nonfans assume goes unnoticed by regular viewers of soap operas.

June: Yeah, you can see the sets moving . . . and everything, when you have the door shutting. Oh, yeah.
(Laughter)
Ada: You do. The sets shake.
(Laughter)
June: Sometimes you find things, you know, from up above hanging down.

Fans, of course, are aware that production values are often different in soap operas than other forms of television. They acknowledge this and usually find it funny. Although popular discourse about soap opera fans implies that fans can't tell the difference, their laughter indicates their lack of gullibility. Plot limitations and acting also fall into this category.

Doris: Liz still think she's married to Don?
Vicki: Yeah, that's for sure. Something will happen such as a fright or else she'll have a fall or a brain tumor.
(Laughter)

The statement that Liz may have a fall or a brain tumor is a comment on the extreme plot twists that can happen on soap operas. Fans often find these possibilities as funny as nonfans find them bizarre. Plot predictability is a source of pleasure here rather than a symbol of soap opera's inferiority.

Part of the pleasure of soap opera fanship is the fact that there is a shared body of knowledge among the group. Often this is in the form of shared history. Like the shared history of friendship, the shared history of soap opera plots both gives comfort and also sometimes reminds one of ambivalent situations, whether soap opera plots or real life. The pleasure of mutual knowledge comes out in the following interview segment:

Ada: Hope was crying. Bo was just about crying. Everyone else in the whole thing was crying.

MEB: Because they thought it had caused him to have a heart attack? And then?

Ada: And then he fell down the stairs, and—

Mary: Oh, he fell down the stairs?

Ada: Oh, no, he didn't actually. On the top of the stairs—you know in Bo's apartment?

June: Who fell down the stairs?

Ada: Doug. When he had his coronary.

June: Paige fell down the stairs when she lost the baby. Remember Paige?

Ada: The Young and the Restless?

June: Yeah.

Corie: Jill climbed up a ladder and jumped.

    (Laughter)

Ada: Jumped.

Mary: Oh, look, I really wish I'd seen that.

    (Laughter)

The laughter here has to do not only with remembering past soap opera plots but with the absurdity of the situation, in this case in parallel soap operas. In *Days of Our Lives,* Doug, who is Hope's stepfather, has had a heart attack after discovering that Bo and Hope had made love. He falls down a flight of stairs. This event reminds the others of a common time when characters in soap operas fall down stairs, which is when a pregnancy needs to be terminated. Because characters must be gotten rid of and pregnancies terminated often in soap operas, certain expected plot twists take on the metonymic representation of the actual event. The event here would be a serious one in any woman's life. Part of the irony here is that in life such an issue has no easy and predictable solution.

Fans experience a large amount of pleasure when those in charge are thought not to be in tune with their viewers. Hence follies on the part of the producers or distributors are the subject of much humor. The one that I document here happened in Western Australia several years before these interviews but is still the subject of much humorous discussion.

Corie: Did you hear about the year when they lost all the episodes at channel 7?

June: Yeah.

Mary: And they printed the whole year on one page of the newspaper.

Corie: And Barry Barker got on TV and told everyone what happened.

June: How beautiful!

Mary: That would have been history.

Ada: And so they missed that whole year. They put it in the paper. It's just a page!

The irony of a whole year of episodes of *Days of Our Lives* fitting onto one page of the newspaper highlights the relative importance of soap operas in relation to news, particularly if we consider news to be a masculine form. However, the fact that it is mentioned at all by mainstream sources is also a bit of a surprise, because in another way it acknowledges that often invisible constituency, the soap opera audience. The humor also lies in the absurd situation of Barry Barker, a local television personality, and the local newspaper featuring a plot summary for a year's worth of the soap opera when each knows little about what their words mean. This story acknowledges the differences between the feminine discourse concerning the soap opera and the masculine discourse, of the newspaper and television power structure and the different knowledges accessible to either group.

Similarly, ironies of time are also a big issue in the us/them disputes between fans and producers/distributors in Western Australia, where the daytime soap operas are taken off the air for the three summer months when the children are home from school. It is presumed by the fans that they are discontinued for the summer to "protect" the children. In any case, because of the never-ending nature of the soap opera, a nonfan would have trouble deciding where in the plot to break for the summer.

Ada: And we're just at the climax, the thing we've been waiting for the past year and a half. We're halfway through the benefit concert and they closed it off for the year!!
(Laughter)

Here is yet another acknowledgment of conflicting discourses. The television station stops a soap opera right before what might be considered in dominant discourse a climax. Lack of knowledge of how a soap opera works is exhibited here, as well as a lack of sensitivity to the female audience. A bit of irony about the position of females in our culture, like Bakhtin's droll laughter, is in evidence in these conversations.

Likewise, even the hallowed institution of the soap opera Christmas, when thrown off schedule (another producer's folly), is the subject of a certain amount of ridicule.

June: Yeah, but I didn't even think it took an order to the people who program them about the seasons, like if you haven't seen them they play them. Like whatever comes next.
Corie: We don't have Christmas when it's Christmas and stuff. Do you have that?

June: Oh, we have Christmas in June. I think that they have Christmas about
every three months.
Ada: No, they don't.
June: They are always having it, that's why.
Ada: I've never seen Christmas.
June: Haven't you?
MEB: Well, normally it only happens once a year.
   (Laughter)

In the United States the seasons on soap operas parallel the actual seasons
of the year. These Australian viewers are commenting on, again, the lack
of sensitivity and knowledge of how soap operas work when episodes are
played back in a somewhat random fashion. The extreme carelessness that
this indicates is both ironic and funny. The confusion as to how many
times, if ever, Christmas has passed in these viewers' viewing history
makes fun of the inability of the whole system to get a simple idea like
the flow of the seasons right. This particular group of teenagers finds
pleasure in painting establishment institutions in general as inept, but here
the values of women's culture are also involved, which adds to the
pleasure. Their insider's knowledge of soap opera and women's culture
shared among the group keep them in the empowered position of insiders.
They understand the codes.
   A fan's own position in discourse and actual life as a member of a soap
opera audience is a source of laughter. Being a fan does not necessarily
mean that one has an absolutely positive regard for the show.

Corie: Prisoner. Did you ever watch *Prisoner*?
Ada: Prisoner's sad.
Mary: Oh, Corie, you and I used to be addicted to that. We used to watch it every
week.
Corie: It got worse.
Mary: It got worse.
Ada: We were always home by 11 o'clock to watch it.
Mary: It got really bad toward the end.
June: These horrible, ugly, fat women were swearing at each other and beating
each other up all the time.
   (Laughter)

In the first quotation, the members of the group are looking back from the
wisdom of years and later deciding that something they liked in their
childhood may have been reevaluated later. But it also points out that they
were involved together just as they are now. They enjoy the fact that their

various soap opera fanship activities have extended over a long period of time.

Ada: I can't believe how much a part of my life this business is.
(Laughter)

It appears that discussing soap operas with the group has reminded a fan of how much time she has spent with the genre. The laughter seems to balance a kind of ambivalence about having spent an excessive amount of time watching soap operas, perhaps ones that she feels negatively about now, and thinking that one should have one's mind on higher ideals, a reflection of the hegemonic notion that women should be busy, discussed in Chapter 5.

A way of speaking that is common in the groups I looked at was the stating of absurdities with deadpan seriousness in the midst of other conversational information. Such conversations could sound like this:

Corie: In *Neighbours,* they've got quite a few nondescript houses, haven't they.
June: Neighbours?
Corie: I can't picture the houses actually. Oh, you can picture the Robinson's a bit, the kitchen.
June: That's the main house, the lounge [lounge room, living room]?
Ada: I can also picture Kylie's house as well.
June: They've got those two lounges.
MEB: What about the opening, you know, when they show all the houses? Can you tell from the opening which one is which?
Ada: I don't know which one's which. Oh yeah, I know that the one with the thing out the front, with the plumbing truck out the front is, with the Merc out the front.
Mary: Is where Shane lives.
June: Is it? The other Merc? The Ramseys?
Ada: No, he's just a chauffeur. You know Home James, that company?
June: Has he still got that job?
Ada: No, he quit because he couldn't drive because of that. You know he killed that woman.
(Laughter)

In this conversation, what seemed to be a conversation about ordinary, everyday occurrences suddenly makes a radical turn. The irony of the way things happen on the soap operas, and perhaps a feeling that this could happen in life, makes the ordinary way in which it is discussed seem funny. The tension between soap opera plots and real life, like the tension between the serious and the mundane, adds to the sense of the absurd.

Talking among each other about soap operas events as if the events they are discussing were real is also a source of amusement. Here's an example.

Ada: I don't know who that is.
Mary: Oh, he's a new guy.
Ada: But I've watched it.
Mary: He was at the wedding.
Ada: Whose wedding?
Mary: At Liz and Neal's.
Ada: I didn't go to Liz and Neal's wedding.
    (Laughter)
Ada: I couldn't make it!
    (Laughter)
Ada: I didn't watch it.

In this case, the speaker gets carried into the fiction and then has fun with the situation. The conversation highlights the importance of the fictional for women in relation to the realism that is valued in dominant culture. There is a fine line between fiction and reality, particularly for subordinated groups.

Ada: I'm naming my kids Bo and Hope.
    (Laughter)
Ada: I'm not being stupid. I'm dead serious.
    (Laughter)
Ada: I don't carry around pictures in my wallet for nothing. I love them. Unreal.
Mary: Have you got their picture in there? Can I see it?
(Ada shows picture)
Mary: I think that's great.
    (Laughter)

When one parodies one's own fanship, it indicates a degree of control over the situation that one is parodying an ability to step back and evaluate one's own fanship behavior. It is thus a source of personal empowerment.

One fan had recently met one of the actors in *Neighbours*. Here is how she talked about it:

MEB: And so, what did you say to him? I mean did you talk to him like he was—
Ada: I just talked to him.
MEB: —like he was his character?

Ada: Yeah, I honestly felt that I knew him because I'd seen him on *Neighbours*.
Mary: You would do.
Ada: It wasn't like I had never met anyone. I was just talking to him like I would
   talk to a friend. Oh, so what have you been doing, yeah, yeah.
   (Laughter)
Ada: I couldn't believe it. It was really quite funny.

Even though soap opera fans frequently play with reality, when they
actually meet a soap opera actor the juxtaposition between character, actor,
and reality, can seem strange, and funny. It is another example of the rejection
of absolute dichotomies between fictional and real. For subordinated groups,
what is considered absolute reality by dominant groups can seem fictional
or constructed in the interest of the dominant and therefore unreal.

The distinctions that one makes between soap opera storytelling and
actual incidents are sometimes funny in that there is a comparison implied
by the fact that one has to clarify which is actual and which is fiction.

Corie: It's like, remember the Burnies? The Burnies, you know they killed those
   five children? This is no soap: this is real life here.
   (Laughter)

The speaker realizes that extreme behavior in real life might be mistaken
for a soap opera plot. The juxtaposition of the two appears to be one of
the pleasures of talking about soap operas as if the characters were real.
When one switches back to other conversations, one needs to flag it as an
actual event for the listeners. The irony of this reversal strikes this audience
as funny. The irony of subordinate positioning in society often sparks
parodic laughter.

Soap Opera and Women's Lives

When women gather and discuss soap operas, other aspects of women's
lives also come up. These include social assumptions about women. In
the first, the assumption is that the speaker will go home and cook dinner
as is socially expected of her.

Judith: I've got to get home and cook my family some dinner.
Vicki: Well, buy them fish and chips.
   (Laughter)

The dominant expectation is that women are always responsible for cooking
the meals. Vicki's comment is on the relative importance of cooking dinner

as compared with the importance of what the group was doing—talking about soap operas. In Vicki's view, soap opera talk is more important. The laughter has to do with women's ambivalent position in relation to the assumption that they are to assume domestic responsibilities in marriage and their momentary lack of ambivalence about soap opera fanship.

Another example of social comment is a statement usually made about women, used here to describe a male character on *Days of Our Lives*.

Sharon: I suppose he's been married for a while now, so he doesn't have to do all those things.
Jackie: Very ordinary now. He doesn't keep himself up.
(Laughter)

"She doesn't keep herself up" is a comment often made in our society about women after they marry. The knowledge behind this is that a woman must rely on beauty to attract a man, but once she is married she can let herself go because she has already "caught" a husband. This comment reverses the position of the sexes and pretends that it is men who must rely on their beauty, a statement that is quite political in terms of sexual politics.

The following example acknowledges the unrealistic expectations of beauty for women.

Jackie: Isn't she lovely.
Vicki: She's a beautiful looking girl, isn't she.
Jackie: She's beautiful. She used to be so bad, didn't she?
Doris: Do you think I'll grow up to look like that?
(Laughter)

This comment shows an awareness of the problem for women of self-image in a world constructed around molding all women to an ideal of beauty that no one can really achieve, thus benefiting the beauty industry and not women. Doris's putting herself into the position of a child in this comment further accents the idea that from childhood women must contend with these expectations—that girls are being brought up with the idea that they must grow up to look beautiful.

Absurdities of subordination are also brought out in the following comments:

Judith: I won't believe it. They weren't there sitting watching the football, were they? That's different.

Doris: When they came home, he'd been out to another bloke's place to sit and watch the football. Take's a little plate of goodies. When the game's here—the Eagles' game's here—they watch the game. But every—whenever it is—when they are away, they go and watch it on television. . . . and they take a plate. The wife makes the plate!

This quotation directly addresses the issue of domestic servitude and male privilege. When the Aussie Rules Football game is away, the men gather to watch it on television and the men's wives make the plate of food they take to share. This custom is being complained about in this interview. This would fall into the gossip category of bitching about subordination, in a directly political way. In contrast, the pleasure of talking about soap opera characters as if they were real is often less direct.

Sometimes there is an implied criticism of dominant hierarchies like those in conventional politics, and sometimes the criticism parodies the way that women are critiqued in society. Here is an example.

Ada: Who else is on *Dynasty*?
Mary: There's only Adam . . .
MEB: John Forsythe to start out with.
June: Oh, he looks like Bob Hawke [Australia's then prime minister].
Corie: I don't know how you get your comparisons.
June: He's got the same haircut, it's blue, and it sort of waves. Blue!
Corie: Blue!
June: Blue rinse.
    (Laughter)

It is women who are usually criticized as blue rinse users. Another example is ironically critical of the power of masculine sexuality.

Doris: Yes, I remember when Julie arrived—when she'd been sent by her parents from Europe.
Jackie: Oh, well now, I didn't see that.
Doris: And she was at school with Susan and there was a problem with that.
Jackie: Oh, I remember her being with Susan, I remember Susan.
Doris: Because Susan adopted the baby, didn't she? Julie murdered Susan, because Susan married David because Susan was pregnant.
Jackie: Oh, I saw all that. Yes, I remember that part.
Sharon: Was that David's father?
Doris: No, David's father—yes, David's father was the real David, because he got Julie pregnant as well, but then she married Scott Manning. He got around, didn't he? Very virile for a 17-year-old.
    (Laughter)

The absurdity of the plot when looked at over time is brought out here, the casualness with which characters both murder and marry each other, but the implied cause of the trouble (male trouble) is viewed here with a certain amount of irony and disdain.

One's own or others' actions concerning soap opera fanship is a frequent topic of laughter. Sometimes one's actions and reactions involve issues of political importance to women.

Ada: She [her mother] won't let me watch it.
MEB: Oh, right, she takes the TV set away from you?
(Laughter)
Mary: My Mum hates it too. She can't stand it. Says it's a waste of time.
Ada: My Mum's addicted to *Neighbours* and she got really emotional during that time when Scott and Charlene . . . she was really angry at it that he was so narrow minded, and for days she would go on about it—"Men are so narrow minded!"
(Laughter)

By way of background, Scott and Charlene of *Neighbours* had decided to go to bed together, and each had revealed his or her previous sexual experiences. Scott had had many and Charlene had had one, and that with a person she was once engaged to. When Scott heard this, he became upset and broke off the relationship.

Part of the laughter here is connected to the mutual acknowledgment among these friends that one of their mothers is serious about the issue of the double standard between men and women, that such issues are important to mother as well as daughter. The contrast between the two mothers is notable. While one displays an extreme anti-soap opera position, the other is completely absorbed and has strong political views on the subject. Another aspect of the interaction has to do with the idea that university-age teens would be told they couldn't watch a particular television show. The interaction contains a thick combination of incongruities and also a serious political stand, a mutually important one for mother and daughter to acknowledge to each other. The spoken text brings together these elements and highlights the issue that mothers can't always protect their daughters either by acknowledging the problem or by forbidding their daughters to watch TV. Laughter gives them ways to deal with the issues but doesn't make the issues go away. The stories that fans in these groups laughed at often carried acknowledgments of subordination. Part of the pleasure in telling these stories was the freedom within the group to speak freely, avoiding many constructed versions of femininity, parodying some and rejecting others. These aspects can also be seen around the issues of women and power, and romance.

One way that this happens is in the imitation of soap opera characters. What follows is a conversation with a British fan who describes how one goes about imitating soap opera characters:

MEB: When you meet somebody else, do you start talking about them [the soaps characters] as if they were real characters, real people?

Ellen: No, you don't. What I do with other fellows—the only way, I don't talk about them. What you do is that you talk in the accent and you pretend to be one of the characters.

MEB: You actually pretend?

Ellen: Well, no, but in conversation, you put on a, say, Bet Lynch voice, or ah, what's her name?

MEB: Different ones? It doesn't matter? I mean do you always put on the same one?

Ellen: I mean there was a time—I wouldn't do it now because I'm not in that situation with others—and I'm not watching it now but there was a time when I was around friends who would watch it regularly, there's Mavis Reilly who is the new old maid.

MEB: She has short hair and works in the corner shop—kind of mousy?

Ellen: You put on your Mavis voice—

MEB: Well, what's the significance of who you choose?

Ellen: Just for pleasure. Just for fun. Just for fun.

MEB: Would you be talking directly about the show?

Ellen: No, you'd be talking about things in general and you'd suddenly throw in a line from Mavis.

MEB: A real line that she had said, or one that was in character.

Ellen: You'd say something in a Mavis voice. I mean there's great lines from Bet Lynch that you—things like put-downs mainly, mainly probably put-downs to men, which is why she is popular in her role as a barmaid, how she puts people down, because I don't know whether you've seen it, but there was this barman Fred Gee, a great big fat obnoxious bloke, who really fancies himself—you know what "fancies himself" means? I didn't know whether it means the same thing in America.

MEB: He was full of himself.

Ellen: Really fancies himself, thinks he's a real hit with the women, but isn't actually and is extremely unpleasant—and obnoxious generally. Most women find him that, and he would always get into situations when he would dress up and put on after-shave and perhaps a cravat and look absolutely ridiculous, and then he would try and get off with someone.

MEB: And then Bet would come in.

Ellen: And he'd be preening in front of the mirror very pleased with himself and he'd say, "How do I look then, Lynch?" and she'd say, "Oh, you look like a well-scrubbed pig." So you'd use that line—or you'd just really appreciate that line.

Such play parodies life with its more restricted behavior. Many women are familiar with similar situations involving men. Usually because of social conventions or fear, women are not able to comment with the directness that Bet has used. By imitating these characters, fans can put themselves in perhaps a more assertive position than they can occupy in actual life.

There are many varieties of this type of play. The one described in the following conversation among Australian university-age women involved *The Restless Years,* an early Australian soap opera. In this case, elaborate codes were developed using the characters' names.

Mary: Restless Years' language—we used to say "Oh, Raelene" whenever we meant really angry.
June: Oh, I was hooked on that. That was just the best show.
MEB: What do you mean you had a language?
Mary: We wouldn't say "really," we'd say a character from *The Restless Years*— we used to say "Oh, Raelene," 'cause Raelene was one of the characters on it.

The above form of play is involved with developing insiders' language codes and is more concerned with style than content. It enforces the boundaries of soap opera networks, giving these fans a point of reference and even a language not accessible to nonfans.

One fan from this group was the person, mentioned earlier, who carried a picture of Bo and Hope of *Days of Our Lives* in her wallet and showed it to people as if Bo and Hope were members of her family. The young woman who carried a picture of Bo and Hope is parodying the fact that dominant discourse suggests that fans can't tell the difference between life and fiction, hence she pretends that she not only thinks Bo and Hope are real but that they are also her friends. Later, when she claims that she is going to name her children after them, she further elaborates on the theme. Hence she ups the ante by involving her own kinship system in her parodic play.

The voice imitation of characters, discussed in some detail earlier, is a constant source of amusement exemplified by the following quotes from the interviews:

Corie: Remember when he was going with Sandy? "I know you're holding back on me and I know you're hurtin' real bad, real bad." [imitating a Southern

American accent]
(Laughter)
Mary: That's such a Chris line, isn't it?
Corie: Yeah.
   * * *
Corie: Hope's a pretty bad actress.
Ada: Oh, Hope's shocking.
Mary: I think she's awful.
June: "I'm 18, I'm 18." That's all she ever says.
(Laughter)
June: "Oh, Larry, I just love champagne."
(Laughter)

In the above quotations, the actual voice of the character is being mim-
icked. With this group of older teenagers, much of the fun comes from
mimicking the show itself. They seem to watch it in order to make fun of
it. In this case, these Australian teenagers are watching an American soap
opera that is in many cases as much as 6 years old. In addition to the much
commented on lack of quality acting on the soap operas and the fact that
it is idiosyncratically American, it is also quite dated. British university
students treated the Australian *Neighbours* in much the same way. They
made fun of *Neighbours* but were often respectful of British-produced soap
operas. Substance as well as style is being parodied in these instances.

Rule Breaking

Laughter is used here in a way that seems to mean that these audiences
are aware of the absurdities in society as it exists. For them, it contradicts
the serious position of those who paternalistically want to take care of
soap opera audiences. Carnivalesque laughter with its droll view of the
world produces a position of defiance for women within discursive networks, and it is such discursive networks that ultimately define reality.
When women talk and joke in recognition of their subordination, they
break boundaries and assert their power. This inversion of power can be
a threat to dominant institutions and transgress the barriers of polite
society.

Bakhtin (1965) uses the example of the carnivalesque to show how
laughter can indicate an ambivalent but aware position in which the world
can be seen in a kind of relativity. I have shown how soap opera gossip
networks playfully imitate characters, develop codes based on soap opera

characters, and, in general, parody life and subordination in their conversations relating to soap opera themes. Laughter becomes an empowering position here partly because it indicates an awareness of and distancing from the power of the media. Although at the moment of viewing the pleasure may rest on what one sees and hears, at the moment of the construction of the spoken text—where the elements of the soap opera get entangled with discussions about life—these same ideas become humorous. The power to laugh from a position of subordination is what Bakhtin noted in relation to carnival. Although the underclasses obeyed the rules of society in their lives in general, for one day life was different. They were able to parody and insult those in power on that day. Turner (1977a) suggests that rituals are a process by which individuals and groups come to understand their world. Some television viewing is just such a ritual process. The process contains a liminal, or in-between stage, when one is neither in nor out of social structures. Like the beach that is neither on land nor in the sea, such spaces allow rules to be broken, roles to be reversed, categories and restrictions to be ignored. According to Turner, these experiences enable societies to create alternative ways of thinking and acting.

Bakhtin's (1965) use of the term *carnivalesque* has been criticized in literary theory (Eagleton, 1981; Stam, 1982) as nostalgic and overoptimistic in terms of resistive activity on the part of oppressed peoples. It has been defined as a kind of licensed release that serves to distract people from their oppression and is thus not resistive at all. On the other hand, the carnivalesque has also been viewed as having a kind of demystifying potential in its earthy, raucous perspective, which can be viewed as resistive. In soap opera gossip networks, such demystification is often of conventional cultural practices concerning women. However, if we can move beyond the debate over whether the original and continuing carnivals were and are politically conservative or progressive and see carnival as operating beyond the confines of popular festivals and as a concept "intrinsic to the dialectics of social classification" (Stallybrass & White, 1986, p. 26), we can use this concept to gain a much more productive understanding of how carnivalesque elements can operate in the process of "symbolic inversion" between high and low culture, particularly that involving the body (Babcock, 1978; Stallybrass & White, 1986). Symbolic inversion, according to Barbara Babcock, is "often symbolically central, and if we ignore or minimize inversion and other forms of cultural negation, we often fail to understand the dynamics of symbolic processes generally" (p. 32). Bakhtin (1965) distinguishes between the classical body and the grotesque body, the high form, according to Stallybrass and White (1986), represented in official culture by statues and the like, and the low form of the body represented in popular festivity like carnivals— the two forms embodying contradictory registers of being. Such binary oppositions can be seen to represent a politics of transgression in which low culture transgresses upon high culture. This is a process that, according to Babcock (1978), happens at the margins, the borders, and the edges rather than at the accepted centers. Soap opera fanship networks are such marginal spaces.

The idea of transgression through inversion is particularly well illustrated by the woman's peace encampment at Greenham Common near the British town of Newbury, where women gathered to protest the U.S. cruise missile base. According to Malise Ruthnen (1984, in Stallybrass & White, 1986):

> All the women arouse a degree of hostility far in excess of any inconveniences they may cause to soldiers, policemen or residents living near the base. Shopkeepers and publicans refuse to serve them; hooligans unexpectedly joined forces with the establishments and actualize the verbal insults by smearing the benders (homemade tents) with excrement and pig's blood. . . . This spontaneous and voluntary association of females, without formal leadership or hierarchy, seems to threaten the soldiers, the local gentry, the bourgeoisie of Newbury and even its hooligans far more than the missiles, although the latter would be a prime target in the event of nuclear war. (p. 1048a)

Peter Stallybrass and Allan White (1986) go on to argue that it is the chaos and disruption of the carnivalesque like the situation at Greenham Common that define an "other" for middle-class values. According to Stallybrass and White (1986), a challenge to the hierarchy of sites of discourse from groups and classes "situated" in marginal positions by the dominant "carries the promise of politically transformative power" (p. 201). The participants in soap opera gossip networks who have chosen trashy television as their cultural capital can constitute such a marginalized and liminal group.

It is here in the ludic, carnivalesque context that internalized ideologies are broken through and here in the liminal in-between state of freedom where the reworking takes place. This group reworking can be seen in the midst of laughter and parodic pleasure over a male character being compared to "a well-scrubbed pig." It is present when a group member's mother "goes on" about how "men are so narrow minded"; when Vicki responds to her friend Judith's need to get home to cook her family dinner with,

"Well, buy them fish and chips"; or when Jackie comments, "He doesn't keep himself up." These and similar comments are direct comments on life. The comments indicate both an awareness of the speakers' subordinate positions as women and also potential challenges to that position. This stance has serious consequences not restricted to watching soap operas. It is a common element with humans dealing with oppression.

Women, in their soap opera groups, are allowed the privilege more often than Bakhtin's carnivalesque revelers while perhaps indulging in a less radical form of carnival. Nevertheless, they refuse to take seriously for a short time the social constraints they must deal with on a regular basis. Like Bet, the barmaid, they may insult the powerful and get away with it.

8

Resistive Readings

From the previous chapters, we can see that soap opera knowledge supports largely feminine friendship and gossip networks by allowing for a system where those who have such knowledge are supported and where such knowledge is legitimated. In addition, we can see the beginning of a tendency to break the rules—both narrative and social—and to question established boundaries through parody and laughter. In this chapter we shall look more carefully at how the text itself is brought into dialogues where it can be used to structure a resistive reading or where a potentially resistive reading can be rejected. In all cases, the resistance is measured in terms of the subordination of women in our culture, hence the facets of female power can be seen as a crucial factor in the creation of resistive meaning.

Female Power

A negotiation of female power evidences itself in both text and audiences. There is evidence in these interviews to suggest that female characters are judged in terms of power; that power is, in many cases, indicated by a female character's ability both to speak and to be seen, as suggested in Chapter 6. In the following conversation, we see this idea taken a step further:

Ellen: Coronation Street is famous also because it has great bawling-out, standup fights between women.
MEB: The first time I saw that was on *Coronation Street.*
Ellen: Between Ena Sharples —
MEB: But she's so old.
Ellen: Between Ena Sharples and —
MEB: Annie would be too sophisticated.
Ellen: Well, no. Annie has got a good bag for that.
MEB: She's got a good mouth on her!
   (Laughter)

Here we see that women willing to literally fight it out can be viewed as powerful. The women being depicted on *Coronation Street* in the above conversation are older women (Ena Sharples was in her nineties at the time), hence the pleasure of seeing two women fight is not in seeing them as sexual objects but as fighting women, able to use their bodies in this way. On *Coronation Street*, older women are considered to have interesting lives and sometimes to be daring and courageous. In this case, there is a bit of resistance embedded in the text itself.

In another case, when a female character is not as strong as she could be, these *Days of Our Lives* fans take note of it.

Sue: How do you feel about the women?

Emma: Well, Marlena, she's the doctor, the psychiatrist. She was at the hospital. She had her office and had patients and then she suddenly gets involved with Roman and police work. She just slipped out of character. Now she is going back [Roman is dead at this point], of course.

Sue: Do you think she is a strong woman character?

Emma: Fairly.

Sue: That's what I feel, fairly. I'd like to see her really get stronger as a person.

Emma: She's very well liked. Seems to be very popular.

Sue: I think she's real popular, but I'd still like to see her be a little more independent or something. I don't know.

Karen: You know who is the best? Gwen. Wasn't she wonderful when she refused to lean on Larry? She has some good lines.

Marlena's popularity means that she may well continue to be a character on the show, but this group of fans would like to see her make use of the power she should have by virtue of her position as a psychiatrist. Gwen, on the other hand, is popular because of the strength of her character and also because she has been given "some good lines." Gwen's power is, at least partially, in what she is able to say. Within the discussion the shifting emphasis between producer, character, actor, and audience in terms of the source of power for these female characters is evidence of the dialogic nature of conversations about soap operas. The power of the female voice seems to be recognized and appreciated by these fans. Another example of this affirmation follows:

Ellen: That's definitely a lot of the pleasure in watching it. It's the way things are said.

MEB: Particularly the put-down, I take it.

Ellen: The put-downs, the rudeness. It's kind of stylized rudeness.

MEB: Well, the power of the women seems to have to do with their—

Ellen: Their mouths.
(Laughter)

But evidence of female power is not the only marker of resistive reading. We have already seen how groups of women constantly negotiate their position within traditional families and romantic relationships in the context of soap opera networks. Now let us look at two groups of teenage soap opera viewers—one, a group of young teenage girls who are fans of the Australian *Sons and Daughters*, and another, British fans of *Neighbours* and *Brookside*. The *Sons and Daughters* fans are mainly working-class, high school friends whose formal contact with the feminist movement is slight. They are close to the age where Australian teens, like British teenagers, will choose whether to continue their education beyond the age of 16. The second group of teenagers are college-age young people from a British university studying in the United States, some of whom are committed feminists. With each group it is possible to distinguish the way that a resistive reading hinges on the social, cultural, and political positions of audience members.

Strategies and Tactics

Patricia Palmer's study *Girls and Television* (1986a) tells us a bit about the general television viewing practices of Australian teenage girls. The viewers in her study, from working-class schools are, she finds, devoted and enthusiastic and watch more television than boys. Girls' viewing, according to her findings, peaks between the ages of 13 and 14. Although two out of the five schools Palmer used in her study were coeducational, talk about television programs by girls was almost always with other girls. Girls, according to Palmer's finding, "had a detailed knowledge of programs their friends watched and liked and the favorite show of their group at school" (p. 32). In fact, according to Palmer, girls often form their friendship groups based on which television programs are their favorites. Girls did not, as a rule, discuss their television involvement with parents, teachers, or other adults; however, as Palmer notes: "It was certainly gratifying to girls if parents viewed their programs, as long as they did not interrupt by talking or asking for translations, in the case of parents who did not speak English" (pp. 43-44).

An attitude of ownership of certain programs was usual and the young women often referred to their favorites as "my programs." Parents in Palmer's study were quite flexible about allowing television viewing of programs of which they did not approve; however, they sometimes were critical of their daughters' viewing practices, criticizing them for watching soap operas in particular. The girls reported an overwhelmingly negative perspective on most television by their teachers, but when a teacher was a television fan, these girls felt supported. As one of Palmer's group members remarked:

> Cheryl: My science teacher likes it, she watches all the "Prisoner" programs and things like that. It's good to come to school and have, you know, a good conversation with the teacher. You feel you are in the right, then, you know. (p. 51)

Although Palmer concludes that girls' use of television contributed to their narrowing their future choices by the educational decisions they made during early teenage years, she also acknowledges the pleasure that the girls she interviewed experienced in talking about television. "While their talk is often intense, it is also punctuated by laughter. What girls learn from television can have serious, and negative, consequences but there is no doubt that the process of doing so affords them great enjoyment" (p. 67). In my view, the laughter and enjoyment of television may themselves be appropriations of television's strategies, and their gathering together to share this enjoyment means that they may be doing more than simply absorbing the ideology that these shows seem to represent. A close look at responses to a specific program can help to clarify how the process of reading takes place within a particular group of girls.

The teenagers whom we look at here are longtime fans of *Sons and Daughters*,[1] two of them having watched it since its inception in 1981. The act of watching this particular soap then put these teenagers in the position of choosing as their cultural capital a particularly trashy soap—an initial act of defiance usually of their parents and teachers in itself and a common one among teenagers. Although sharing many similarities with the American daytime soap operas, also noted for their excessive trashiness, *Sons and Daughters* also has significant differences. The plots on *Sons and Daughters* move exceptionally fast (thus counteracting the universal teenage complaint of boredom), and they emphasize different aspects of the narrative than do plots of American daytime soap operas. This can be seen by the way the show deals with weddings.

The major wedding on *Sons and Daughters* during the period when I interviewed the teenagers was that of Wayne and Susan. When Wayne, the villain, and Susan (a good, honest, and strong young woman) are married,

Wayne has kidnapped Susan's younger brother to persuade her mother to influence Susan to marry him. In addition, he has framed Glen, Susan's real love, so that Susan will think Glen has betrayed her. The wedding itself is, of course, a gathering of all of the show's characters. It features a fistfight between Wayne and Glen and a last-minute appeal to Susan by Glen for a chance to prove his innocence. All of this is similar to what might happen at an American daytime soap opera wedding, but the remarkable thing about this wedding is that the program shows less than a minute of the actual ceremony. As one of the young women in the interview group put it, there was no necessity to show it because "everyone knows what goes on at a wedding." This is markedly different than the usual portrayal of weddings on American daytime soap operas. On *Days of Our Lives*, Roman and Marlena's first wedding lasted three days, giving the entire "real time" text of the wedding ceremony. Wayne and Susan's wedding on *Sons and Daughters* provides us with an example of the way that the text itself contributes to teenage resistive readings of romantic sentiment, of which the wedding is the culminating symbolic act.

To look at specific examples of the ways that teenage girls talk about *Sons and Daughters* in light of commonly held beliefs that audiences do not question dominant ideological assumptions in relation to soap operas, let us turn to the recorded conversations.

The first aspect to be noted is that this group evidenced a decided preference for individualistic characters, particularly those who defied social norms.

Diana: I like the people or the characters. They do things that people we know wouldn't do. Sort of, we've been told, no I could never do that to another person, but they go right out to hurt another person's feelings, or something like that. And we just like to see what happens when it does happen.

The conflicts of teenage girls mentioned by Taylor (1987), noted in Chapter 2, in relation to the expectation that they be proper young ladies rather than seek their independence as boys do, seem to be played out in the admiration of a character who is not a nice person. Contrary to notions of being good, their favorite characters tended to be villains.

MEB: Which characters do you like?
Jan: Wayne.
MEB: What is it about Wayne?
Jan: Because he is such a little devil and is like a split personality: like to his wife he is such an angel and then when she is out of the room he turns and his

whole face changes. And the type of clothes he wears changes and he goes right out, you know, to hurt other people. Like he uses old family friends, like his next-door neighbor Charlie and all that, for their money. She doesn't have a clue what her money's invested in but he uses her anyway.

Diana: I think he's good because he does it without anyone knowing what he's doing.

The pleasure here seems to be appreciation of Wayne's ability to get away with things, to use people without getting caught, but also to get along in the world. Thus Wayne is a kind of role model for resistance. Female villains are also admired for, among other things, being at the center of the action.

MEB: Well, Jan said that Alison is a winner, but Caroline's not. Do you agree with that?

Diana: She doesn't play as major a role and you know, she doesn't get involved in as many activities that Alison does, type of thing. Not as adventurous type of thing. Alison gets into more trouble.

Jan: Yeah, I think it's because Alison's got more drive and more ambition to do things and she knows who to contact to get in touch with people and get about what she wants to do. Whereas Caroline just sort of fumbles her way toward it and whatever she does isn't really a big thing to the series at all . . . so you know . . .

Diana: She's just taking every day as it comes type of thing . . . whereas Alison, she plans ahead.

Alison is admired as a role model in avoiding the passive expectations of women. Decisive action, then, is a high priority with these viewers, one that contrasts sharply with the statement by a 15-year-old girl in Hudson's (1984) study, "Whatever we do, it's always wrong" (p. 31). The idea of simply taking every day as it comes, which is the fear of many educators about girls limiting their economic choices by early decisions on school options, is not the admired characteristic among these fans, whereas planning ahead and knowing what one wants are appreciated. This would seem to broaden young women's options rather than decrease them. Of course, there are also other influences in these young womens' lives, but if we consider television viewing and fanship a contributing factor, then these conversations must be looked at as seriously as the content of the program.

With the exception of the strong matriarch, the saintly characters are disliked by this group of fans. However, those characters who exhibit socially aberrant behavior, or who at least behave or act defiantly, are admired.

MEB: I expected you to like the teenage characters.

Diana: Like Andy and Craig and . . .

Jan: I like Andy. He's good.

Diana: I don't know, I suppose Craig—he's all right, but he's such a goody-goody—he's always doing good things for everyone, you know. I suppose in that teenager there would be a good adventurous side and that would be Andy, and there'd be the really nice side, and that would be Craig. They've sort of split the individual up into two characters. There's not just one—I suppose Ginny would be the character where she is really nice to people and adventurous. Ginny would be the . . .

MEB: I'm trying to remember which one Ginny is.

Jan: She is the one who wears the really odd clothes, she puts together with the long—sort of hair.

MEB: She's the one that's just had that thing fall on her.

Jan: Yeah.

MEB: So she's the one that you like?

Diana: She's all right. She doesn't like blend in with the rest of the *Sons and Daughters'* characters, but she uses her language differently. Her odd clothes make it more interesting to listen to her and everything, but that's about it.

Jan: Her character's really outstanding.

MEB: What do you mean, she uses language?

Jan: Like soft-spoken and everything, she doesn't care what she says, she's outgoing and . . .

Diana: Loud . . .

It is clear in the above example that the manner in which the characters are constructed is clear to these viewers. The idea expressed here that Craig and Andy are two sides of a single character construction is indicative of the group's awareness that the characters in soaps are constructs, that these girls were able to like characters seemingly without the process of identification clearly demanded by narratives with a single hero or heroine whose ability to be identified with is coded for the audience by her or his well-roundedness. Although the latter type of character relationship with audiences is clearly rewarded in terms of dominant viewership, its invitation was not accepted by these teenage girls. Andy and Craig were clearly, to the speaker, only parts of a character construction.

Moreover, the power of speech is evident in the above excerpt from the interview. This quoted section is complex in the group members' understanding of how, for example, the codes of dress that Ginny is given affect how we code her speech ("She uses her language differently. Her odd clothes make it more interesting to listen to her and everything"). That visual codes and oral codes can be related seemed clear to these readers.

In addition, the power of Ginny's speech (she uses language) was quite clear to this particular *Sons and Daughters* fan. That power is used by the character of Ginny to contradict what "nice" girls might be allowed to say. ("She doesn't care what she says, she's outgoing and . . ."—"Loud"). These fans valued characters for their power over hegemonic discourse (niceness for girls) and for the freedom to use voice quality to assert a position of strength in nonconformity. Ginny makes herself heard, and this is a valued behavior.

The following example, the first part of which appears in Chapter 6, is an instance of how the conversation about *Sons and Daughters* slips between analysis of the construction of the soap's plot and storytelling or performance on the part of the speakers of the group, including the "filling in" process that brings the others up to date on the current plot:

Jan: Most of what happens is based on revenge for what someone's done to them or working around greed for money, I think, and someone else's wife.

Diana: Or husband, as Alison.

Jan: Love of money and revenge. I think it is going to be pretty, um, shall we say dramatic for a while seeing as Alison is in such a critical condition at the moment in hospital.

Diana: Is she in hospital?

Jan: She's in a coma.

Diana: Well, I haven't seen it for three days.

Jan: She got stuck in the freezer with David.

Diana: Yes, I saw that bit.

Jan: Yeah, well they had no air and she went into a coma.

Diana: Oh no!

Jan: Yes and, um—Craig's mother drew the people out into the open and arrested them and Craig got off the hook.

Diana: Good one!

Although the conversation begins with an analysis of the plot possibilities, it slips into the process of storytelling ("seeing as Alison is in such a critical condition"), and when it is discovered that one member of the group has not watched for 3 days, the intensity of the conversations heightens while the drama of Alison's coma and the courage and cleverness of Craig's mother are disclosed. The act of storytelling, recounting complicated and unpredictable plot structures, catching one's friends up on missed episodes, obviously is a major source of pleasure for these soap opera fans. Within the boundaries of such storytelling groups, these young women are verbally powerful.

Teenage girls' gossip networks and friendship systems centering on soap operas and other television programs, as Palmer has pointed out, are often systems in which girls take the power to exclude both boys and adults. Even when boys and adults are tolerated, it is only on the girls' terms. As Palmer's interviews indicated, girls often are happy to have others watch with them as long as they don't "interrupt." This is a reversal of the usual gender and adult-child power relationships. As de Certeau (1986) and many others have pointed out, the power to speak, control of the speech act, regulation of who may speak and under what conditions, is one of the central strategies by which the dominant system maintains control.

The hegemonic necessity to win over subordinated groups to particular ideological stances that in turn support their own subordination seems to be at least partially tactically subverted by the rich oral culture that Australian girls enjoyed around *Sons and Daughters*. Some romantic notions, like the wedding ceremony as life goal, are challenged by the text itself and these teenage viewers consume the text in ways that begin to distinguish power relationships within the construction of the text. Their awareness of the narrative constructions of these relationships and their willingness to challenge dominant notions of feminine dependency may indicate that these young women are using soap operas in ways that may support a resistance to the ideology of dependence and romance discussed earlier.

The following is excerpted from a conversation with British fans in their early twenties who watch soap operas primarily with their friends. At the time of the interview, Jen, an outspoken feminist member of the group whom I have quoted extensively, was studying in the United States for 6 months but would shortly return to Britain to finish her education at a polytechnical institute near London. She is from a working-class family and grew up in Manchester. In the following conversation, she is clearly attuned to the politics of the character she describes. The politics, in the first example, concern labor unions rather than women's issues.

Jen: You know . . . that when *Brookside* first started it was a lot more political than it is now, and it had a lot of following because of it. And they had one particular character in there who was married to Sheila, Bobby Grant, who was a member of his union and also a member of Militant—do you know Militant? It's a faction of the Labour party, extreme left faction of the Labour party. And every week, without fail, there used to be an opportunity for him to make some kind of political speech. And then they kept moving him up in the series, his job kept getting better, and then he went into management, but he was still in the union. And the guy who plays Bobby Grant actually was a member of Militant and the reason he was in that program was because he saw it as an opportunity to get across his political message.

Steve: Phil Redman, who came up with the idea for that program, started it specifically because he wanted a forum for these ideas in a way that could reach everybody.

MEB: So it was really political?

Jen: There is a lot of political sermon in it, and then they tried to really dilute his character. And when he became an executive of something, they tried to portray him as somebody who'd sold out the shop floor members of the union to make a deal with the bosses. And the guy who plays Bobby Grant quit the series because he wouldn't portray a union boss in that light, because it was when the union was getting really bad press, and everything, and he didn't want to add anything to that. And also, he just didn't want to be a party to that. So they just killed off his character, because he refused to play that part.

Jen, in the passage above, is comfortable with the political position expressed in the early episodes of *Brookside*. A preferred reading is one in which the audience member agrees with the ideological stance presented and thus has no trouble accepting the point of view portrayed in the piece. If we look at Stuart Hall's (1980) classification of viewers' possible responses to television as preferred, negotiated, or oppositional readings, we can see that some soap operas present a preferred reading in some aspects for some people. Thus these viewers are not reading against the grain when they view and interpret soap operas, but with the grain.

An antiunion audience member, on the other hand, might reject the positive reading entirely and thus read against the grain. His or her reading would be termed *oppositional* using Hall's criteria because the ideological message is so offensive that the reading is interpreted completely negatively. A negotiated reading would fall somewhere in between. An audience member could also approve of unions in general but find Militant too extreme. Or another viewer might interpret Bobby Grant's actions not as selling out but as a reasonable compromise. Any number of possibilities can be incorporated in a negotiated reading.

Sometimes reading with the grain can produce a preferred and resistive reading because the soap opera itself appears to take such a stand. This is the case earlier when young teenagers read the wedding as pretty routine and of little interest in and of itself. It is apparent that the soap opera itself can support a nondominant reading, which in the case of the union story in *Brookside* would be antimanagement and in the case of *Sons and Daughters* would be antimarriage. However, we can see clearly in the union story the retraction or "clawing back" of the story. When it goes so far as to threaten hegemonic stability, the character is made to compromise the union's position in the story. When the ideological point of view in the story changes, the audience doesn't automatically change with it. Instead, the viewer may change her reading strategy to a negotiated or oppositional one.

The younger group of viewers of *Sons and Daughters*, in the following conversation, fail to read the text in an oppositional manner and give a preferred reading instead. In general, their readings of the text are not as overtly political as are Jen's, and in this case their reading is consistent with the dominant one.

Sara: I think that's because they don't relate them to, like we are, they just relate them as characters, they have made these characters up and put them on tele, that's why they didn't sort of . . . like we don't really know what sort of work Gordon and that's in, except that they invest their money and they've got a business, we don't know exactly what sort of business they've got . . . so we can't really say oh, he couldn't have that much money with that sort of job, you know, or maybe he should go into that sort of job, we don't sort of . . .

Diana: . . . you know wondering what he works at, to get so much money and everything; how Caroline gets so much money.

Jan: Yeah, because it's not important to the program, it's not important how they get their money, just they have the money and they are what they are and what happens to them being what they are.

MEB: How come?

Sara: Because most people don't work sort of 24 hours a day once they finish their job they stop and that's it. That's the end of their job and then, you know, you're not really fussed about it. You don't want to switch on the tele and watch someone else work, it probably would be boring.

Diana: Because the only important thing is the characters and what they do. Like the money only comes into it if Wayne is blackmailing someone for money or trying to get more money invested or something like that and then the money is brought into the program, you know what they do, but otherwise it's not mentioned because the program's based on the relationship between people rather than what people do.

Such lack of interest in money is often a part of dominant female conditioning, so much so that women sometimes fail to take the responsibility for their own finances or make poor judgments in relation to money. In this case, the audience member's preferred reading supports dominant notions that soap operas reinforce women's subordination relating to money issues—at least some of the time.

It is the ideology in question that constitutes the opening for a resistive reading. Such ideology can be contained within the narrative itself or it can be contained in the way viewers use the narrative in the context of their own social positioning. It is therefore impossible to say that all soap operas provoke a resistive reading just as it is also not always possible to predict how a resistive reading will take place. Ideologies change their inflection as do soap operas and as do the people who participate in soap opera networks. Many inflections of various ideologies exist within a given audience structured as it is by their social, cultural, or racial position, for example.

Just as it is rare to have a mainstream film address women's issues as directly as *Thelma & Louise* does, it is also rare that a soap opera addresses social issues as precisely as did *Brookside* in its early programs. Consequently, let us turn to situations that present less specific resistance within the soap opera itself.

In the following two examples, a soap opera's treatment of female characters is brought into question. The first is about *Neighbours* in its British run.

Jen: You know what's really interesting about Jane, I think, because she was always portrayed as Jane, Jane, she's the brain. She was really, really intelligent when she's at school, but very awful in a conventional sense. When she left, she became very beautiful overnight. She got that job as a secretary. And yet she's supposed to be super, super brains, and the best she could get was [a job] as a secretary. She did not mind, though, did she?

This viewer is offering a critique both of the soap opera and also of society in general, where intelligent women are able to secure only conventionally female jobs. A similarly smart and educated man might be employed in a job with greater status and pay. And if a man were underemployed for his talents, he would surely mind, she implies. Thus the capping statement, "She did not mind, though, did she?" conveys sadness on the part of the speaker and an acute personal awareness of the pain of such a position. Also in this statement is an implied criticism of the school system when Jen says that Jane is intelligent "in the conventional sense," presumably in the sense that the knowledge that schools convey is knowledge that doesn't question established rules. The fact that Jane has become beautiful overnight indicates to the speaker that, for women in the world of work, the real value is beauty—not intelligence, and that Jane is now doing socially acceptable women's work and can be rewarded for this by being seen as beautiful. Thus we can see that this conversation is a critique of the portrayal of women on the program and of a system where conventions oppress women in a number of ways. Still, Jen seems to negotiate this meaning in relation to her own identity.

In the next quotation about the British soap opera *EastEnders,* the character of Angie, once married to Den, has adopted his daughter, who, it turns out, had also been adopted earlier by Den. The conversation is about Angie.

Jen: She adopted his daughter. She was adopted when she was very young, and she didn't find out she was adopted until she was quite old. She tried to get in touch with her biological parents, and that was so real. They came around in the end. It was so outrageous the way they did it because her birth mother, when she finally found her, had exactly the same hair, same dress. What are they trying to say here? I mean that was really powerful. I thought, that they were trying to say family ties, the way you turn out to be, is not a socialized thing, it's the naturalized thing. . . . I was actually considering writing to them about not looking for Angie, now, because it was really out of order.

This passage questions a number of assumptions that are evident in the visualization of the program as well as the plot. Jen questions the biological basis for socialization but also the value that the program (and society) place on the birth mother over the adoptive mother. This skepticism brings up the question of maternity rather than the often expressed problem of paternity frequently at issue in the American daytime soap operas, discussed in Chapter 3. Concern with whom one's mother is could be seen to imply an interest in matriarchal descent. This time Jen does not accept with resignation the situation as she did in looking at Jane's work situation, but is obviously angry that the program has overstepped the boundaries that she considers appropriate in dealing with women's issues even for a popular media form. Here she gives the program an oppositional reading.

Commenting about the lack of politics in *Neighbours,* the same British fan sees it as only political enough to add a bit of interest.

Jen: They just live out their roles. Scott's the boy next door and Kylie is the girl next door with a bit of rebellion put in for good measure, you know, but not too much, just enough to make mommy and daddy slightly angry. Enough to make people think. There's a little edge, but not enough to tarnish the image.

She has obviously not bought into the untarnished image of the girl next door. Thus there are clear distinctions made by the audience about what constitutes resistance to dominant ideology on the soaps and what doesn't. Jen obviously watches but finds it necessary to negotiate quite frequently. Sometimes, oppositional readings become funny. In discussing *Neighbours* again, the same person says:

> I cried when Marge married "The Bish." I did, I cried. I was so embarrassed, I cried. She married the Bishop Harold. I don't know why. I've always cried at weddings. I don't think it's for the reasons most people cry—another one bites the dust.

Here the traditional feminine response at a wedding, crying, gets turned around as an ironic expression of sorrow that another woman has succumbed; the tears show disappointment at defeat rather than joy. Thus we see that this resistive reading, like many in Chapter 7, involves the appropriation of certain behavior for an ironic reading of a dominant institution, in this case marriage.

Jen is looking, of course, at these examples of British and Australian soap operas as a feminist. And needless to say, some fans of soap operas are feminists (see also Ang, 1985). However, most of the women and girls we look at in this study would not call themselves feminists; but when confronted with specific situations, either on a soap opera or in actual life, they often speak from a perspective that acknowledges their partial rejection of domestic role expectations, gender-defined double standards, in favor of feminine empowerment. For example, in Chapter 5, we saw Rita, from her position in the Australian outback, negotiate a position for her own viewing preferences within her family by incorporating her husband into her viewing network if he wished to spend that viewing time with her. At the same time, she continued to rely for support on her long-distance women's network, which incorporated her soap opera network. In this context, Rita has set up a more egalitarian position for herself within her family.

Resistance

For such a resistive reading to reach outside the boundaries of the soap opera network and thereby transgress into areas of overt politics, thus becoming adopted as a political stance of the viewer in life situations, several variables need to come into play. These are

a. the political economy of the patriarchal family, which may be more or less exploitative in different contexts;
b. a genre that caters to women and the emotional tone of their lives;
c. the alternative interaction networks that soap operas facilitate;
d. the development of solidarity bases that give women support outside of the patriarchal family;
e. the development of a fund of strategic knowledge, not just about the genre itself but around the language of the genre and the life context of women;
f. the carnivalesque atmosphere of the genre, that is, the release from the dogmatism of the social norms surrounding the patriarchal family and broader social institutions; and
g. finally, the emergence of resistive readings, the conscious questioning of the existing structure of domestic roles and a rethinking of how these roles may be structured.

In the case of soap opera fanship, it is where all of these variables are present in the spoken text that a reading is likely to be resistant.

There are many critics who negate the possibility of a resistive reading of any type of television. Their position is that society reproduces itself in the repetitive stories of television—in the systems of reward and punishment shown, in the patterns of heroism and villainy, in the absence of nonhegemonic political positions. In other words, television can only be seen to legitimate the existing social order (Newcomb & Alley, 1983, p. 21). Similarly, it is often assumed that women must leave their feminine pleasures behind in order to become liberated; but, in fact, these feminine pleasures may give them space to evaluate their lives in light of existing dominant notions of femininity as well as some nondominant strategies with which to challenge the system on another level.

There are four areas that are important in the generation of resistive readings: talk, boundaries, strategic knowledge, and the lowering of normative controls. There is *first* the necessity for the talk to take place. Not only are soap operas constructed in such a way that they elicit talk, but it is also obvious that a large amount of the pleasure that women derive from soap operas is in talking about them. It is in this *spoken text* that most of the meaning generation concerning everyday life and the construction of identity for audiences takes place.

The second important area is the developing of boundaries within which it is safe to talk freely—that is, to speak in feminine discourse. Many soap opera gossip networks are loose knit but others are more formalized neighborhood-based "video clubs." Often relatives, particularly mothers and daughters, or close friends are a part of one's gossip network. Australian teenage networks frequently have large informal groups of fans. But no matter how the groups are organized, the important thing seems to be that these fan groups set boundaries and within these boundaries one is free to speak as one pleases.

The third area is strategic knowledge. Regular soap opera viewers not only know the codes and conventions of soap operas, which gives them a way of talking that outsiders don't understand, but they can also access strategic knowledge, that is, knowledge of women's oppression.

The fourth area is the lowering of normative controls and this is expressed in carnivalesque laughter, or laughter that involves the inversion of the normal order of things—particularly in the way that soap operas are defiantly considered by many women as valuable cultural capital when dominant culture finds them trash or rubbish, that is, not acceptable in official designations of high art or what might be taught in school, for example.

At this point, let us list evidence that supports the notion that the young teenagers negotiate their reading actively rather than passively when they consume *Sons and Daughters*, at least part of the time. First, the television program that these teenagers chose to watch was itself defiant of hegemonic notions of the "proper" text. It earned its trashy reputation because of its simple plots, its low production costs, its melodramatic morality, and its narrative structure. Second, these young women discussed the narrative structure in some detail, acknowledging the constructedness of the narrative itself. Third, they preferred characters who defy social norms, and they liked this characteristic in women as well as in men. In addition, they liked characters who took control of their voices, who "use language differently," that is, who use dominant structures on their own behalf. Although there were times when the group did not resist the expectations of feminine behavior as it is constructed in dominant terms, there were also times when they did. These conversations seem to indicate that these young women understand at some level the constraints of subordination. All of these points are supported by both the pleasure they experience and the freedom they feel to speak seriously and in fun about these soap opera narratives within their friendship networks, networks in which they themselves are in control (Brown, 1991). In the group of college-age British viewers, we have seen that the nature of resistive reading practices, when the readers are ideologically feminists, is still to some degree controlled by what goes on in the text. We can only think differently when our social and cultural positions are compared with those in a given text, when rather than being sucked in by the text we are challenged to think for ourselves to the extent that there is room within dominant discourse to do this. This space to think for ourselves is in a constant state of flux, governed by our own emotional closeness or distance from its politics and our fluctuating capacity to think rationally outside of our conditioning, controlled as it is by the discourses to which we are each subjected.

Feminism and the Soap Opera Text

The work of Foucault (1975) on archeology, discussed in more detail in Chapter 6, delineates the power of discourse to shape what is considered truth in a given discursive tradition. He defines discourse by its parameters of containment, by which he refers to those discursive practices that surround a social practice and ultimately construct a dominant "reality" for the practice under consideration. Foucault (1982) relates the power to make one's own meaning within dominant discourse to a will to power combined with a will to knowledge. He sees all power relationships as containing within their structure the possibility of resistance: "Every power relationship implies, at least in potential, a strategy of struggle, in which the two forces are not superimposed, do not lose their specific nature, do not finally become confused. Each constitutes for the other a kind of permanent limit, a point of possible reversal" (p. 225).

Thus when I refer to an element of popular culture as a site of struggle, I mean that, although popular culture is embedded in ideology, the possibility of struggle is always there for subordinated groups. Soap operas contain their own ideological contradictions because they are a product of hegemonic culture that embodies the very contradictions it seeks to disguise. Fiske (1988) has called the site of potential resistance "a personified cultural process held in a moment of temporary stability when shifting social allegiances come together at the moment of semiosis" (p. 246). If we picture the moment of the reading of a particular text as the point where specific aspects of our lives come together with the issues and ideological notions inherent in a text, then certain possible stances of resistance can manifest themselves in our individual readings. Then when we bring the meanings garnered from those readings to bear in conversations, the spoken text can become a way of expressing resistance. If one is then in a position to have his or her resistances acknowledged and validated by a group of people, it may be possible for one to begin to work politically at the level of everyday life.

Not all women's talk is resistive, but that which recognizes, rather than denies, oppression is very likely to be able to question prevalent ideological assumptions and therefore women's own construction in discourse, thereby making it potentially resistive. In soap opera texts, there is usually no clear feminist message although the issues brought up are of interest to women, whether they are feminists or not. Other political issues such as those having to do with class can also come up, particularly in British soap operas like *EastEnders* or *Brookside*. Thus audience members can either appreciate the politics of the soap opera or not, or they can struggle with the ideas presented in order to negotiate an ideological position for themselves.

Let us return briefly to the text mentioned at the beginning of this volume, the movie *Thelma & Louise*. The following statement was made by a fan after viewing the text: "My women friends and I have gone over that cliff together so many times." There are three aspects of this resistive reading that are particularly important and that, in fact, make this particular moment a moment of resistive pleasure. The first is "my women friends and I"; the second is going "over that cliff"; and the third is "so many times." The first emphasizes solidarity among women. The "going over the cliff" accomplishes a symbolic transgression of boundaries necessary to rock the stability of the status quo. It is an impossible and deadly act, at the same time courageous and open ended. And the repetition of this feeling "so many times" confirms the existence and duration of the problem.

For me, the third party in the transaction, to hear it from a friend who overheard it provided a particularly resistive reading because many of us are now involved. Thus resistive pleasure comes not only with an understanding of the political implications of the mere existence of such a film, of its availability in mainstream movie houses and on videotape, and of its political messages for many women, particularly feminists, but also with our acknowledging its existence by talking about it. In other words, part of the pleasure here is the allowing into the discourse of mainstream film a position and space known only to the subordinated. Additionally, the recognition of the conversation with others as a powerful force in relation to subordination is of great value.

Although women have historically been subordinate, the meaning of women's friendship groups has changed in the eyes of dominant culture. In the nineteenth century, women's supposed asexuality meant that they could have close and loving relationships with their female friends without such friendships being considered threatening (Faderman, 1981; Smith-Rosenberg, 1975). It has been suggested that such relationships were problematized after the 1920s with the popularization of theories of Freudian and neo-Freudian psychoanalysis because these saw female relationships as sexual, bringing up possible sanctions against lesbianism because these theories considered it normal behavior to be heterosexually active. This led to the popular image of the older single woman as not normal (Walby, 1990). Some writers see this as an attack on first-wave feminism because it involved strong bonding among women (Jefferys, 1985; Millett, 1977). Thus the political, cultural, and social atmosphere in which we live determines how we construct our gendered identity. Seen in a society that stresses individuality as a mark of mature functioning, the politics of connectedness can be discursively turned into a resistive and powerful position.

Soap opera provides images and plots that are of special interest to women, that are sufficiently open and sufficiently related to a woman's life context to be worked on by women together to generate symbols of resistance and ways of rethinking the role definitions of women, and consequently those of men also. The fact that groups of women do this together gives them a space where they can be enabled to fully work out issues and then to work them into their consciousness. It then provides the social support to carry these decisions out in practice. In addition, a soap opera group does not bring down on itself the anathema that the suffragists or the women's groups in the 1970s women's movement did because its purpose is overtly *nonpolitical* in the traditional sense of the word. However, as we have seen, politics can be reconceptualized on the level of culture where soap opera gossip networks can be thought of as not only political but perhaps even subversive.

Note

1. *Sons and Daughters* is an Australian teenage soap opera. The first U.S. teen soap opera, *Swans Crossing,* began in June 1992 on the Fox network. These soap operas are aimed at children aged 11-13 and a little older, often called the "tween" market. In the United States, I have seen young girls' peer networks centered on soap opera viewing start as young as 7, and of course children watch at much younger ages.

9

Conclusion: A Never-Ending Story

A popular entertainment genre like soap opera can contribute to the process of change at two levels. The first level is that of generating a rethinking of the role of women. The interdependent factors that I have suggested operate together to facilitate such rethinking are boundaries, knowledge, and the power to resist cultural conditioning and to break rules. These aspects of soap opera networks transform essentially neutral or polyvalent images of soap opera into resistant meanings. We have seen that the possibility for resistive meaning generation is present and that the discursive struggle happens to a large extent in the process of conversation within the networks generated by soap opera knowledge that challenge dominant discourses about the roles of women within the family, on the silencing of women's voices and laughter, on the social expectations of women's behavior, and about the power of women's relationships with other women. At the same time, within such discursive networks, the cultural capital of women's traditional roles is not necessarily rejected. Aspects like the pleasure in close-knit families, the pleasure of rituals and emotional stability provided by the family, the pleasure in looking at clothing styles and elaborate wedding spectacles, or the pleasure of gossip continue to have meaning in women's lives. These resistive readings are clothed in subtle contradictions and are thus not obvious to a casual observer. But it is in this way that the seeds for subversion of a system can germinate.

Despite the public negative valuation of soap operas, many women find a space for them in their lives, both because they value the pleasure they bring and because they value the space that soap opera gossip networks provide for the experiencing of that pleasure. For this to happen, pleasure needs to be theorized outside of the space of desire formulated in psychoanalysis (Mulvey, 1975) or the space of false consciousness formulated by Marxists (Rutsky & Wyatt, 1990). Psychoanalytic film criticism contends that film language like all language is structured around masculine desire to the extent that the narrative structure uses various structural devices to "suture" or embed the spectator within the constraints of that narrative form. Marxist ideas of false consciousness construct a position for consumers of mass media in which, once a type of consciousness is formed, all other aspects of media use are held to be "false" as well. Both perspectives allow the user little power. The space that soap opera networks provide for "illegitimate" pleasure in women's lives provides one kind of boundary for feminine pleasures in which feminine discourse can be spoken of and appreciated. In addition, soap opera viewer networks constitute affective alliances (Grossberg, 1984a, 1984b, 1992) or alliances based on shared emotional responses. These exist outside of and often unacknowledged by hegemonic culture. In many ways, the maintenance of this space refuses hegemonic control. Such networks tap into female friendship networks that exist outside dominant hierarchic arrangements. These networks are not organized with leaders and rules that reinforce hierarchic concerns. It is grassroots and informal groups that soap opera discussion networks tap into. These groups can be socially invisible, intentionally and subversively. In this chapter we draw together the aspects of group consciousness-raising that stand out in the previous chapters in order to synthesize their meaning for media studies, and we look at parallels between women's gossip networks that sometimes form around soap operas and the small group consciousness that took place in the 1970s women's movement.

The Pleasure of Resistance

My account of soap opera audiences conceptualizes the pleasure of resistance as happening on several levels. The context of resistive pleasure must be one in which a subordinated group recognizes its oppression and reacts to that oppression. I call this *reactive pleasure* as opposed to *active pleasure*. Active pleasure is similar to Barthes's (1975a) notion of *plaisir*, in which one's sense of identity is confirmed. However, active pleasure for women in soap opera groups affirms their connection to a women's culture that operates in subtle opposition to dominant culture. It is this culture of the home and of women's concerns, recognized but devalued in patriarchal terms, that provides a notion of identity that values women's traditional expertise. Reactive pleasure, on the other hand, while not rejecting the connection women often feel toward women's cultural networks and concerns, also recognizes that these concerns often arise out of women's inability to completely control their own lives. Thus they are able to recognize and to feel at an emotional level the price of oppression.

Resistive pleasure for women in soap opera groups involves talking. Women's talk has traditionally been devalued in our culture, but it is through oral networks that women have maintained some of their cultural priorities. The very act of talking implies that someone is being talked to and thus requires a listener who is present, though possibly at a distance as is the case in telephone conversations (see Rakow, 1992). This in turn indicates the importance of connectedness to others, particularly other women, recently discussed in feminist psychology (Gilligan, 1982; Gilligan et al., 1990). Although women's talk has persisted, its devaluation has meant that individual women do not feel empowered to talk, or by talk, in many situations. Indeed, language itself limits what women are able to say about their own concerns and experiences. Talking itself, but particularly to sympathetic listeners, is a real source of pleasure to the women I encountered in soap opera groups.

Resistive pleasure around soap operas has also had to do with the fact that the genre was designed and developed to appeal to women's place in society. Whatever one may think of that place and the concerns it involves—home, relationships, emotional dependency—it is the place constructed for women in patriarchal and capitalistic discourse. Hence, in the cultures of which I speak, whether or not we live in this space, we are still hailed by it; that is, we recognize a kind of subjectivity, or space into which we are supposed to fit, constructed by our culture for us even though we do not occupy it. In Althusserian (1976) terms, the dominant social construction of women is a part of our consciousness. We recognize it, understand it, and must deal with it. In fact, soap opera texts work very hard at disguising the contradictions of hegemonic femininity but that does not mean that they actually do it in any complete sense. Although soap operas work at isolating women in their homes and keeping them buying household products, in fact my observations indicate that they actually bring women together. The marginalized position of women when they are conceptualized as "belonging" in the home fits with the marginalized position of soap operas broadcast at home during the day in order to "fill up the time." The fit seems relatively unproblematic in dominant culture, where women's talk is dismissed as easily as soap operas have been dismissed in communication studies. As Henry Jenkins (1992) points out in his work on fanship:

> The irony, of course, is that fans have found the very forces that work to
> isolate us from each other to be the ideal foundation for creating connections
> across traditional boundaries; that fans have found the very forces that trans-

form many Americans into spectators to provide the resources for creating a more participatory culture; that fans have found the very forces that reinforce patriarchal authority to contain tools by which to critique that authority. (p. 284)

The genre of soap opera has provided a space for women's resistive pleasure even while it attempts to keep women in their "place." De Certeau (1986) has distinguished between the place of dominant institutions, where strategies work to keep resistive consciousness in line, and the spaces where people take their own pleasures, despite pressure to conform, and create their own meanings as they go about their lives. Soap opera gossip networks can operate in this way.

Resistive pleasure theorizes audiences as being powerful in themselves and requires that the methodology of research allow such theorization. Much of the debate about audiences in cultural studies and communication studies in general has to do with the concept of active rather than passive audiences. Obviously those critics doing ethnographic work conceptualize the audience as active. The ethnographer, to some degree, shapes the way that audiences are perceived to speak; however, ethnographers also allow audiences to talk back to the critic. Many strands of audience theory and criticism still view the audience as what is usually called passive. Actually the conceptualization is more that of audiences being subject to powers that are out of their control. Out of the five types of critical approaches to the audience described by Martin Allor (1988), only one, which he labels "cultural studies," conceptualizes the audience as active.[1] Both the critical perspectives and the methodologies of research about television audiences determine whether audiences are conceptualized as active. This has been particularly true of soap opera audiences. Until both the genre and the audiences could be looked at with respect and studied in a way that allows their voices to be heard, it was impossible to note the existence of resistive pleasure in soap opera audiences. Recent feminist research in cultural studies reader response criticism has made this shift possible.

Resistive pleasures require a safe place where audiences can express that pleasure. In the case of soap opera audiences, this space is acquired by setting up boundaries or contexts of discourse where people can speak in illegitimate ways. Such boundaries, although sometimes quite flexible, are important in identifying a social space where women's pleasure not only is not ignored but is also valued. Soap opera networks allow for the testing of social boundaries. They provide fantasy spaces where the behavioral possibilities within patriarchy are explored. The most important political aspect of soap opera fanship is the creation of oral networks. To the extent that soap operas do this, then they may be considered important for women's cultural survival in dominant culture. These networks can merge with other women's underground networks like those that presently preserve women's religions or women's healing information. Or they can potentially become networks that specifically function to subvert dominant ideology as did consciousness-raising networks. In terms of the politics of liberation, it seems important that more systematic analytical networks emerge, but in their absence soap opera networks may be important points of contact for women and women's politics.

Resistive pleasure requires strategic knowledges. These strategic knowledges manifest themselves in the intricate levels of soap opera knowledges available to this audience because they have adopted a form of cultural capital that is out of the mainstream in terms of either leftist or rightist cultural politics. Disguised as the most ordinary of activities, soap opera fanship is allowed while it is devalued. The discourse of patriarchal capitalism produces several ways that an audience member can picture herself as a soap opera fan. If one is working class, one is characterized as lazy and perhaps as sexually perverse. If one is in the middle class, one gets reproduced as not keeping her (assumed virtuous) mind on appropriate matters and in addition becomes associated with the working class or, as Lee and Cho (1990) point out, with a different (and lower) caste. This process, for women, however, replicates other contradictions to be found in the ideological construction of women. An example of this sort of contradiction is to be found in the virgin/whore dichotomy, which works to profoundly deny women's sexuality. Thus what might seem to some a rather severe deterrent to soap opera fanhood is no more extreme than what ordinary women are confronted with in their everyday lives. Yet, although the resistive nature of this cultural activity is constructed in discourse outside of the boundaries of soap opera networks as hardly worthy of notice, on the other hand it is strongly critiqued. Women who choose soap operas as cultural capital are thus able to play on these contradictions. Their soap opera knowledges help them to use these contradictions as a resistive statement. The audiences accept these contradictory positions as their own, which provides a critique from the margins accessible to themselves and other fans. It is the strategic knowledges that create the boundaries for fanship rather than conventional membership roles or styles of dress. This makes soap opera networks invisible in much the same way as the grassroots woman's movement.

Resistive pleasure involves an affective response. As Ien Ang (1990) has noted, women's response to their cultural positioning and to the contradictions that such cultural construction involves can be painful to them. Ang's analysis uses responses to the character of Sue Ellen on *Dallas*, who is unable to conceptualize herself except in relation to the character of J. R. Melodramatic characters respond to women's position in society as it is rather than as it should be in a more egalitarian society. According to Ang, this allows a space for the experiencing of the pains of subordinate conditions. In a similar way, I have found that women in soap opera groups have a space to experience great joy through laughter at both soap operas' excessive portrayal of women and the excessiveness of the contradictions in women's actual lives. This raucous laughter is an affective response that becomes a transgressive act. It forms a contradictory and knowledgeable position from which to offer an emotional critique. In effect, these fans speak with their bodies, which is a tangible experience of their resistive pleasure.

Resistive pleasure often involves resistive reading practices in which the reader becomes a cultural critic and an instigator of social change. Some soap opera audiences experience resistive pleasure on an intellectual level and some feminists are soap opera fans. Even though feminist discourse in the late 1980s and early 1990s is thought to be somewhat repressed, there is evidence to suggest that it has merely gone underground. The emergence of resistive discourse in my recorded conversations about soap opera is not unusual. People who have chosen not to identify themselves with the feminist political movement are quite comfortable, when speaking in a safe environment, with identifying individual spaces where they are oppressed. Such underground resistive discourse is an important element in eventual political change. Pilar Riaño (in press), for example, states the case for women's use of grassroots communication systems.

> The presence of alternative indigenous communication systems (oral tradition, informal information networks) that are at the very center of women's activities and define their roles as communicators in a social community has tended to be ignored. Women in the Third World producing grass roots media recognize women's subordinate condition and also their connections with other oppressions of race and class. The consciousness evidenced identifies gender oppression but also their belonging to a collectivity which shares social and class oppression. (p. 1)

Riaño and her collaborators outline an important way in which women's oral networks can be converted into direct political action. In other social settings and among other women, the reaction may be more or less public, more or less radical, and the issues involved may be different, but the impetus to emancipation or, as Foucault (1980b) would put it, the insurrection of subjugated knowledge, is evident.

In terms of mainstream analysis, Angela McRobbie (1992) has rightly suggested that femininity and feminists are no longer a binary opposition. The "old domestic settlement" has, according to McRobbie, come unhinged without a new one being put in its place. With the opening up of positions in the labor force that place women in positions to make policy decisions, like editorial positions on women's magazines or television producer positions, feminism has become a counterhegemonic force *within* the culture industries. McRobbie maintains that the production of culture in teenage magazines like *Just Seventeen* is not excessively concerned with romance. This, she feels, is due to the professional ideologies of the editorial boards being in contestation with dominant culture. The editors' support of girls who don't want a diet of romance and, above all, don't want to be portrayed as silly is seen by McRobbie as a major factor in the changes from romance-laden photo stories to magazines more concerned with independent style for girls.

We can see other examples of overt challenges to the dominant culture. McRobbie (1992) also sees support for notions of feminine self-interest and independent thought in her analysis of Rave subculture in Britain. According to McRobbie, working-class boys consume the drug ecstasy and refuse stylish dressing while the girls not only do not participate in the drug culture but carefully adopt clothing styles making their own statements of feminine independence using consumer culture. Girls also create style from recycled clothes, which McRobbie considers to be in resistance to the ready-made clothing industry. In doing this, they provide a critique of existing images of femininity while staying outside of mainstream economy. In the process, according to McRobbie, these girls learn skills that function as an alternative to art school while allowing them to exercise entrepreneurial independence. Further, their styles are sometimes copied by the fashion industry. The *production* of culture here becomes a sight of cultural contestation. Many kinds of resistance are possible on the cultural level, and it is here and in our everyday lives that much of the struggle takes place.

Before the women's movement of the 1970s (speaking here of the United States, Britain, and Australia), talking about women's oppression was done with great difficulty. It is the discourse of feminism that has enabled women to speak about the contradictions inherent in their gender roles. The feminist movement of the 1970s was a grassroots political movement. It used as a political tool the technique of consciousness-raising. Consciousness-raising might be thought of as a form of gossip although more formal and purposeful. Women gathered in small groups and took turns talking about their personal issues. In this way they discovered the power of the idea that the personal is political. Their personal stories, when taken collectively, outlined the parameters of their oppression. In other words, these are not personal problems but structural limitations built into a system that oppresses them.

These groups of women talking together were the backbone of the women's movement, and many women who participated in them remained autonomous, acting on their feminism by participating in the founding of women's centers, creating events for media education, developing feminist studies courses at universities, staging marches, creating underground railroads for battered women, and the like. When I say "remained autonomous," I refer to the fact that many women who were ardent and militant feminists during the women's movement of the 1970s did not belong to any of the national organizations of women that sprang up at the same time as part of the more organized women's movement that followed. Thus, in this case, women operated politically in unconventional and largely undocumented ways. There was, because of the absence of formal groups, no way that membership in the movement could be measured accurately, which was a subversive move in itself.

Feminism and Women's Talk

In this particular aspect of the women's movement, talk was crucial and served multiple functions. Through talk, women were able to verify that their own personal experience fit into preexisting structures of oppression. Where women were ideologically conditioned not to trust other women and to compete with each other for a man (and thus economic survival), talking together built trust among women. Women, through consciousness-raising groups, established conversations and places for enunciating and testing ideas and theories about oppression. Women had the opportunity to gain their voices, to hear themselves speak and be heard—skills needed for more conventional politics. However, consciousness-raising groups were themselves political in nature and systematic in their analysis of oppression. Participants in them were speaking feminist discourse as well as feminine discourse. As the grassroots consciousness-raising movement spread to more and more women, its success against hegemonic ideology became clear and profound.

The 1970s women's movement, like all grassroots political movements, began, and in many ways continues, outside of mainstream politics. What I have earlier referred to as radical feminism brings into the arena of political analysis issues that have not been conventionally considered as part of the analysis in terms of social inequality. Many women have gone on to develop a political critique that involves both the critique of patriarchy developed in the grassroots women's movement and a more theoretical analysis of the relationship of patriarchy to capitalism, what I have earlier referred to as dual-systems theory. However, the importance of the change in consciousness from what some Marxist analysts would call "false consciousness" to what feminists have called "raised consciousness" on the part of individual women is still considered to be a vital element in feminist consciousness. In other words, a radical change in consciousness precedes theoretical sophistication.

It is at the level of consciousness that the strength of the women's movement lies. As Gramsci (1971) has pointed out, to maintain hegemonic consciousness, people have to be won and rewon to that position. In the course of their everyday lives, people are inundated with conversations and systems that support dominant notions of how the world operates. The dual systems of patriarchy and capitalism support their own ideology, which is built into all of the communication systems that function in our society. Thus it is largely through oral networks that the raised consciousness of the feminist movement has survived on the grassroots level.

It is true that there is a great deal of writing and literate activity among feminists in the academy and that currently it is fashionable to have "name" feminists on various university faculties. However, these activities, and the academic women's studies programs that have emerged as well, are under constant pressure to accept hegemonic notions of acceptable behavior. It is in large part the alternative discourse that circulates in the feminist community that allows committed feminists to verify their resistive position. It is also this discourse that fortifies nonacademic feminists who are actively engaged in struggles over women's rights to nonviolent lives and control over their bodies. Within the feminist movement, there are constant struggles over the nature of the discourse, but the issue of "raised consciousness" is never lost sight of. It is this raised consciousness that allows feminists to apply what bell hooks (1992) calls the oppositional gaze.

hooks speaks of the gaze in relation to colonized black people, but her observations can apply to other subordinated groups.

> Subordinates in relations of power learn experientially that there is a critical gaze, one that "looks" to document, one that is oppositional. In resistance struggle, the power of the dominated to assert agency by claiming and cultivating "awareness" politicizes "looking" relations—one learns to look a certain way in order to resist. (p. 116)

What makes us able to apply the critical, oppositional look, to become a spectator in the position of agency, is the existence of an oppositional consciousness.

The Gaze and the Voice

So much of the discourse in feminist media criticism has been taken up with concerns involving the power of the look or the "gaze." The use of psychoanalytic criticism, particularly in film criticism, has weighted our discussion in that direction. Such emphasis relies on a viewer conceptualized as an individual dealing with the look in very private ways. hooks suggests that we can wrest the power of the look away from its position in dominant culture and make it work for us. I would suggest that such an act only becomes politically powerful when it becomes a collaborative act. A person may use a critical gaze independently, but its power is in sharing that perspective with others, to develop a concept of agency that works toward new levels of empowerment. A feminist view of the power to act in terms of "emancipatory consciousness" has been developed by Erica Sherover-Marcuse (1986). She defines such subjectivity as "the forms of subjectivity that tend towards a rupture with the historical system of domination" (p. 1). In other words, emancipatory subjectivity involves the beliefs and attitudes conducive to radical social change.

To understand this process, one first has to recognize the phenomenon of internalized oppression, which means that the effects of systematic mistreatment are internalized by the oppressed. Over the course of time, these effects seem natural and acquire a life of their own to the extent that the mistreatment is passed on even by the members of one's own oppressed group. Thus "there is an 'adherence' on the part of the oppressed to the prevailing order of unfreedom" (Sherover-Marcuse, 1986, p. 5). Such an adherence has to be systematically unlearned. The process of breaking with internalized oppression includes breaking with the structures of feeling and affective involvements inherent in the existing consciousness. Many oppositional movements have recognized the importance of the transformation of consciousness as an element of their radical practice. The civil rights movement in the United States, the women's movement, and the liberation theology movement in South America have recognized this aspect of the process of resistance. This recognition exists in the writings on social change as well (see particularly Freire, 1977/1985). Herbert Marcuse (1969), for example, comments that "radical change in consciousness is the beginning, the first step in changing social existence" (p. 53). Affective change is necessary for the change of consciousness that can bring about social change; however, it is not solid and pure but still subject to the influences and pressures of dominant culture. Thus female subjectivity is in a constant state of struggle. There is then no clear-cut or permanent place where one can say, "I am completely emancipated," due to the contradictory position of women in the wider world. But one can perform acts of resistance that help us to think in oppositional ways.

Thus, rather than entering the process of resistance at the macro level— the rethinking of women's roles—the second level of resistance often enters into the cultural negotiation of the process of resisting hegemony at the level of the private sphere. Here the content, style, flow, and narrative conventions of soap operas, by holding one in a complex relationship to the discourses of femininity, feminism, and dominant culture, can be responsible for the particular reaction that women experience. Researchers and theorists who both theorize and count themselves as subjects can perhaps best characterize the process as that of emancipation through the constant awareness of contradiction and the struggle to secure a space for the voice of the female spectator who speaks as well as sees.

Note

1. His remaining categories are political economy, in which audience practices are subordinated to Marxist analysis of labor relations; poststructuralist film theory, in which the analysis of the audience becomes a matter of filling subject positions created by the text; reader response criticism, which, in his view, predominantly theorizes the activity of the reader rather than addressing actual audiences; and postmodernism, whose critique of the audience returns us to the totalizing view of the audience of the Frankfort School's critique. In Allor's analysis, feminist ethnographic work is spread over two categories: reader response criticism and cultural studies. If we group separately the feminist works he mentions, it is not hard to note that all of the feminist ethnographic work has dealt with resistive pleasure—Radway's (1984)

study of romance novels, Ang's (1985) analysis of *Dallas* viewers, Walkerdine's (1986) observation of family television viewing, or McRobbie's (1984) theorization of the resistive position of dance for young women.

Appendix
Methodology

I interviewed 30 soap opera fans, 26 women and 4 men; 11 were adults, 9 were young adults (early twenties), and 10 were teenagers. To find the participants in this study, I used a version of snowball sampling (Press, 1991; L. B. Rubin, 1986; Stacey, 1987; Sudman, 1976; Sudman & Bradburn, 1983). In this type of sampling, one starts with a member of the desired group and then asks for recommendations of friends, neighbors, or relatives to be included in the group. In this way, I was able to tap into kinship and friendship groups as well as fanship groups.

In addition, I sought out mother-daughter combinations who both watched the same soap opera. Group 1 includes both adults and teenagers who live in the United States and are fans of the American daytime soap opera *Days of Our Lives*. What I am calling Group 2 consists of a British fan of the British *Coronation Street* temporarily living in Australia. Group 3 is composed of young teenage fans of the Australian soap opera *Sons and Daughters*. Group 4 comprised adult Australian fans of *Days of Our Lives*. Group 5 is an extension of Group 4 to include a fan who lives in the Australian outback. Group 6 consists of college-age Australian fans of both *Days of Our Lives* and the Australian soap *Neighbours*. The research was conducted from July 1985 to July 1988. Group 7, British college-age fans of the Australian soap opera *Neighbours*, was added in December 1991.

TABLE A.1 Age, Sex, Occupation, Education, and Status of the Participants in the Study

	Age	Sex	Occupation	Education	Status*
Group 1: American Fans of *Days of Our Lives* (July 1985)					
Emma	70-80	F	Retired nurse	HS, Nursing School	W
Sue	40-50	F	Former teacher, accountant	M.A.	M
Karen (Sue's daughter)	10-20	F	Student	HS, Studying English Lit. in college	M
Laura	20-30	F	Student/interior design	HS, Studying interior decorating in college	M
MEB (researcher)	40-50	F	Student/college teacher	M.A., Studying communication in graduate school	M
Carl	10-20	M	Student/lab assistant	HS, Studying physics	M
Fern** (Laura's cousin)	40-50	F	Real estate agent	HS	M
Melanie** (Fern's daughter)	10-20	F	Horse groomer	HS, Studying art in college	M
Chris**	10-20	M	Student	Below HS (mother and father teachers)	M
Group 2: British Fan of *Coronation Street* (September 1986)					
Ellen	20-30	F	Former housing authority office worker/houseworker	College degree	M
Group 3: Australian Fans of *Sons and Daughters* (October 1986)					
Jan	10-20	F	Student/fast-food server	HS	M
Sara***	10-20	F	Fast-food server	Left school to work	W
Diana***	10-20	F	Fast-food server	Left school to work	W
Anna***	0-10	F	Student	(father truck driver)	W
Group 4: Australian Fans of *Days of Our Lives* (June 1987)					
Sharon	40-50	F	Houseworker	HS	M
Judith (Vicki's daughter)	40-50	F	Houseworker (avocation—plays the stock market)	HS, Business college	M
Sally	50-60	F	Shopwork	O Levels (U.K.)	W

(continued)

	Age	Sex	Occupation	Education	Status*
Vicki	70-80	F	Houseworker/child minding	HS	W
Jackie	20-30	F	Teacher special education	B.A., B.Ed.	M
(Sharon's daughter)					
Doris	30-40	F	College lecturer/ department chair	M.A.	M
(Jenny's daughter)					
Jenny****	50-60	F	Shop owner	HS	M
Group 5: Australian Fan of *Days of Our Lives* (June 1987)					
Rita	30-40	F	Houseworker/station (ranch) manager	B.A., LLB	O
Group 6: Australian Fans of *Days of Our Lives* and *Neighbours* (November 1987)					
Ada	10-20	F	Student	HS, Studying general liberal arts	M
Mary	10-20	F	Student/waitress	HS, Third-year law student	M
June	10-20	F	Student	HS, Studying commerce, primary school	M
Corie	10-20	F	Student	HS, Second-year law school	M
Group 7: British Fans of *Neighbours* (December 1991)					
Jon	20-30	M	Student/tutor	HS, Third-year college, studying media (university lectures)	W
Ronald	20-30	M	Student	HS, Third-year college, studying media	M
Steve	20-30	M	Student	HS, Third-year college, studying media (radio production)	M
Ann	20-30	F	Student	HS, Third-year college, studying journalism	M
Jen	20-30	F	Student	HS, Third-year college, studying media	W

NOTE: All names are fictitious.
*W = working-, M = middle-, and O = owning-class status.
**Not present at group interview.
***Sara, Diana, and Anna are sisters.
****Present at the group interview but did not answer the questionnaire.

Of these 30 participants in the study, 4 were not interviewed. In Group 1, Fern, Melanie, and Chris were not able to attend the interview session. In Group 3, I excluded Anna's part of the interview because she was not a group member and was present because her sisters were baby-sitting for her. In Group 4, Jenny did not complete the questionnaire because she was not a soap opera fan but was present as the mother of a fan.

The ethnographic component of this study consists of three research strategies: participant observation, unstructured interviews, and questionnaires. The participant observation segment, which was contiguous with the other segments, consisted of my becoming a fan of the American daytime soap *Days of Our Lives,* which is also broadcast in Australia, and the Australian soap opera *Sons and Daughters.* When *Sons and Daughters* was taken off the air, I became a fan of its successor, *Neighbours.* I also watched the British soap operas *Coronation Street* and *East-Enders.* This often involved watching soaps with other fans, usually members of one of the ongoing groups of fans in this study. I kept notes on the process and have referred to them in drawing conclusions.

The interviews consisted of unstructured group discussions and, in situations where group discussion was not possible, in unstructured individual interviews. I recorded the interviews and later analyzed the material. During the interviews the conversation was allowed to flow naturally, but I asked questions freely as issues arose. Group interviews lasted 2 to 3 hours. Individual interviews (also 2 to 3 hours) were conducted by me and by one other member of one of the groups. The interview that Doris conducted was with a group participant who lived on a remote station in Western Australia whose mother (Sally) participated in Group 4. The individual interview between Doris and Rita is listed as Group 5. Group 7 was added after the rest of the study in order to flesh out the British reception of *Neighbours,* which was transported to Britain in 1987. This group consisted of interviews only.

The interview transcriptions were keyed into a computer where a software package called *The Ethnograph* (Seidel, Kjolseth, & Seymour, 1988) was used to code and sort the data. There are 51 coding possibilities. Some of these were decided upon by what I was looking for—that is, an analysis of pleasure in the context of involvement with a group of soap opera fans—and some were decided upon in relation to the data—that is, the directions that the conversations took suggested additional methods of analysis or points of view in looking at the data. The codes are arranged under the general headings of *soaps fanhood, fanship practices, soap opera knowledge,* and *pleasure.*

The questionnaire, consisting of 80 items, was administered at the end of the group interviews to three interview groups. The questions in the questionnaire were arrived at after three initial interviews were completed. They reflect the issues that arose in the taped discussions of the American, British, and Australian audience groups in the first three interviews. The questionnaires were then reviewed by a member of Group 4 and modified according to her feedback. The questionnaire also included some questions brought up by recent research on soap opera.

The Soap Operas

In Western Australia, the Australian-produced soap operas broadcast in 1986 were *The Sullivans* (in rerun at 6 a.m. weekdays), *Prisoner* (at 10 p.m. on Saturdays), *A Country Practice* (8:30-9:30 p.m. Tuesdays and Thursdays), and *Sons and Daughters* (7-7:30 p.m. Monday-Thursday). The American daytime soaps available in Western Australia were *The Young and the Restless* (noon-1 p.m., weekdays), *Days of Our Lives* (1-2 p.m. weekdays), and *Another World* (2-3 p.m. weekdays). The nighttime soaps were *Dallas, Dynasty, Knots' Landing,* and *Falcon Crest.* The British soap operas *Coronation Street* (11 a.m. in Western Australia), *East-Enders* (6 p.m.), and *Brookside* (6 p.m.) began being broadcast (or in the case of *Coronation Street,* rebroadcast) in Australia in 1986 and 1987.

The Questionnaire

Name: _____

Address: _____

Phone Number: _____

  1. Which soaps do you watch?

  2. Do you keep the TV set on while you are working around the home?
  3. If so, what types of tasks do you do?

  4. Do you do other things while you are actually sitting to watch TV?

     Like what?

  5. Do you do any of these while watching *Days of Our Lives*?
  6. Do you talk to other people when you watch TV? If so, who? Is it the same if you are watching during the day as at night?

  7. Do you talk about TV with people (brothers, sisters, friends, daughter, grandmother, etc.)?

  8. Do you talk about *Days of Our Lives*?
  9. To whom?
 10. Son(s)?
 11. Daughter(s)?
 12. Lover?
 13. Husband?
 14. Women friend(s)?
 15. Men friend(s)?
 16. How many people do you know who follow *Days of Our Lives*?

17. Do you discuss *Days of Our Lives* with any or all of these people?
18. Out of this group, how many are women and how many are men?
19. When do you usually talk about soaps?

20. Do you do most of the housework?
21. Do you live with—
    Children _____ How many _____
    Ages _____ Female _____ Male _____
    Other woman or women _____
    Man or men _____
22. Do your children watch soaps? Which one?
23. What do you like about soaps?
24. What is the first soap you remember watching or listening to?

25. Who introduced you to it?
26. Did you watch it or listen to it together with this person?
27. What sort of books or magazines do you read?
28. Do you ever read soaps fan magazines?
29. Do you have a favorite series of books?
30. Who are some of your favorite authors?
31. Who are some of your favorite TV characters?
32. When a group of people is watching TV at your house at night, who controls the TV set?
33. In the day who controls the TV set?
34. Do you have a videotape recorder?
35. If so, do you record your soap when you can't see it?
36. If this is the case, when and how do you watch your soap?
37. Do you know your friends' favorite soap?

38. Do you refrain from telephoning her (them) when you know it is on?

39. Do you think that soaps' characters are like real people? Why?

40. Do you ever laugh when you are watching *Days of Our Lives*? When?
41. Do you ever cry? When?
42. Could you sketch out a family tree for the families on *Days of Our Lives*?
43. Do soaps' plots in general seem believable to you?
44. Are they generally sad, funny, happy, sentimental, or what other word would you use?
45. Do the men on soaps (or some of them) seem sexy to you?

46. Who, currently, is the sexiest?

47. Do you have a favorite woman character on *Days of Our Lives*? If so, who?

48. Why do you like her?

49. If you saw her on the street tomorrow, what sort of questions would you ask her?

50. Do you and friends sometimes talk about the characters as if they were real?

51. Who do you think is the most tragic character on *Days of Our Lives*?

52. What events in her or his life make her/him tragic?

53. Is there something other than the events in their lives that makes these characters tragic? If so, what?

54. Who do you think is the worst villainess on the show?

55. Do you get pleasure out of hating her?
56. Do you think the characters talk too much on *Days*?

57. Do you enjoy listening to them talk?

58. Do you sometimes listen to the TV set when *Days of Our Lives* is on and turn to look when there is an intense moment?
59. Which do you like best, the intense emotional scenes (sad), the intense emotional scenes (romantic), the family togetherness scenes (like Christmas)?

60. Do you also like the other two?

61. Do you ever act out or repeat a phrase from someone's conversation on *Days of Our Lives*? If so, what?

62. Who is your favorite male character? Why?
63. Do you think that the characters on *Days of Our Lives* have too many problems? _____ Why do you think this?

64. Do people you know make fun of soaps and people who watch them?
65. Are they usually men? _____ Are they usually women?
66. What is the usual criticism?

67. Are soap operas like real life or not?

68. Do all of the women in your family watch soaps?

69. Do all the women in your family watch the same soap?

70. How long have you been watching *Days of Our Lives*?

71. When you work out the possibilities of what could happen next on *Days of Our Lives,* what sorts of things do you consider?

72. Does it bother you when a character comes back after having been considered dead for a long time? Why or why not?

73. Some would argue that some things that happen on soaps are not rational.
    Does this bother you?
    Do you think it is funny?
74. Does it provide a topic of conversation about the soap?

75. Do you compare the problems on the soaps with what you would do in your own life?
76. If so, can you give an example?
77. Profile

Sex	Age Range	Presently paid employment?
F	10-20	
M	20-30	Nature of job
	30-40	
	40-50	Inside or outside the home?
	50-60	
	60-70	
	70-80	
	80-90	

78. Do you spend more than 2 hours per week on other formal activities (charity work,
    child minding, etc.)? _____

    _____

    Please describe. _____
79. Highest level of formal education reached._____
80. Do you still have children at home? _____ Ages? _____

Thank you very much.

Interview Codes

The codes used to classify the interview data in this study are listed below.
Next to each is the research question associated with the code word. In most cases
the specific code word is used (those listed A, B, C, and so on), but in some cases
the content is more general and is coded by the general category (listed 1, 2, 3).

1. Soaps Fanhood: FANHOOD, FANSHIP—What does fanhood mean to these
   fans?
   a. SPFAN-FEEL: How fans feel about being soaps fans?
   b. AUDIENCE: Conception of the construction of the soaps audience?
   c. ADDICTION: What does addiction mean in this context?
   d. FANHOOD-OP: How do other people react to their fanhood?
2. Fanship Practices—VIEW PRACT, PRACTICES
   a. INTEGRATE: How are soaps integrated into daily life?
   b. GOSSIP: How are soaps integrated into gossip?
   c. SITUA-LIFE: Are there situations close to real life in the soaps?
   d. CODES: Are codes used to talk about soaps?

    e. FRIENDS: How do friends figure in soaps networks?

    f. MOM-DAUGHT: How are mothers and daughters involved in soaps practices?

    g. SOAP FAMILY: Are soaps characters discussed as if they were members of the family?

    h. ACT: Do these fans act out segments of soap operas?

    i. JUDGMENT: How do these fans make judgments about soap operas?

    j. LENGTH FAN: How long have some people continued their lives as fans?

3. Soaps Knowledge: SOAPS KN—What are the knowledges that people have because they are fans?

    a. SK-AW PROD: What do these fans say that indicated that they are aware of production considerations?

    b. SK-PREDICT: How do these fans go about predicting what will happen next?

    c. CHARACTERS: What are their perceptions and expectations around the characters?

    d. SK-PLOTS: How do they deal with the plots?

    e. TIME: What are the issues about time within the soaps story line?

    f. TIME-SPT&A: How does soap opera time correlate with the actual time of the viewers?

    g. PLACE: What is the function of place in the soaps?

    h. INTEXT S: What are the intertextual references with other soaps and other television programs?

    i. INTEXT N: What are the intertextual references through the newspaper?

4. Pleasure: PLEASURE—How do these conversations describe and indicate pleasure for the members of these groups?

    a. LAUGH: What things did these fans laugh at in the course of these conversations?

    b. STORY TELL: What were some of their stories about soaps?

    c. READ.VIEW: What do they say about reading versus television viewing?

    d. MEMORIES: What memories do they have about soap opera and their lives?

    e. RELAX: How do they talk about watching without effort or relaxing?

    f. ANTICIPATE: What are these fans' feelings about anticipation, the search for truth, or the hermeneutic code?

    g. ROMANCE: What do these fans say about romance in the soaps?

    h. CLOTHES: What do these fans say about clothes on the soaps?

    i. WEDDING: What do these fans say about soaps weddings?

    j. VILLAIN: What do these fans say about the villains?

    k. GENEALOGY: How do genealogies fit into their conversations?

    l. LOOK: What are their pleasures in looking?

m. PL-PREDICT: What is the pleasure in predicting for these fans?
n. GOSSIP: How does gossip figure into soaps pleasure?
o. TALK: Is talk different than gossip in this context?
p. ORAL V TRD (traditional): Are there examples of oral narrative conventions in the conversations included here?
q. WORK: When the topics of work, class, race, age, or the status of women come up, how are they talked about?

References

Agar, M. (1980). *The professional stranger: An informal introduction to ethnography.* New York: Academic Press.

Allen, R. C. (1985). *Speaking of soap operas.* Chapel Hill: University of North Carolina Press.

Allen, R. C. (1987). *Channels of discourse.* Chapel Hill: University of North Carolina Press.

Allor, M. (1988). Relocating the site of the audience. *Critical Studies in Mass Communication, 5,* 217-233.

Althusser, L. (1976). Ideology and ideological state apparatuses. In *Essays on ideology* (pp. 1-61). London: Verso.

American Heritage Dictionary. (1982). (2nd college ed.). Boston: Houghton Mifflin.

Amesley, C. (1989). How to read *Star Trek. Cultural Studies, 3,* 323-339.

Ang, I. (1985). *Watching "Dallas": Soap opera and the melodramatic imagination.* London: Methuen.

Ang, I. (1987). Popular fiction and feminist cultural politics. *Theory, Culture and Society, 4,* 654-658.

Ang, I. (1989). Wanted: Audiences: On the politics of empirical audience studies. In E. Seiter, H. Borchers, G. Kreutzner, & E. M. Warth (Eds.), *Remote control: Television, audiences, and cultural power* (pp. 96-115). London: Routledge & Kegan Paul.

Ang, I. (1990). Melodramatic identifications: Television fiction and women's fantasy. In M. E. Brown (Ed.), *Television and women's culture* (pp. 75-88). Sydney/London: Currency/Sage.

Ang, I. (1991). *Desperately seeking the audience.* London: Routledge & Kegan Paul.

Ang, I., & Hermes, J. (1991). Gender and/in media consumption. In J. Curran & M. Gurevitch (Eds.) *Mass media and society* (pp. 307-328). London: Edward Arnold.

Arnheim, R. (1944). The world of the daytime serial. In P. F. Lazarsfeld & F. M. Stanton (Eds.), *Radio research: 1942-1943* (pp. 38-45). New York: Duell, Sloan and Pearce.

Babcock, B. (1978). *The reversible world: Symbolic inversion in art and society.* Ithaca, NY: Cornell University Press.

Bacon-Smith, C. (1992). *Enterprising women: Television fandom and the creation of popular myth.* Philadelphia: University of Pennsylvania Press.

Baehr, H. (1980). *Women and media.* Oxford: Pergamon.

Bakhtin, M. (1965). *Rabelais and his world* (H. Iswoy, Trans.). Cambridge: MIT Press.

Bakhtin, M. (1971). Discourse typology in prose. In L. Matejka & K. Pomorska (Eds.), *Readings in Russian poetics: Formalist and structuralist views* (pp. 176-196). Cambridge: MIT Press.

Barbatis, G., & Guy, Y. (1991). Analyzing meaning in form: Soap opera's compositional construction of "realness." *Journal of Broadcasting and Electronic Media, 37,* 59-74.

Barker, B. (1992, October). *Renegotiating the female spectator.* Paper presented at the annual meeting of the Speech Communication Association, Chicago.

Barnouw, E. (1970). *The image empire.* New York: Oxford University Press.

Barnouw, E. (1975). *Tube of plenty.* New York: Oxford University Press.

Barthes, R. (1972). *Mythologies* (A. Lavers, Trans.). New York: Hill & Wang.

Barthes, R. (1975a). *The pleasure of the text* (R. Miller, Trans.). New York: Hill & Wang.

Barthes, R. (1975b). *S/Z* (Richard Miller, Trans.). London: Cape.

Barwick, L. (1985). *Critical perspectives on oral song in performance: The case of Donna Lombarda.* Unpublished doctoral dissertation, Flinders University, Adelaide, South Australia.

Baym, N. (1993). *Women's fiction: A guide to novels by and about women in America 1820-70* (2nd ed.). Urbana: University of Illinois Press.

Blumler, J. (1985). The social character of media gratifications. In K. Rosengren, L. Wenner, & P. Palmgreen (Eds.), *Media gratifications research: Current perspectives* (pp. 41-59). Beverly Hills, CA: Sage.

Bobo, J. (1988). *The color purple:* Black women as cultural readers. In E. D. Pribram (Ed.), *Female spectators: Looking at film and television* (pp. 90-109). New York: Verso.

Bourdieu, P. (1984). *Distinction: A social critique of the judgment of taste* (R. Nice, Trans.). Cambridge, MA: Harvard University Press.

Brower, S. (1990). Inside stories: Gossip and television audiences. In S. Thomas & W. A. Evans (Eds.), *Culture and communication* (Vol. 4, pp. 225-235). Norwood, NJ: Ablex.

Brown, M. E. (1986). The politics of soaps: Pleasure and feminine empowerment. *The Australian Journal of Cultural Studies, 4,* 1-25.

Brown, M. E. (1989a). Soap opera and women's culture: Politics and the popular. In C. Spitzack & K. Carter (Eds.), *Doing research on women's communication: The politics of theory and method* (pp. 161-190). Norwood, NJ: Ablex.

Brown, M. E. (1989b). Teaching about soap opera. *Interpretations: The English Teacher's Journal of Western Australia, 4,* 9-11.

Brown, M. E. (Ed.). (1990a). *Television and women's culture.* Sydney/London: Currency/Sage.

Brown, M. E. (1990b). Motley moments: Soap operas, carnival, gossip and the power of utterance. In M. E. Brown (Ed.), *Television and women's culture* (pp. 183-198). Syndey/London: Currency/Sage.

Brown, M. E. (1990c). Knowledge and power: An ethnography of soap opera viewers. In L. Vande Berge & L. Wenner (Eds.), *Television criticism* (pp. 178-198). New York: Longman.

Brown, M. E. (1990d, Fall). Soap operas and romance novels: Questioning the politics of pleasure and power. *Phoebe: An Interdisciplinary Journal of Feminist Scholarship, Theory and Aesthetics, 2,* 18-28.

Brown, M. E. (1991). Strategies and tactics: Teenage girls and Australian soaps. *Women and Language, 16,* 22-28.

Brown, M. E., & Barwick, L. (1987). Fables and endless genealogies: Soaps and women's oral culture. *Continuum: An Australian Journal of the Media, 1-2,* 71-82.

Brunsdon, C. (1981). Crossroads: Notes on a soap opera. *Screen, 22,* 32-37.

Brunsdon, C. (1983). Crossroads: Notes on a soap opera. In E. A. Kaplan (Ed.), *Regarding television: Critical approaches—an anthology* (pp. 76-83). Frederick, MD: University Publications of America.

Brunsdon, C. (1984). Writing about soap opera. In L. Masterman (Ed.), *Television mythologies* (pp. 82-87). London: Comedia.

Brunsdon, C. (1986). Women watching television. *Medie Kultur, 4,* 100-112.

Brunsdon, C. (1987). Feminism and soap opera. In K. Davies, J. Dickey, & T. Stratford (Eds.), *Out of focus: Writings on women and the media* (pp. 147-150). London: Women's Press.

Brunsdon, C. (1989). Text and audience. In E. Seiter, H. Borchers, G. Kreutzner, & E. M. Warth (Eds.), *Remote control: Television, audiences, and cultural control* (pp. 116-129). London: Routledge & Kegan Paul.

Brunsdon, C. (1993). Identity in feminist television criticism. *Media, Culture and Society, 15,* 309-320.

Buckingham, D. (1987). *Public secrets: "EastEnders" and its audience.* London: British Film Institute.

Buckingham, D. (1991). What are words worth? Interpreting children's talk about television. *Cultural Studies, 5,* 228-245.

Buckman, P. (1984). *All for love: A study in soap opera.* London: Secker and Warburg.

Budd, M., Entman, R. M., & Steinman, C. (1990). The affirmative character of U.S. cultural studies. *Critical Studies in Mass Communication, 7,* 169-184.

Buerkel-Rothfuss, N., with Mayes, S. (1981). Soap opera viewing: The cultivation effect. *Journal of Communication, 31,* 108-115.

Butcher, M. (1993). *Lookin' at country music television: The presentation differences between the country music video and the rock music video.* Unpublished paper, University of Missouri.

Byars, J. (1988). Gazes/voices/power: Expanding psychoanalysis for feminist film and television theory. In E. D. Pribram (Ed.), *Female spectators: Looking at film and television* (pp. 110-131). London: Verso.

Cantor, M., & Pingree, S. (1983). *The soap opera.* London: Sage.

Carragee, K. M. (1990). Interpretative media study and interpretative social science. *Critical Studies in Mass Communication, 7,* 81-96.

Carveth, R., & Alexander, A. (1985). Soap opera viewing motivations and the cultivation process. *Journal of Broadcasting and Electronic Media, 29,* 259-273.

Cassata, M., & Skill, T. (1983). *Life on daytime television: Tuning in American serial drama.* Norwood, NJ: Ablex.

Chesler, P. (1972). *Women and madness.* New York: Avon.

Chodorow, N. (1978). *The reproduction of mothering: Psychoanalysis and the sociology of gender.* Berkeley: University of California Press.

Clark, D. (1989). *Actors' labor and the politics of subjectivity: Hollywood in the 1930s.* Unpublished dissertation, University of Iowa.

Clifford, J. (1983). On ethnographic authority. *Representations, 1,* 118-146.

Clifford, J., & Marcus, G. E. (Eds.). (1986). *Writing culture: The poetics and politics of ethnography.* Berkeley: University of California Press.

Compesi, R. J. (1980). Gratifications of daytime TV serial viewers. *Journalism Quarterly, 57,* 155-185.

Cook, P., Gomery, D., & Lichty, L. (1989). *American media: The Wilson Quarterly reader.* Washington, DC: Wilson Center Press.

Cornell, M., Davis, T., McIntosh, S., & Root, M. (1981). Romance and sexuality: Between the devil and the deep blue sea? In A. McRobbie & T. McCabe (Eds.), *Feminism for girls* (pp. 155-177). London: Routledge & Kegan Paul.

Corner, J. (1988, July). *Looking in on life: The social relations of documentary television in the 1980's*. Paper presented at the 1988 International Television Studies conference, London.

Cowie, C., & Lees, S. (1981). Slags and drags. *Feminist Review, 9,* 17-31.

Coyne, R. F. (1990, November). *Finding a feminist voice*. Paper presented at the annual meeting of the Speech Communication Association, Chicago.

Daly, M. (1978). *Gyn/ecology: The metaethics of radical feminism.* Boston: Beacon.

Daniels, A. K. (1987). Invisible work. *Social Problems, 32,* 403-415.

Dates, J. L., & Barlow, W. (1990). *Split image: African Americans in the mass media.* Washington, DC: Howard University Press.

Davies, J. (1984). Soap and other operas. *Metro, 65,* 31-33.

Davies, J. (1986). Television audiences revisited. *Australian Journal of Screen Theory, 18,* 84-105.

de Certeau, M. (1986). *The practice of everyday life* (S. F. Rendall, Trans.). Berkeley: University of California Press.

de Lauretis, T. (1987). *Technologies of gender.* Bloomington: Indiana University Press.

de Lauretis, T. (1990). Upping the anti [sic] in feminist theory. In M. Hirsh & E. F. Keller (Eds.), *Conflicts in feminism* (pp. 255-270). New York: Routledge & Kegan Paul.

Deleuze, G., & Guattari, F. (1977). *Anti-Oedipus: Capitalism and schizophrenia* (R. Hurley, M. Seem, & H. R. Lane, Trans.). New York: Viking.

DeVault, M. L. (1990). Talking and listening from women's standpoint: Feminist strategies for interviewing and analysis. *Social Problems, 37,* 96-116.

Donovan, J. (1992). *Feminist theory: The intellectual traditions of American feminism* (2nd ed.). New York: Continuum.

DuBois, W. E. B. (1961). *The souls of black folk.* New York: Fawcett.

Dworkin, A. (1987). *Intercourse.* New York: Free Press.

Dyer, R. (1982). *Stars.* London: British Film Institute.

Dyer, R. (1992). *Only entertainment.* New York: Routledge & Kegan Paul.

Eagleton, T. (1981). *Walter Benjamin: Towards a revolutionary criticism.* London: Verso.

Eisenstein, H. (1983). *Contemporary feminist thought.* Boston: G. K. Hall.

Eisenstein, Z. (1981). *The radical future of liberal feminism.* New York: Longman.

Evans, W. A. (1990, June). The interpretive turn in media research: Innovation, iteration, or illusion? *Critical Studies in Mass Communication, 7,* 147-168.

Faderman, L. (1981). *Surpassing the love of men: Romantic friendship and love between women from the Renaissance to the present.* London: Junction.

Fish, S. (1980). *Is there a text in this class? The authority of interpretive communities.* Cambridge, MA: Harvard University Press.

Fishman, P. M. (1978). Interaction: The work women do. *Social Problems, 24,* 397-406.

Fiske, J. (1986). *Cagney & Lacey:* Reading character structurally and politically. *Communication, 13,* 399-426.

Fiske, J. (1987). *Television culture.* London: Methuen.

Fiske, J. (1988). Critical response: Meaningful moments. *Critical Studies in Mass Communication, 5,* 246-251.

Fiske, J. (1990). Ethnosemiotics: Some personal and theoretical reflections. *Cultural Studies, 4,* 85-98.

Fiske, J. (1992). The cultural economy of fandom. In L. A. Lewis (Ed.), *The adoring audience: Fan culture and popular media* (pp. 30-40). New York: Routledge & Kegan Paul.

198   *Soap Opera and Women's Talk*

Fiske, J., & Hartley, J. (1978). *Reading television*. London: Methuen.
Flitterman, S. (1983). The real soap operas: TV commercials. In E. A. Kaplan (Ed.), *Regarding television: Critical approaches—an anthology* (pp. 84-96). Frederick, MD: University Publications of America.
Foucault, M. (1975). *The birth of the clinic: An archaeology of medical perception* (A. M. Sheridan Smith, Trans.). New York: Vintage.
Foucault, M. (1977). Nietzsche, genealogy, history. In D. Bouchard (Ed.), *Language, counter-memory, practice: Selected essays and interviews* (pp. 139-164). Oxford: Blackwell.
Foucault, M. (1980a). *The history of sexuality: Vol. 1. An introduction*. Harmondsworth: Penguin.
Foucault, M. (1980b). *Power/knowledge: Selected interviews and other writings, 1972-1977*. New York: Pantheon.
Foucault, M. (1982). Afterword: The subject and power. In H. L. Dreyfus & P. Rabinow (Eds.), *Michel Foucault: Beyond structuralism and hermeneutics* (pp. 208-226). Brighton: Harvester.
Franklin, S., Lury, C., & Stacey, J. (1992). Feminism and cultural studies. In P. Scannell, P. Schlisinger, & C. Sparks (Eds.), *Culture and power: A media, culture and society reader* (pp. 90-111). London: Sage.
Franzblau, S., Sprafkin, J. N., & Rubinstein, E. A. (1977). Sex on TV: A content analysis. *Journal of Communication, 27*, 164-170.
Frazer, E. (1987). Teenage girls reading Jackie. *Media, Culture and Society, 9*, 407-425.
Freire, P. (1985). *The pedagogy of the oppressed* (M. Bergman, Trans.). New York: Continuum.
Frey-Vor, G. (1990). Soap opera. *Communication Research Trends, 10*(1), 1-16; *10*(2), 1-12.
Frow, J. (1993). Knowledge and class. *Cultural Studies, 7*, 240-291.
Game, A., & Pringle, R. (1983). *Gender at work*. Sydney: Allen & Unwin.
Geraghty, C. (1981). The continuous serial: A definition. In R. Dyer, C. Geraghty, M. Jordan, T. Lovell, R. Paterson, & J. Stewart (Eds.), *Coronation Street* (pp. 9-26). London: British Film Institute.
Geraghty, C. (1991). *Women and soap opera: A study of prime time soaps*. Cambridge: Polity.
Gerbner, G. (1972). Violence in television drama: Trends and symbolic functions. In G. S. Comstock & E. A. Rubinstein (Eds.), *Television and social behavior: Vol. 1. Media content and control*. Washington, DC: Government Printing Office.
Gerbner, G., & Gross, L. (1976). Living with television: The violence profile. *Journal of Communication, 26*, 173-199.
Gerbner, G., Gross, L., Morgan, M., & Signorielli, N. (1980). The "mainstreaming" of America: Violence profile no. 11. *Journal of Communication, 30*, 10-29.
Gilbert, A. (1976). *All my afternoons*. New York: A & W Visual Library.
Gilligan, C. (1982). *In a different voice: Psychological theory and women's development*. Cambridge, MA: Harvard University Press.
Gilligan, C., Lyons, N. P., & Hanmer, T. J. (Eds.). (1990). *Making connections: The relational worlds of adolescent girls at Emma Willard School*. Cambridge, MA: Harvard University Press.
Gilman, C. P. (1915/1979). *Herland*. New York: Pantheon.
Gitlin, T. (1985). *Inside prime time*. New York: Pantheon.
Glaser, B., & Strauss, A. (1967). *The discovery of grounded theory*. Chicago: Aldine.

Gramsci, A. (1971). *Selections from the prison notebooks* (Q. Hoare & G. Nowell-Smith, Trans.). New York: International Publishers.

Gray, A. (1987). Behind closed doors: Video recorders in the home. In H. Baehr & G. Dyer (Eds.), *Boxed in: Women and television* (pp. 38-54). London: Pandora.

Greenberg, B. S., Abelman, R., & Neuendorf, K. (1981). Sex on the soap operas: Afternoon delight. *Journal of Communication, 31,* 83-89.

Greschwender, J. A. (1992). Ethgender, women's waged labor, and economic mobility. *Social Problems, 39,* 1-16.

Gripsrud, J. (1990). Toward a flexible methodology in studying media meaning: *Dynasty* in Norway. *Critical Studies in Mass Communication, 7,* 117-128.

Grodin, D. (1991). The interpreting audience: The therapeutics of self-help book reading. *Critical Studies in Mass Communication, 8,* 404-420.

Grossberg, L. (1984a). Another boring day in paradise: Rock and roll and the empowerment of everyday life. *Popular Music, 4,* 225-258.

Grossberg, L. (1984b). I'd rather feel bad than not feel anything at all (Rock and roll: Pleasure and power). *Enclidic, 1-3,* 1-33.

Grossberg, L. (1987). The in-difference of television. *Screen, 28,* 28-46.

Grossberg, L. (1988). Wandering audiences, nomadic critics. *Cultural Studies, 2,* 377-391.

Grossberg, L. (1992). *We gotta get out of this place: Popular conservatism and postmodern culture.* New York: Routledge & Kegan Paul.

Hall, S. (1980). Encoding/decoding. In S. Hall, D. Hobson, A. Lowe, & P. Willis (Eds.), *Culture, media, language* (pp. 128-138). London: Hutchinson.

Harding, S. (1986). *The science question in feminism.* London: Cornell University Press.

Harlequin Romance Editorial Guidelines. (1991). Don Mills, Ontario, Canada: Harlequin Enterprises Limited.

Hartley, J. (1984). Encouraging signs: Television and the power of dirt, speech and scandalous categories. In W. D. Rowland & B. Watkins (Eds.), *Interpreting television: Current research perspectives* (pp. 119-141). Beverly Hills, CA: Sage.

Hartley, J. (1987). Invisible fictions: Television audiences, paedocracy, pleasure. *Textual Practice, 1,* 121-138.

Hartley, J. (1988). The real world of audiences. *Critical Studies in Mass Communication, 5,* 234-238.

Hartley, J. (1992). *The politics of pictures: The creation of the public in the age of popular media.* London: Routledge & Kegan Paul.

Hartmann, H. (1981). The unhappy marriage of Marxism and feminism: Toward a more progressive union. In R. Dale et al. (Eds.), *Education and the state: Vol. 2. Politics, patriarchy and practice* (pp. 191-210). Lewes, England: Falmer.

Hartmann, H. (1987). The family as the locus of gender, class and political struggle. In S. Harding (Ed.), *Feminism and methodology* (pp. 109-134). Bloomington: Indiana University Press.

Hayden, D. (1984). *Redesigning the American dream: The future of housing, work and family life.* New York: Norton.

Herzog, H. (1944). What do we really know about daytime serial listeners. In P. Lazarsfeld & F. M. Stanton (Eds.), *Radio research: 1942-1943* (pp. 3-33). New York: Duell, Sloan and Pearce.

Hobson, D. (1982). *"Crossroads": The drama of a soap opera.* London: Methuen.

Hobson, D. (1989). Soap operas at work. In E. Seiter, H. Borchers, G. Kreutzner, & E. M. Warth (Eds.), *Remote control* (pp. 150-167). London: Routledge & Kegan Paul.

Hobson, D. (1990). Women audiences and the workplace. In M. E. Brown (Ed.), *Television and women's culture* (pp. 61-71). Sydney/London: Currency/Sage.

Hochschild, A., with Machung, A. (1989). *The second shift: Working parents and the revolution at home.* New York: Viking.

Hodge, R., & Tripp, D. (1986). *Children and television.* London: Quality Press.

Holloway, W. (1984). Gender difference and the production of subjectivity. In J. Henriques et al. (Eds.), *Changing the subject: Psychology, social regulation, and subjectivity* (pp. 227-263). London: Methuen.

Holub, R. C. (1984). *Reception theory: A critical introduction.* London: Methuen.

hooks, b. (1981). *Ain't I a woman: Black women and feminism.* Boston: South End.

hooks, b. (1992). *Black looks: Race and representation.* Boston: South End.

Hudson, B. (1984). Femininity and adolescence. In A. McRobbie & M. Nava (Eds.), *Gender and generation* (pp. 31-53). London: Macmillan.

Iser, W. (1974). *The implied reader: Patterns of communication of prose fiction from Bunyan to Beckett.* Baltimore, MD: Johns Hopkins University Press.

Iser, W. (1978). *The act of reading: A theory of aesthetic response.* Baltimore, MD: Johns Hopkins University Press.

Jauss, H. R. (1982a). *Aesthetic experience and literary hermeneutics.* Minneapolis: University of Minnesota Press.

Jauss, H. R. (1982b). *Toward an aesthetic of reception.* Minneapolis: University of Minnesota Press.

Jefferys, S. (1985). *The spinster and her enemies: Feminism and sexuality 1800-1930.* London: Pandora.

Jenkins, H. (1988a). "Going bonkers": Children, play and Pee-wee. *Camera Obscura, 17,* 169-194.

Jenkins, H. (1988b). Star Trek rerun, reread, rewritten. *Critical Studies in Mass Communication, 4,* 21-36.

Jenkins, H. (1992). *Textual poachers: Television fans and participatory culture.* London: Routledge & Kegan Paul.

Jensen, K. B. (1987). Qualitative audience research: Toward an integrative approach to reception. *Critical Studies in Mass Communication, 4,* 21-36.

Jensen, K. B. (1990). Television futures: A social action methodology for studying interpretative communities. *Critical Studies in Mass Communication, 7,* 129-146.

Jones, D. (1980). Gossip: Notes on women's oral culture. *Women's Studies International Quarterly, 3,* 193-198.

Jordan, M. (1981). Realism and convention. In R. Dyer, C. Geraghty, M. Jordan, T. Lovell, R. Patterson, & J. Stewart (Eds.), *Coronation Street* (pp. 27-39). London: British Film Institute.

Jordan, M., & Brunt, R. (1988). Constituting the television audience: A problem of method. In P. Drummond & R. Patterson (Eds.), *Television and its audience* (pp. 231-249). London: British Film Institute.

Kalcik, S. (1975). Like Ann's gynecologist or the time I was almost raped . . . In C. R. Farrer (Ed.), *Women and folklore* (pp. 3-11). Austin: University of Texas Press.

Kaplan, A. (1987). Feminist criticism and television. In R. C. Allen (Ed.), *Channels of discourse* (pp. 211-253). Chapel Hill: University of North Carolina Press.

Katz, E., & Liebes, T. (1984). Once upon a time in Dallas. *Intermedia, 12,* 28-32.

Katz, E., & Liebes, T. (1986a). Mutual aid in the decoding of *Dallas:* Preliminary notes from a cross-cultural study. In R. Paterson (Ed.), *Television in transition* (pp. 187-198). London: British Film Institute.

Katz, E., & Liebes, T. (1986b). Decoding *Dallas:* Notes from a cross-cultural study. In G. Gumpert & R. Cathcart (Eds.), *Inter/media: Interpersonal communication in a media world* (3rd ed., pp. 97-109). New York: Oxford University Press.

Katzman, N. (1972). Television soap operas: What's been going on anyway? *Public Opinion Quarterly, 36,* 201-212.

Kissane, K. (1988, April). Soaps: More bubble than trouble. *Time* (Australian edition), pp. 50-57.

LaGuardia, R. (1977). *"Ma Perkins" to "Mary Hartman": The illustrated history of soap operas.* New York: Ballantine.

LaGuardia, R. (1983). *Soap world.* New York: Priam.

Land, J. (1987). *Demeter.* Larchmont, NY: Author.

Leal, O. F., & Oliver, R. G. (1987). Class interpretations of a soap opera narrative: The case of the Brazilian novela *Summer Sun. Theory, Culture and Society, 4,* 81-99.

Lee, M., & Cho, C. H. (1990). Women watching together: An ethnographic study of Korean soap opera fans in the U.S. *Cultural Studies, 4,* 30-44.

Lembo, R., & Tucker, K. H. (1990). Culture, television, and opposition: Rethinking cultural studies. *Critical Studies in Mass Communication, 7,* 97-116.

Lemish, D. (1985). Soap opera viewing in college: A naturalistic inquiry. *Journal of Broadcasting and Electronic Media, 29,* 275-293.

Lesko, N. (1988). The curriculum of the body: Lessons from a Catholic high school. In L. G. Roman, L. K. Christian-Smith, with E. Ellsworth (Eds.), *Becoming feminine: The politics of popular culture* (pp. 123-142). London: Falmer.

Levy, M., & Windahl, S. (1985). The concept of audience activity. In K. Rosengren, L. Wenner, & P. Palmgreen (Eds.), *Media gratifications research: Current perspectives* (pp. 109-112). Beverly Hills, CA: Sage.

Lewis, L. A. (1990). *Gender politics and MTV: Voicing the difference.* Philadelphia: Temple University Press.

Lewis, L. (1992). *The adoring audience: Fan culture and popular media.* London: Routledge & Kegan Paul.

Lichter, R., Lichter, L., & Rothman, S. (1986). The politics of the American dream—From Lucy to Lacey: TV's dream girls. *Public Opinion, 9,* 16-19.

Liebes, T. (1988). Cultural differences in the retelling of television fiction. *Critical Studies in Mass Communication, 5,* 277-292.

Liebes, T., & Katz, E. (1986). Patterns of involvement in television fiction: A comparative analysis. *European Journal of Communication, 1,* 151-171.

Lindlof, T. R. (1988). Media audiences as interpretative communities. In J. Anderson (Ed.), *Communication yearbook* (Vol. 11, pp. 81-107). Newbury Park, CA: Sage.

Lindlof, T. R. (1991). The qualitative study of media audiences. *Journal of Broadcasting and Electronic Media, 35,* 23-42.

Lindlof, T., & Meyer, T. (1987). Mediated communication as ways of seeing, acting, and constructing culture: The tools of qualitative research. In T. Lindlof (Ed.), *Natural audiences: Qualitative research of media uses and effects* (pp. 1-32). Norwood, NJ: Ablex.

Livingstone, S. (1989). Interpretative viewers and structured programs. *Communication Research, 16,* 25-37.

Long, E. (1986). Women, reading, and cultural authority: Some implications of the audience perspective in cultural studies. *American Quarterly, 38,* 591-612.

Long, E. (1987). Reading groups and the postmodern crisis of cultural authority. *Cultural Studies, 1,* 306-327.

Longhurst, B. (1987). Realism, naturalism and television soap opera. *Theory, Culture and Society, 4,* 633-649.

Lont, C. M. (1993). Feminist critique of mass communication research. In S. P. Bowen & N. Wyatt (Eds.), *Transforming visions: Feminist critiques in communication studies* (pp. 231-248). Cresskill, NJ: Hampton.

Lowery, S. A. (1980). Soap and booze in the afternoon: An analysis of the portrayal of alcohol use in daytime serials. *Journal of Studies in Alcohol, 41,* 829-838.

Lowry, D. T., Love, G., & Kirby, M. (1981). Sex on the soap operas: Patterns of intimacy. *Journal of Communication, 31,* 90-96.

Lowry, D. T., & Towles, D. E. (1989). Soap opera portrayals of sex, contraception, and sexually transmitted diseases. *Journal of Communication, 39,* 76-83.

Lull, J. (1988). The audience as nuisance. *Critical Studies in Mass Communication, 5,* 239-243.

MacDonald, J. F. (1979). Soap operas as social force. In *Don't touch that dial! Radio programming in American life, 1920-1960.* Chicago: Nelson-Hall.

Marcuse, H. (1969). *An essay on liberation.* Boston: Beacon.

Martin-Barbero, J. (1993). *Communication, culture and hegemony: From the media to the mediations.* London: Sage.

Matelski, M. J. (1988). *The soap opera evolution: America's enduring romance with daytime drama.* London: McFarland.

Mattelart, M. (1982). Women and the cultural industries. *Media, Culture and Society, 4,* 133-151.

Mattelart, M. (1986). *Women, media and crisis: Femininity and disorder.* London: Comedia.

Mattelart, M., & Mattelart, A. (1990). *The carnival of images: Brazilian television fiction* (D. Buxton, Trans.). New York: Bergin & Garvey.

McCormack, T. (1983). Male conceptions of female audiences: The case of soap operas. In E. Wartella & C. Whitney (Eds.), *Mass communication review yearbook* (Vol. 4, pp. 273-283). Beverly Hills, CA: Sage.

McQuail, D. (1987). *Mass communication theory: An introduction.* Newbury Park, CA: Sage.

McRobbie, A. (1984). Dance and social fantasy. In A. McRobbie & M. Nava (Eds.), *Gender and generation* (pp. 130-162). London: Macmillan.

McRobbie, A. (1991). *Feminism and youth culture: From "Jackie" to "Just Seventeen."* Boston: Hyman.

McRobbie, A. (1992, April). *Changing representations of adolescent femininity in U.K. media.* Paper presented at "Are the Kids Alright?" a conference on adolescents and the media, Pennsylvania State University.

Meehan, E. (1986). Conceptualizing culture as commodity: The problem of television. *Critical Studies in Mass Communication, 3,* 448-457.

Meehan, E. (1987). Recentering a television-centered television criticism: A political-economic response. In J. Anderson (Ed.), *Communication yearbook* (Vol. 11, pp. 183-193). Newbury Park, CA: Sage.

Mellencamp, P. (1986). Situation comedy, feminism and Freud: Discourses of Gracie and Lucy. In T. Modleski (Ed.), *Studies in entertainment: Critical approaches to mass culture* (pp. 80-95). Bloomington: Indiana University Press.

Metcalf, A., & Humphries, M. (Eds.). (1985). *The sexuality of men.* London: Pluto.

Miller, J. B. (1976). *Toward a psychology of women.* Boston: Beacon.

Millett, K. (1977). *Sexual politics.* London: Virago.

Modleski, T. (1982). *Loving with a vengeance: Mass-produced fantasies for women.* London: Methuen.

Morin, E. (1962). *L'esprit du temps, I: Nevrosé.* Paris: Grasset.

Morley, D. (1980). *The "Nationwide" audience: Structure and decoding.* London: British Film Institute.

Morley, D. (1981). The "Nationwide" audience: A postscript. *Screen Education, 39,* 3-14.

Morley, D. (1986). *Family television: Cultural power and domestic leisure.* London: Comedia.

Morley, D. (1989). Changing paradigms in audience studies. In E. Seiter, H. Borchers, G. Kreutzner, & E. M. Warth (Eds.), *Remote control: Television, audiences, and cultural power* (pp. 16-43). London: Routledge & Kegan Paul.

Morley, D. (1993). *Television, audiences and cultural studies.* London: Routledge & Kegan Paul.

Morris, M. (1990). Banality in cultural studies. In P. Mellencamp (Ed.), *Logics of television: Essays in cultural criticism* (pp. 14-43). Bloomington: Indiana University Press.

Mulvey, L. (1975). Visual pleasure and narrative cinema. *Screen, 16*(3), 6-18.

Mumford, L. S. (1991). Plotting paternity: Looking for dad on the daytime soaps. *Genders, 12,* 45-61.

Newcomb, H., & Alley, R. (1983). *The producer's medium.* New York: Oxford University Press.

Newman, K. (1988). On openings and closings. *Critical Studies in Mass Communication, 5,* 243-246.

Nightingale, V. (1990). Women as audiences. In M. E. Brown (Ed.), *Television and women's culture* (pp. 25-60). Sydney/London: Currency/Sage.

Nochimson, M. (1992). *No end to her: Soap opera and the female subject.* Berkeley: University of California Press.

Norwood, R. (1985). *Women who love too much.* New York: St. Martin.

NPR (National Public Radio). (1991, January 13). *All things considered.*

Oakley, A. (1979). *Becoming a mother.* Oxford: Martin Robertson.

Oliker, S. J. (1989). *Best friends and marriage: Exchange among women.* Berkeley: University of California Press.

Ong, W. (1982). *Orality and literacy: The technologizing of the word.* London: Methuen.

O'Sullivan, T., Hartley, J., Saunders D., & Fiske, J. (1983). *Key concepts in communication.* London: Methuen.

Palmer, P. (1986a). *Girls and television.* Sydney: New South Wales Ministry of Education.

Palmer, P. (1986b). *The lively audience: A study of children around the TV set.* Sydney: Allen and Unwin.

Palmgreen, P., Wenner, L., & Rosengren, K. (1985). Uses and gratifications research: The past ten years. In K. Rosengren, L. Wenner, & P. Palmgreen (Eds.), *Media gratifications research: Current perspectives* (pp. 11-37). Beverly Hills, CA: Sage.

Parkin, F. (1979). *Marxism and class theory: A bourgeois critique.* New York: Columbia University Press.

Passalacqua, C. (1991, June 23). Will all my children search for tomorrow? *The New York Times,* pp. 27-32.

Pendergast, S., & Prout, A. (1980). What will I do . . .? Teenage girls and the construction of motherhood. *Sociological Review, 28,* 517-535.

Pendley, C. (1991). Brownian motion: Women, tactics, and technologies. In C. Pendley & A. Ross (Eds.), *Technoculture*. Minneapolis: University of Minnesota Press.

Presnell, M. (1989). Narrative gender differences: Orality and literacy. In C. Spitzack & K. Carter (Eds.), *Doing research on women's communication: Perspectives on theory and method* (pp. 118-136). Norwood, NJ: Ablex.

Press, A. L. (1991). *Women watching television: Gender, class and generation in the American television experience*. Philadelphia: University of Pennsylvania Press.

Propp, V. (1968). *Morphology of the folktale* (L. Scott, Trans.). Austin: University of Texas Press.

Rabinovitz, L. (1990, July). *The bride wore white: Women, weddings and watching soaps.* Paper presented at the annual meeting of the International Communications Association, Dublin.

Radway, J. (1984). *Reading the romance: Women, patriarchy and popular literature.* Chapel Hill: University of North Carolina Press.

Radway, J. (1988). Reception study: Ethnography and the problems of dispersed audiences and nomadic subjects. *Cultural Studies, 2,* 359-376.

Rakow, L. F. (1992). *Gender on the line: Women, the telephone, and community life.* Chicago: University of Illinois Press.

Reid, E. (1989, July). Television viewing habits of young black women in London. *Screen, 30,* 114-128.

Riaño, P. (Ed.). (1994). *The role of women in grassroots communication.* Newbury Park, CA: Sage.

Richardson, K., & Corner, J. (1986). Reading reception: Mediation and transparency in viewers' accounts of a TV program. *Media, Culture and Society, 8,* 485-508.

Riessman, C. K. (1987). When gender is not enough: Women interviewing women. *Gender and Society, 1,* 172-207.

Roman, L. G. (1988). Intimacy, labor and class: Ideologies of feminine sexuality in the punk slam dance. In L. G. Roman, L. K. Christian-Smith, with E. Ellsworth (Eds.), *Becoming feminine: The politics of popular culture* (pp. 143-184). London: Falmer.

Rosengren, K., Wenner, L., & Palmgreen, P. (Eds.). (1985). *Media gratifications research: Current perspectives.* Beverly Hills, CA: Sage.

Rubin, A. W. (1985). The uses of daytime television serials by college students: An examination of viewing motives. *Journal of Broadcasting and Electronic Media, 29,* 241-258.

Rubin, J. (1992). *The making of middlebrow culture.* Chapel Hill: University of North Carolina Press.

Rubin, L. B. (1986). *Worlds of pain: Life in the working-class family.* New York: Basic Books.

Ruthnen, M. (1984, September 21). Cassandras at camp. *Times Literary Supplement,* p. 1048a.

Rutsky, R. L., & Wyatt, J. (1990). Serious pleasure: Cinematic pleasure and the notion of fun. *Cinema Journal, 30,* 1, 3-19.

Scanzoni, J. (1986, June). *Changes in gender patterns: Harbinger of a paradigm shift?* Paper presented at "Being Female and Male: Traditions, Changes and Dilemmas—Changing the Family," a conference held at the University of Iowa, Iowa City.

Scott, R. (Director), & Scott, R., & Polk, M. (Producers). (1991). *Thelma & Louise* [Film]: C. Khouri (Screenplay), S. Sarandon (Louise), G. Davis (Thelma), H. Keitel (Hal), M. Madsen (Jimmy), C. McDonald (Darryl), S. Tobolowsky (Max), & B. Pitt (JD). MGM-Pathé.

Seaman, W. R. (1992). Active audience theory: Pointless populism. *Media, Culture and Society, 14,* 301-311.

Seidel, J. V., Kjolseth, R., & Seymour, E. (1988). *The ethnograph: A user's guide.* Littleton, CO: Qualis Research Associates.

Seiter, E. (1982). Promise and contradiction: The daytime television serial. *Film Reader, 5,* 150-163.

Seiter, E., Kreutzner, G., Warth, E. M., & Borchers, H. (1989). "Don't treat us like we're so stupid and naive": Towards an ethnography of soap opera viewers. In E. Seiter, H. Borchers, G. Kreutzner, & E. M. Warth (Eds.), *Remote control: Television audiences, and cultural power* (pp. 323-347). London: Routledge & Kegan Paul.

Shatz, T. (1981). *Hollywood film genres: Formulas, filmmaking, and the studio system.* Philadelphia: Temple University Press.

Sherover-Marcuse, E. (1986). *Emancipation and consciousness: Dogmatic and dialectical perspectives in early Marx.* London: Blackwell.

Silverstone, R., Hirsch, E., & Morley, D. (1991, May). Listening to a long conversation: An ethnographic approach to the study of information and communication technologies in the home. *Cultural Studies, 5,* 204-227.

Smith, J. (1987). Transforming households: Working-class women and economic crisis. *Social Problems, 34,* 416-435.

Smith-Rosenberg, C. (1975). The female world of love and ritual. *Signs, 1,* 1-29.

Soares, M. (1978). *The soap opera book.* New York: Harmony.

Spacks, P. (1985). *Gossip.* New York: Knopf.

Spender, D. (1985). *Man made language.* London: Routledge & Kegan Paul.

Spradley, J. P., & McCurdy, D. W. (1988). *The cultural experience: Ethnography in complex society.* Prospect Heights, IL: Waveland.

Stacey, J. (1987). Sexism by a subtler name? Postindustrial conditions and postfeminist consciousness in the Silicon Valley. *Socialist Review, 17,* 7-28.

Stallybrass, P., & White, A. (1986). *The politics and poetics of transgression.* Ithaca, NY: Cornell University Press.

Stam, R. (1982). On the carnivalesque. *Wedge, 1,* 47-55.

Stam, R. (1988). Mikhail Bakhtin and left cultural critique. In E. A. Kaplan (Ed.), *Post-modernism and its discontents: Theories, practices* (pp. 116-145). London: Verso.

Stedman, R. W. (1981). *The serials: Suspense and drama by installment.* Norman: University of Oklahoma Press.

Steeves, L. H. (1987). Feminist theories and media studies. *Critical Studies in Mass Communication, 4,* 95-135.

Steiner, L. (1983). Finding community in nineteenth-century suffrage periodicals. *American Journalism, 1,* 1-16.

Steiner, L. (1988). Oppositional decoding as an act of resistance. *Critical Studies in Mass Communication, 5,* 1-15.

Stern, L. (1978). Oedipal opera: "The restless years." *Australian Journal of Screen Theory, 4,* 39-48.

Stern, L. (1982). The Australian cereal: Home grown television. In S. Dermody, J. Docker, & D. Modjeska (Eds.), *Nellie Melba, Ginger Meggs and friends: Essays in Australian cultural history* (pp. 103-123). Malmsbury, Victoria: Kibble.

Stoessl, S. (1987). Women as TV audience: A marketing perspective. In H. Baehr & G. Dyer (Eds.), *Boxed in: Women and television* (pp. 107-116). London: Pandora.

Sudman, S. (1976). *Applied sampling.* New York: Academic Press.

Sudman, S., & Bradburn, N. M. (1983). *Asking questions: A practical guide to questionnaire design.* San Francisco: Jossey-Bass.

Suleiman, S. R. (1980). Introduction: Varieties of audience-oriented criticism. In S. R. Suleiman & I. Crosman (Eds.), *The reader in the text: Essays on audience and interpretation* (pp. 3-45). Princeton, NJ: Princeton University Press.

Taylor, E. (1989). *Prime-time families: Television culture in postwar America.* Berkeley: University of California Press.

Taylor, S. (1987). *The tender trap: Teenage girls, romantic ideology and schooling.* Unpublished paper, Educational Studies Department, Brisbane College Advanced Education, Kelvin Grove Campus.

Tedesco, N. S. (1974). Patterns in prime time. *Journal of Communication, 24,* 119-124.

Thorne, B., Kramarae, C., & Henley, N. (1983). *Language, gender, and society.* Rowley, MA: Newbury House.

Timberg, B. (1987). The rhetoric of the camera in television soap opera. In H. Newcomb (Ed.), *Television: The critical view* (4th ed., pp. 164-178). Oxford: Oxford University Press.

Tuchman, G., Daniels, A. K., & Benet, J. (1978). *Hearth and home: Images of women in the mass media.* New York: Oxford University Press.

Tulloch, J., & Moran, A. (1986). *A Country Practice: "Quality soap."* Sydney: Currency.

Turner, V. (1969). *The ritual process.* Chicago: Aldine.

Turner, V. (1977a). Frame, flow and reflection: Ritual and drama as public liminality. In M. Benamon & C. Caramello (Eds.), *Performance in post-modern culture* (pp. 33-55). Madison, WI: Coda.

Turner, V. (1977b, Summer). Process, system and symbol: A new anthropological synthesis. *Daedalus,* pp. 67-73.

van Zoonen, L. (1988). Rethinking women and the news. *European Journal of Communication, 3,* 35-53.

van Zoonen, L. (1991). Feminist perspectives on the media. In J. Curran & M. Gurevitch (Eds.), *Mass media and society* (pp. 33-54). New York: Edward Arnold.

Waggett, G. J. (1989, May). Let's stop turning rapists into heros. *TV Guide,* pp. 10-11.

Walby, S. (1990). *Theorizing patriarchy.* Oxford: Blackwell.

Waldrop, J., & Crispell, D. (1988, October). Daytime dramas: Demographic dreams. *American Demographics, 10,* 28-32.

Walkerdine, V. (1986). Video replay: Families, film and fantasy. In V. Burgin, J. Donald, & C. Kaplan (Eds.), *Formations of fantasy* (pp. 167-199). London: Methuen.

Warner, W. L., & Henry, S. E. (1948). The radio day time serial: A symbolic analysis. *Genetic Psychology Monographs, 37,* 71.

Webster's New World Dictionary of the American Language. (1964). Cleveland, OH: World.

Welch, S. D. (1985). *Communities of resistance and solidarity: A feminist theology of liberation.* New York: Orbis.

West, C., & Zimmerman, D. H. (1983). Small insults: A study of interruptions in cross-sex conversations between unacquainted persons. In B. Thorne, C. Kramare, & N. Henley (Eds.), *Language, gender and society* (pp. 86-111). Rowley, MA: Newbury House.

Whetmore, E. J., & Kielwasser, A. P. (1983). The soap opera audience speaks: A preliminary report. *Journal of American Culture, 6,* 110-116.

White, R. (1991, April). *Media reception theory: Emerging perspectives.* Paper presented at Le Programme Pluriannuel en Sciences Humaines Phone-Alpes: Société et Communication, Lyon, France.

Whittenberger-Keith, K. (1992). Understanding fandom rhetorically: The case of *Beauty and the Beast.* In A. King (Ed.), *Postmodern political communication* (pp. 131-151). New York: Praeger.

Whittenberger-Keith, K., & Lutfiyya, M. N. (1992). *Fans' constructions of how TV works.* Unpublished manuscript, University of Louisville.

Williams, R. (1976). *Key words: A vocabulary of culture and society.* London: Fontana.

Williams, R. (1977). *Marxism and literature.* Oxford: Oxford University Press.

Willis, S. (1990). Work(ing) out. *Cultural Studies, 4,* 1-18.

Winship, J. (1987). *Inside women's magazines.* London: Pandora.

Woodiwiss, K. E. (1972). *The flame and the flower.* New York: Avon.

Index

About the Author

Mary Ellen Brown teaches television criticism, cultural studies, and feminist media theory in the Department of Communication at the University of Missouri, Columbia. She is editor of *Television and Women's Culture: Politics and the Popular* and has published widely, both in this country and internationally, on feminist cultural studies, soap opera and other women's genres, reader response criticism, the concept of resistive reading, orality, and women's culture. She has also been invited to present her research findings at international colloquia on television, melodrama, and popular culture in Spain and Italy. Her current research interests include identity and postmodern television audiences, women's use of the video version of *Thelma & Louise*, and the cultural politics of Hillary Rodham Clinton's image.